DEBATING
AMERICAN
IMMIGRATION,
1882–PRESENT

Debating Twentieth-Century America
Series Editor: James T. Patterson, Brown University

DEBATING AMERICAN IMMIGRATION, 1882–PRESENT

ROGER DANIELS
and
OTIS L. GRAHAM

Introduction by James T. Patterson

ROWMAN & LITTLEFIELD PUBLISHERS, INC.
Lanham • Boulder • New York • Oxford

ROWMAN & LITTLEFIELD PUBLISHERS, INC.

Published in the United States of America
by Rowman & Littlefield Publishers, Inc.
4720 Boston Way, Lanham, Maryland 20706
http://www.rowmanlittlefield.com

12 Hid's Copse Road
Cumnor Hill, Oxford OX2 9JJ, England

British Library Cataloguing in Publication Information Available

Library of Congress Cataloging-in-Publication Data

Daniels, Roger.
  Debating American immigration, 1882–present / Roger Daniels and Otis L. Graham ; introduction by James T. Patterson.
    p. cm. — (Debating 20th Century America)
  Includes bibliographical references and index.
  ISBN 0-8476-9409-7 (alk. paper)—ISBN 0-8476-9410-0 (pbk. : alk. paper)
    1. United States—Emmigration and immigration—Government policy—History.
  2. United States—Emmigration and immigration—Government policy—History—
  Sources. 3. Emigration and immigration law—United States—History. 4. Emigration
  and immigration law—United States—History—Sources. I. Graham, Otis L. II. Title.
  III. Debating twentieth-century America.

JV6483 .D35 2001
325.73—dc21   00-062654

Printed in the United States of America

♾ ™The paper used in this publication meets the minimum requirements of American National Standard for Information Sciences—Permanence of Paper for Printed Library Materials, ANSI/NISO Z39.48–1992.

CONTENTS

FOREWORD

Debating Twentieth-Century America is a series of books aimed at helping readers appreciate an important aspect of the writing of history: there is no simple, wholly agreed-on "truth" that captures what has happened in the past. Our understanding of the events of history depends considerably on the way that individual historians interpret them.

With this in mind, each book in the series features two essays, written from varying perspectives, about an important issue, event, or trend in twentieth-century American history. The essayists, who are well-known writers and teachers in their fields, bring to this task considerable expertise. They have delved into the primary and secondary sources and have arrived at personal interpretations of their subjects. Their conclusions, however, reflect different approaches or conclusions. Placed side by side, as in this book, the essays frequently engage in "debate" over the past.

The sources for the essays in this book are far too numerous and varied to reprint in full here. Still, the writers of the essays in *Debating Twentieth-Century America* wish to give readers a sense of the evidence for their generalizations. They therefore include a small number of documents that have influenced their thinking. Readers may find it challenging to evaluate the relevance and importance of these documents.

We hope that the essays and documents will help readers understand the complexity of the past, as well as the subjective process of writing history that carries the past to the present.

James T. Patterson

INTRODUCTION

James T. Patterson

In the course of his stimulating essay "The Unfinished Reform: Regulating Immigration in the National Interest," Otis Graham cites an observation by journalist Theodore White about the Immigration Act of 1965. The law, White asserted, was "noble, revolutionary—and probably the most thoughtless of the many acts of the Great Society [of President Lyndon Johnson]."

Graham agrees with this judgment. "The passage of time," he writes, "may position the 1965 immigration law as the Great Society's most nation-changing act, especially if seen as the first of a series of ongoing liberalization of U.S. immigration and border policy extending through the end of the century and facilitating four decades (so far) of mass immigration."

The results since 1965 of this historic law seem to support this conclusion. During the lifetime of the so-called "national origins" system of immigration (between the 1920s and 1965), population movements to the United States were hardly noticeable, averaging 178,000 per year. Thereafter, these totals swelled—to 400,000 in 1973 and to 600,000 in 1978. By the 1990s the number of new immigrants ran at about 900,000 a year, to which number must be added hundreds of thousands of illegal immigrants. During the decade, immigration accounted for about a third of American population growth.

None of the people who fashioned the law of 1965 anticipated immigration growth of this magnitude. Nor did they imagine that non-Europeans—notably Latin Americans and Asians—would be the most numerous among the newcomers. On the contrary, they thought that they were reforming a racially discriminatory national origins system and that the

1

number of immigrants would rise only moderately. Their liberal intentions, enacted without considering carefully the results of what they were doing, were what Theodore White meant when he praised the nobility of law-makers but emphasized how "thoughtless" they had been. Indeed, the 1965 immigration law is a prime example of legislation that has led to huge and unforeseen consequences.

Given the significance of these consequences, it is hardly surprising that immigration law and policy—the focus of the essays by Graham and Roger Daniels—have aroused considerable argument in recent years. As in many European nations since the 1980s—it is necessary to remember that vast demographic changes are deeply affecting the planet, not just in the United States—debate in North America about the wisdom of accepting many millions of people, most of them from crowded, impoverished areas of the so-called Third World, has engaged citizens and politicians alike, es-pecially in those states such as California, Texas, and Florida, where the number of newcomers has been especially high. Graham may well be cor-rect in stating that immigration laws since 1965 have become the most "na-tion-changing" acts of the contemporary era.

Both Daniels and Graham are prominent historians of American his-tory, and they pay considerable attention to these developments since 1965. However, they do much more than that in their essays here. Look-ing at these changes through the lens of history, they set them in a broader perspective, which reveals that Americans have long debated immigration policies. Graham briefly explores events during the seventeenth and eigh-teenth centuries to remind us that newcomers to American shores have not always been the ones discriminated against: early European immigrants to North America managed virtually to eradicate the Native Americans with whom they came in contact.

Both Graham and Daniels do an especially thorough job of describ-ing and analyzing the periodic spates of anti-immigration feeling in the mid- and late nineteenth century. Fear of certain immigrant groups, such as the Chinese, led to exclusionary laws and agreements as early as 1882. By 1900 the "immigration question" was becoming a highly contested is-sue in national politics.

Immigration then peaked; approximately 1 million immigrants were admitted to the United States each year between 1900 and 1914. These were enormous numbers—much higher as a percentage of total population than the numbers in our own times. Worried by trends such as these, interest groups formed to dam the flow. Other groups, including employers who welcomed cheap labor, mobilized to keep the stream moving. After years of struggle, the anti-immigration lobbies succeeded in 1924, and the restrictionist national origins system, destined to last until 1965, came into being.

Graham and Daniels offer similar perspectives on some of these historical events, as well as on the more recent laws and policies that have once again helped to make immigration a political issue in the United States. Readers of these essays, however, will soon notice that Graham and Daniels approach the subject from different angles (hence the title of this volume: *Debating American Immigration*). In the process they spar over a number of key points. Have large scale influxes of overseas migrants—whether a hundred years ago or today—been generally beneficial for the United States? By what measures? Have foes of substantial immigration tended to be racists or nativists hostile to alien cultures, or have they normally advanced other sorts of arguments? Which groups have led the fight for and against restriction? Have the costs of immigration (necessitating public support of education, welfare, and other services) outweighed the benefits (such as providing needed labor and greater cultural diversity)?

The authors debate other questions, too. Have blue-collar workers and blacks had good reason—in the past as well as today—to worry about job competition from migrants who work for very low wages? Was what Graham calls the "breathing spell" afforded by immigration restrictions between the 1920s and 1965 mainly good for American society? Is there a point at which high levels of ethnic diversity can threaten the political or cultural cohesiveness of a nation? What will be the impact in the future of substantial population growth (much of it from immigration) on the environment of economically developed countries such as the United States?

In recent years, as controversy over immigration has grown (in Europe as well as in the United States), I have found myself devoting more and more of my teaching to the issue. These two essays—elegantly written and forcefully argued—do an admirable job of debating, and thereby elucidating, a whole range of questions associated with this historically significant subject.

TWO CHEERS FOR IMMIGRATION

Roger Daniels

M odern American immigration policy may conveniently by divided into
five periods: (1) high immigration and growing restriction (1882–
1924), (2) low and decreasing immigration and severe restriction (1924–43),
(3) low but increasing immigration and decreasing restriction (1943–65), (4)
high and increasing immigration and relatively low restriction (1965–80), and
(5) high and increasing immigration and increasing but essentially ineffective
restriction (1980–present).

Before discussing each period, it is appropriate to indicate both the size
and incidence of immigration to the United States since the 1880s: in demographic matters if you don't get the numbers right you just don't know
what you're talking about. Table 1.1 shows the number of immigrants
recorded in official government statistics by decade; table 1.2 shows the incidence of foreign-born persons, whether citizen or alien, as recorded in
each decennial census; and tables 1.3 and 1.4 show, in general terms, the
global regions from which immigrants came. Taken together, the data in
these four tables give the best possible "snapshot" of the volume of immigration, the incidence of immigrants in the American population, and the
countries of origin of most immigrants.

Taken together, the first two tables demonstrate two things: the percentage of foreign-born individuals in the population has been constant despite the enormous increases in the volume of immigration in the decades
after 1880 (about 14 percent of the population between 1860 and 1920),
and in the more recent decades the percentage of foreign-born individuals

Table 1.1
NUMBER OF IMMIGRANTS, 1880–1997

Decade	No. of immigrants (rounded)
1881–90	5,247,000
1891–1900	3,688,000
1901–10	8,795,000
1911–20	5,736,000
1921–30	4,107,000
1931–40	528,000
1941–50	1,035,000
1951–60	2,515,000
1961–70	3,322,000
1971–80	4,493,000
1981–90	7,338,000
1991–97	6,943,000
Total	53,747,000

Source: U.S. Immigration and Naturalization Service, *Statistical Yearbook of the Immigration and Naturalization Service, 1997* (Washington, DC: Government Printing Office, 1999).

Table 1.2
FOREIGN-BORN POPULATION AND INCIDENCE, 1880–1990

Year	U.S. Population (in millions)	No. of foreign-born (in millions)	% of foreign-born
1880	50.2	6.7	13.3
1890	63.0	9.3	14.7
1900	76.2	10.3	13.6
1910	92.2	13.5	14.7
1920	106.0	13.9	13.2
1930	123.2	14.3	11.6
1940	132.2	11.7	8.8
1950	151.3	10.4	6.9
1960	179.4	9.7	5.5
1970	203.3	9.6	4.7
1980	226.5	14.1	6.2
1990	248.7	19.8	7.9

Source: U.S. Bureau of the Census, *Statistical Abstract of the United States, 1999* (Washington, DC: Government Printing Office, 2000).

Table 1.3
IMMIGRATION BY CATEGORY, 1925–30

Year	Total	Quota	Family	New World	Other
1925	294,314	145,971	7,159	139,389	1,795
1926	304,488	157,432	11,061	134,305	1,690
1927	335,175	158,070	18,361	147,339	11,345
1928	307,255	153,231	25,678	123,534	4,812
1929	279,678	146,918	30,245	97,547	4,967
1930	241,700	41,497	32,105	63,147	4,951
Total	1,762,611	903,119	124,609	705,259	29,560

Source: U.S. Bureau of the Census, *Historical Statistics of the United States, Colonial Times to 1970*, Series C 139–151 (Washington, DC: Government Printing Office, 1975).

is still well below traditional levels. Yet, from the 1880s to the present day, many have perceived that the numbers of immigrants is overwhelming.

These perceptions have been repeated by many if not most writers of history texts, who have persisted in using what I call hydraulic metaphors to describe the immigration process. Immigration is almost habitually described as a "flood" or an "inundation," and immigrants are described as coming in "waves," "torrents," and "streams." It is not necessary to be an expert in semantics to understand that one result of the habitual use of such language is to stigmatize immigrants as the "other," rather than as the ancestors of us all. These numbers and their interpretation should be kept in mind during the following discussion of immigration policy by period.

Table 1.4
THE ORIGINS OF AMERICAN IMMIGRANTS, 1900 AND 1990
(IN PERCENTAGES)

Country of Origin	1900	1990
Europe	84.9	22.0
Latin America	1.3	42.5
Asia	1.2	25.2
All other (mostly of Canadian and European origin)	12.6	10.3

Source: U.S. Bureau of the Census, *We, the Foreign Born* (Washington, DC: Government Printing Office, 1993).

HIGH IMMIGRATION,
GROWING RESTRICTION (1882-1924)

THE EXCLUSION OF ASIAN IMMIGRANTS (1882-1924)

The period 1882–1924 is set off by two statutes, the Chinese Exclusion Act of 1882 and the Immigration Act of 1924. The latter act all but ended the immigration of Asians, whereas the former was the first real regulation of immigration. Prior to the passage of the Chinese Exclusion Act of 1882, there had been no effective restriction of free immigration. An ineffective 1875 statute, the so-called Page Act, prohibited the entry of criminals and prostitutes, barred bringing in "any Oriental person" involuntarily, but established no immigration bureaucracy. The 1882 Exclusion Act, which stemmed both from economic fears of white working men in the Far West and from the blatant anti-Asian racism that most Americans shared, did not exclude all Chinese but prohibited the entry of Chinese laborers who had not previously been in the United States. Businessmen and their families were exempted from the ban and were referred to in administrative regulations as "treaty merchants," reflecting the fact that the rights of merchants in both the United States and China had long been guaranteed by treaty.

Chinese exclusion is usually treated in texts as a minor matter affecting only Chinese Americans. (In effect, it froze the demographic structure of the Chinese American community in a "bachelor society" mode typical of the early stages of ethnic group immigration for half a century.) However, it is now apparent that it became the pivot upon which all American immigration policy turned, the hinge on which the "golden door" of immigration began its swing to a nearly closed position.

The aftermath of the brief Spanish-American War of 1898 brought into the American orbit three new territories with largely non-white populations. Congress treated them in very different ways. Citizens of Hawaii immediately became American citizens, and persons born in Hawaii became birthright citizens. Citizens of Puerto Rico would receive the same status by 1917, but no such rights were granted to citizens of the Philippines.

During the early years of the new century meaningful immigration restriction continued to focus on Asians. Japanese immigration, much of it by way of Hawaii, triggered the same kinds of negative reactions from white Americans along the Pacific Coast as had Chinese immigration. If Japan had been a weak country, as China was, a victim rather than a predator, it is clear that something like a "Japanese Exclusion Act" would have been legislated in the first decade of the twentieth century. However, Japan was a rising power and the executive branch of the U.S. government was intent on reaching an accommodation, which meant finding an alternative to exclusion that Tokyo could live with without totally alienating western voters who were overwhelmingly against further Japanese immigration.

Theodore Roosevelt and the U.S. State Department found an acceptable modus vivendi, at least for the short run, in 1907–8. The so-called Gentlemen's Agreement of those years (a series of executive agreements between the United States and Japan that did not require senatorial ratification) was designed to stop immigration and save Japan's face. Its primary elements were that Tokyo agreed to stop issuing passports valid for passage to the United States or Hawaii to male laborers, and Washington agreed not to enact legislation barring Japanese immigrants. Tokyo was amenable to this somewhat one-sided agreement because it was convinced that overtly anti-Japanese legislation would militate against Japan's achieving recognition as a great power.

The negotiators agreed that laborers already in the United States could leave and return, as had been true for Chinese laborers, and that close family members in Japan could join them in America. This resulted in the immigration of the so-called "picture brides," Japanese women who entered into arranged marriages with Japanese laborers in Hawaii or on the American mainland. The pair would exchange photographs, a proxy marriage would take place in Japan, and the brides would embark for America. Although this was not a uniquely Asian practice—heavily male immigrant communities in America had been importing marriageable women since the Jamestown colony was founded in the early seventeenth century— never before had so many come in such a short period: more than 20,000 Japanese women, not all of them picture brides, emigrated to the mainland and Hawaii between 1909 and 1921. These women helped create a Japanese American community with a relatively balanced gender ratio, one in which, by 1940, native-born citizens would outnumber foreign-born aliens by about 2 to 1. (Asian immigrants were "aliens ineligible to citizenship" in American law, which, after 1870, limited naturalization to "white persons" and those of "African descent." Under the Fourteenth Amendment anyone born in the United States was a birthright citizen.)

To western white Americans in general and Californians in particular, the picture brides seemed evidence of an unholy collaboration between Tokyo and Washington. The Gentlemen's Agreement had been presented to them as tantamount to exclusion, and yet Japanese population on the mainland continued to grow, from 72,000 in 1910 to 111,000 in 1920, and the rising Japanese American birthrate allowed nativists with more than a touch of what Richard Hofstadter called the paranoid style to speak of a coming "yellow majority" in California. This episode of immigration restriction serves to highlight two factors that have to be figured into the immigration policy equation: the effect of foreign policy on immigration decisions and the failure of immigration policy makers to consider the likely consequences of their actions. What some political scientists have called the "law" of unintended consequences had and continues to have much validity for immigration policy.

In the first years of the twentieth century other Asians began to immigrate to the United States and Hawaii, particularly Koreans, Filipinos, and Asian Indians. None of these groups was particularly numerous in the years before World War I, but a concerned Congress passed the so-called "barred zone" or "Asia-Pacific triangle" provisions of the act of 1917, which outlined an area of Asia from which immigration was forbidden. The legislators believed that they were stopping all Asian immigration except for that from Japan and China, which was already largely blocked. However, the courts soon ruled that Filipinos were "American nationals" and thus entitled to unrestricted entry to the United States even though they were ineligible for naturalization (because they were neither white nor of African descent). This provided a window of opportunity for Filipinos to fill empty niches in the agricultural labor forces of California and Hawaii, a window that would be closed in the 1930s.

The final episodes in the saga of Asian exclusion came in the 1920s and 1930s. Some authorities had questioned the meaning of the racial parameters of the naturalization statutes, but two Supreme Court decisions in the 1920s confirmed the right of Congress to discriminate on the grounds of race. The first, *Ozawa v. U.S.* (1922), denied the application for naturalization of an otherwise qualified immigrant from Japan, Takao Ozawa, purely on the grounds of his race. The Court held, without objection, that the disputed words in the statute, "white person," meant a "person of the Caucasian race." The second, *U.S. v. Thind* (1923), denied a similar application from an otherwise qualified immigrant from India, Bhagat Singh Thind, even though it granted that Thind was what ethnologists then called a "Caucasian." In a unanimous decision, the Court simply switched its interpretation of what the word "white" in the 1870 statute meant, ruling that " 'white persons' are words of common speech, to be interpreted in accordance with the understanding of the common man."

These decisions made it safe for Congress to rely upon the naturalization statute in its penultimate measure affecting Asian exclusion. The Gentlemen's Agreement in general and picture bride immigration in particular had come under increasing attack from American opponents of Japanese immigration, and the Japanese government had voluntarily stopped the picture bride immigration in 1920, but those Japanese men resident in the United States who could afford it could still go to Japan, get married, and bring their brides back with them. Those in Congress who had long wanted to abrogate the Gentlemen's Agreement were able to do so by inserting a clause in the Immigration Act of 1924 barring the immigration of "aliens ineligible to citizens." This ended not only the largely female immigration from Japan, but also the immigration rights of Chinese treaty merchants. Students from Asia, travelers for pleasure, and businessmen could enter with the proper temporary visas, but they could not become legal immigrants or permanent residents.

This left Filipinos, as American nationals, the only Asian group still allowed to come to the United States to work. Nativists in Congress used the 1934 law that promised the Philippines independence in 1945 as a vehicle to all but eliminate Filipino immigration. As will be discussed below, after 1921, immigration from all eligible nations was on a quota system, with 100 admissions a year the smallest possible quota. Asians had no quotas after 1924. In 1934 the Philippines was given a quota of just fifty persons annually. Anti-Asian restrictionists rejoiced: there was now, for all intents and purposes, total exclusion of Asians. That exclusion lasted nine years.

The restriction and eventual virtual exclusion of Asian immigrants was the first and, for contemporaries, the least controversial aspect of evolving American immigration policy. Race (what W.E.B. DuBois liked to call "the color line") was the first line to be drawn. Even as that was being done, however, many were waging a campaign to restrict all immigration, a campaign that eventually focussed on ethnicity.

THE RESTRICTION OF WHITE IMMIGRATION (1882–1924)

The Founding Fathers had a positive view of immigration. They knew, as the Argentine statesman Domingo Faustino Sarmiento (1811–88) put it, that, for a largely empty country, "to govern [was] to populate." Although the word "immigration" does not appear in the Constitution, the fathers clearly envisaged it. They mandated "a uniform system of naturalization" (Art. 1, Sec. 8) and provided that immigrants could hold all offices under the Constitution except for president and vice president (Art. 2, Sec. 1). The Supreme Court would rule, in 1849, that immigration was "foreign commerce" and, as such, could be regulated only by Congress. Congress did very little, however. It ended the importation of slaves in 1808, provided that immigrants be counted at the ports in 1819, and did nothing else before 1875.

Except for the politically inspired anti-immigrant and antiradical scare in the dying days of the Federalist Era, a pro-immigration consensus prevailed in the early decades of the republic. President John Tyler's June 1841 message to Congress described it well: "We hold out to the people of other countries an invitation to come and settle among us as members of our rapidly growing family . . ."

However, that consensus was under attack by the time of Tyler's message. In the 1840s Massachusetts and other eastern seaboard states legislated against incoming immigrants only to be frustrated by the Supreme Court. The major target was Irish Catholic immigration, which, in the aftermath of the potato famine of the mid-1840s, was largely of desperately poor immigrants including many whose emigration had been assisted by the British government in a process one British official referred to as "shoveling out paupers." Continued heavy immigration in the early 1850s, largely of Irish, Germans (a minority of whom were Catholic), and Scandinavians, coupled with the growing crisis over slavery, led to the first anti-immigrant mass movement in American history.

Sparked by a Protestant fraternal organization, the Order of the Star Spangled Banner (popularly known as the Know-Nothings), anti-immigrant groups in 1854–55 elected eight governors; more than 100 congressmen; the mayors of Boston, Philadelphia, and Chicago; and thousands of other local officials. In Massachusetts Know-Nothing forces got the state constitution changed to deny the vote to naturalized citizens until two years after they had become naturalized. At the national level unfulfilled goals included an extension of the waiting period for naturalization from five to fourteen years, various proposals to limit immigration, and a constitutional amendment barring foreign-born persons from holding any public office. After an unsuccessful attempt to elect ex-President Millard Fillmore on an "American Party" ticket in 1856, the anti-immigrant movement collapsed. According to its historian, Tyler Anbinder, the collapse was caused by its attempt to straddle the slavery issue and the fiasco of Fillmore's presidential candidacy, which carried only Maryland.

Historians have come to call all anti-immigrant movements "nativist": the term stems from the false claim made by anti-immigrant spokesmen that General George Washington, at a crucial point in the War of Independence, had ordered that "only native Americans" be put on guard. (Washington was anything but a nativist, and foreign officers were crucial in shaping the American army.) The term nativist covers a wide spectrum of opinion. In the nineteenth century nativists were all but universally white supremacists, along with most of the population, and generally anti-Catholic. Contemporary nativists often disavow bigotry in all its forms, and some actually mean it. As used in this essay, the term simply means a person or movement whose objectives are pointedly anti-immigration. (Keep in mind, however, that a person who holds that there should be certain limits to immigration is not necessarily a nativist.) Nativists also usually stress that foreigners (or certain foreigners) are "un-American," "unassimilable," or genetically unsuited to American life.

Nativist movements continued during and after the Civil War, but the patent demonstration of patriotism by the hundreds of thousands of immigrants who fought in the Union Army, often in ethnic regiments, while millions of native-born white Americans attempted to destroy the nation, made a generally anti-immigrant agenda inappropriate for the immediate postwar years, although nativist cartoonist Thomas Nast never desisted from his apelike portrayals of the Irishman.

By the 1880s times had changed. The great growth in the volume of immigration in the Gilded Age made some kind of organized administration necessary. In the same year that it enacted Chinese exclusion, Congress also passed the first general immigration law. It created the first immigration bureaucracy, supervised by the Secretary of the Treasury, but with most functions contracted out to states. For example, New York State ran the main immigrant depot, Castle Garden at the tip of Manhattan, but was subsidized by the federal government. A fifty-cent head tax placed on each incoming immigrant was collected from the steamship companies to defray the cost of immigration administration. This tax, really a user fee, would rise, in stages, to eight dollars by 1917. In most years the government collected more in head taxes than it spent on administration. The law also created a new category of inadmissible aliens, those "likely to become a public charge." This so-called "LPC clause" originally only kept out persons who were obviously unable to support themselves, but in the twentieth century the executive branch broadened it, first to keep out poor Asian Indians and Mexicans and then to keep out poor people generally, unless they had affidavits of support from financially responsible persons or organizations.

In 1885 Congress passed the first of many laws that made "contract labor" illegal. From that time to the present the statutes have made it "unlawful to import aliens into the United States under contract for the performance of labor or services of any kind," but they have provided exceptions for various kinds of labor, including (most significantly) agricultural labor in times of shortages, real and imaginary, and, most recently, various kinds of persons with "high tech skills."

In 1891, as immigration climbed, administration was strengthened and minor general restrictions were added. Congress established a Bureau of Immigration in the Treasury Department under a Superintendent of Immigration. The superintendent got a salary of $4,000 a year (cabinet officers got $8,000) and supervised a staff of twenty-seven, including one inspector for each of twenty-four inspection stations. The 1891 statute also barred a variety of persons from entering the country: mentally disturbed persons, persons suffering from a "loathsome or contagious" disease, paupers, persons convicted of a felony or infamous crime or misdemeanor of moral turpitude, and polygamists. (The last was aimed at immigrant Mormons, not against Muslims.) None of these restrictions kept very many people out, but they did establish a second pattern of restriction, a pattern aimed at keeping out individuals deemed deficient or dangerous.

During the economically depressed 1890s increased anti-immigrant sentiment developed. In 1894 a group of Harvard graduates established the Immigration Restriction League, which became the premier anti-immigrant pressure group for three decades. In the 1890s its chosen goal was the passage of a literacy test for immigrants. Congress passed a bill requiring that immigrants be literate, but Grover Cleveland vetoed it in 1897 as "unAmerican" and stressed that the "stupendous growth" of the nation had been "largely due to the assimilation and thrift of millions of sturdy and patriotic adopted citizens." The literacy test continued as a live political issue for the next twenty years. Congress passed it three more times, in 1913, 1915, and 1917, only to have it vetoed by William Howard Taft and Woodrow Wilson. Congress overrode Wilson's second veto, and the literacy test became law in 1917.

Although many of the measure's proponents had wanted a statute that specified literacy in English, the enacted law required only an ability to read a brief text in any "language or dialect, including Hebrew or Yiddish" by immigrants over sixteen years of age. In addition, wives, mothers, grandmothers, widowed or unmarried daughters of a literate male alien, or one already living in the United States need not be literate. Thus, the law had little effect. In 1920–21, when more than 800,000 immigrants were admitted, about 1.5 percent (13,799 persons) were rejected for one reason or another. Only 1,450 of them were barred for illiteracy. Nevertheless the enactment of the literacy test was an important symbolic victory for the forces of nativism, and its obvious failure to restrict immigration meaningfully was used as an argument for further restriction by such spokespersons as the Immigration Restriction League's Prescott F. Hall (1868–1921).

During the administrations of William McKinley (1897–1901) and Theodore Roosevelt (1901–9), growth in the immigration bureaucracy was rapid. By 1906 the staff had grown to 1,200, an increase of 4,200 percent in fifteen years. Many of them were based at the new government immigration station at Ellis Island, opened in 1892. The immigration service has been unlike most other federal bureaucracies in one important regard: whereas most of the personnel of such bureaucracies serve as advocates for their constituencies (e.g., agriculture for farmers, labor for working people), most of those in the immigration bureaucracy have, from its very beginnings as an agency primarily concerned with keeping out Chinese and contract laborers, seen it as their mission to protect America from the harmful effects of immigrants and immigration.

No individual was more important in imprinting this attitude than McKinley's appointee, Terence V. Powderly, the second commissioner general of immigration who served from 1897 until 1902. Powderly, best known as the Grand Master Workman of the reformist Knights of Labor in its heyday, is the only person ever appointed as chief immigration bureaucrat who was a well-known figure before he was appointed (as a reward for his vigorous campaigning for McKinley during the 1896 campaign). Powderly was a persistent advocate of all kinds of immigration restriction, and although he repeatedly denied any form of prejudice toward European immigrants, time and again he stated his belief that British, German, and Scandinavian immigrants made the best Americans. (Note that in two generations, immigrant groups that once had been the chief targets of nativists were now generally seen as pillars of the republic. This shifting pattern of prejudice has been repeated to this day.) To be sure, Powderly often preceded or followed such statements by making positive remarks about some North Italians or some "Polanders."

Powderly's tenure set a precedent: all subsequent Republican presidents until Nixon appointed labor leaders as commissioners general of immigration or secretary of labor, or both. Unlike Powderly, most were time-serving hacks.

Thus, as the new century began in a time of relative prosperity, national policy still permitted white immigrants virtually unrestricted entry to the United States. The more significant changes were not new laws but administrative regulations promulgated by a growing immigration bureaucracy. These patterns continued with no major changes until 1917. In 1903 separate statutes transferred the Bureau of Immigration to the newly established Department of Commerce and for the first time enacted legislation regarding the political opinions of immigrants. In the wake of the assassination of President McKinley by an American-born individual with a foreign-sounding name, Congress excluded the entry of "anarchists, or persons who believe in, or advocate, the overthrow by force and violence of the government of the United States, or of all government, or of all forms of law, or the assassination of public officials." In 1906 Congress gave immigration officials responsibility for naturalization and changed the name of the bureaucracy to Bureau of Immigration and Naturalization, and, for the first time, made "knowledge of the English language" a requirement for naturalization.

Despite much pressure from groups and popular demand for legislation that would limit European immigration significantly, no such statute was passed until after World War I. In part as a way of justifying inaction, in 1907 Congress created the United States Immigration Commission, the first large-scale government investigation of the conditions of immigration and immigrant life. Sometimes called the Dillingham Commission (for its chair, Republican Senator William P. Dillingham of Vermont, 1843–1923), it produced a massive forty-one-volume report in 1911. Although the volumes are filled with valuable data that scholars use today, its political conclusions were all but preordained: there was too much immigration and much of it came from the "wrong places." Referring to immigrants from Southern and Eastern Europe, who were predominantly Catholics, Jews, and Greek Orthodox, the report claimed:

> The old immigration movement was essentially one of permanence. The new immigration is very largely one of individuals, a considerable proportion of whom apparently have no intention of permanently

changing their residence, their only purpose in coming to America being to temporarily take advantage of the greater wages paid for industrial labor in this country.

The commission recommended that American immigration policy take a new direction, and it proposed two general principles:

1. That some kind of numerical limit be placed on the previously unrestricted immigration from Europe and
2. That immigration from Northwestern Europe—principally from the British Isles, Germany, and Scandinavia—be favored.

Obviously such a policy discriminated against Italians, Poles, and Eastern European Jews. The 1911 report bore no immediate fruit. Dillingham did introduce a bill in 1913 to limit immigration by establishing national quotas, quotas that would set maximum but not minimum numbers. Although hearings were held, it was not acted upon in 1913. However, quotas became a major factor in the important immigration acts of 1921 and 1924, and thus the commission report helped to establish major parameters of American immigration policy for more than half a century, until the Immigration Act of 1965.

As noted previously, anti-immigration partisans, in Congress and out, continued to focus on the literacy test as a major means of curbing immigration. That object was achieved in the Immigration Act of 1917, which also created the barred zone/Asia-Pacific Triangle, expanded the grounds for exclusion on the grounds of mental health, and made deportation easier. By 1917, the outbreak of World War I in Europe had caused immigration to drop sharply. In the year immediately before the war began 1.2 million persons, more than four out of five of them Europeans, had entered the United States. The combined immigration of the next five years did not quite equal that number. The immediate postwar years (1919 and 1920) saw immigration rise to 430,000 and 805,000 (well below prewar numbers).

There seemed to be little rational need for a drastic change in immigration rules, but the postwar climate of opinion was hardly rational. Americans were shocked by the Bolshevik Revolution of 1917, disillusioned by the apparent failure of American war aims, worried about postwar unemployment, and alarmed by sensational stories about hordes of penniless Europeans, many of them dangerous radicals, lining up to come to America. Historians who have sampled the postwar climate of opinion have tended to overstate the actual impact of immigration by focussing on consular and newspaper reports rather than the actual immigration statistics. The postwar Red Scare, what Assistant Secretary of Labor Louis F. Post called the "deportation delirium of 1920," helped to create the preconditions for the broader restrictionist movement to come.

Before describing the critical congressional debates and actions between 1920 and 1924, it might be worthwhile to recapitulate the status of immigration law as of 1920. By that time the once free and unrestricted immigration policy of the United States had been limited, and eight categories of people were barred from immigrating: contract laborers, Asians (except for Japanese and Filipinos), criminals, persons who failed to meet certain moral standards, persons with various diseases, persons likely to become a public charge, certain radicals, and illiterate individuals.

Although there are no reliable public opinion polls for this era, there is every reason to believe that a majority of Americans felt that their country was letting in too many of the "wrong" kinds of people. It was not just the tiny minority of organized nativists who held this view. Organized labor had long supported immigration restriction, as had a whole variety of civic organizations and representatives of well-established immigrant groups. Conversely, many industrialists (but few of the much more numerous small businessmen) argued that immigration was necessary to provide them with labor or with labor that they could afford. The social stresses of what John Higham has dubbed the "tribal twenties" had the rift between "older stock" Americans and recent immigrants as one of its major fault lines.

The election of 1920, which swept away temporarily discredited Wilsonian internationalism and progressive reform in favor of Warren Harding's "normalcy," served as a stimulus for congressional action. The lame duck session of Congress (from December 1920 until Harding's inauguration in March) took speedy and rapid action. In the House, dominated by radical anti-immigration forces, precipitate action was taken. The House Committee on Immigration, chaired by Albert Johnson (1869–1957), a Republican who represented a largely rural district in western Washington, quickly proposed a two-year suspension of all immigration to give the lawmakers time to recast the immigration laws. Within one week the full House adopted the suspension idea overwhelmingly (296–42) but cut it to one year.

This extreme proposal found little sympathy in the Senate. Senator Dillingham dusted off and adapted his 1913 bill, which the Senate quickly substituted for the Johnson bill, also as a one-year emergency measure. Dillingham's measure, although clearly aimed at reducing immigration from eastern and southern Europe, did contain elements of fairness and equity. His bill would not affect the existing exceptions for Asians (the Chinese treaty merchants and the Japanese family members). There would be limits for Europeans, which would allow the migration of only 5 percent of the number of foreign-born from each country that had been listed in the 1910 census. This would have produced a maximum annual quota of 600,000 persons, although the assumption was that many of the quota spaces—some of those allocated to the British Isles, for example—would not be used.

Despite complaints from hard-core restrictionists that the bill was too generous, it passed the Senate easily. The House reluctantly accepted the quota principle but lowered the annual percentage to 3 percent, thus reducing the number of annual quota spaces to some 350,000. The Senate agreed to the House reduction, and the measure went to President Wilson just before he left office. Wilson killed it with a pocket veto, but only sixty days later the special session of the new Congress called by Harding passed it again. It was so uncontroversial that it went through the House without recorded vote and passed the Senate by 78–1. Harding signed it without demur: clearly his notion of "normalcy" did not extend to immigration. The 1921 act was an innovation: for the first time a numerical cap had been legislated.

The cap was variable rather than absolute, however; there were large numbers of exceptions, exceptions that most journalists and textbook writers have ignored. Aliens under the age of eighteen who were children of U.S. citizens were exempt from quota limitation, and other close relatives of citizens or resident aliens who had filed for citizenship papers received preference within the quotas. Intellectuals, artists, members of learned professions, and domestic servants received special status: if there were quota spaces, they used them, but if there were not they could enter anyway. Most important in terms of numbers of future immigrants, it exempted from numerical limitation persons who were natives of independent countries of the Western Hemisphere or had resided in one of those countries for at least one year preceding their application for entry. (These residence provisions were lengthened to five years in 1922.) They not only enabled Western Hemisphere natives (chiefly Canadians and Mexicans) to increase their share of immigration but also enabled a number of Europeans to get around the quotas.

It proved more difficult for Congress to agree on a permanent law, and the 1921 act (in theory a one-year act) had to be extended until 1924 when a "permanent" restrictive immigration law was passed. The 1921 act was relatively brief (five pages in the compilation of immigration statutes that I use), but the 1924 act was prolix (thirty-five pages in the same volume). The arguments over what became the 1924 law were long and bitter, and a summary of them is a good way to depict some of the forces and arguments used to defend and attack the role of immigration in American life in general and the 1924 law in particular.

The 1924 debate was never a matter of whether immigration should be restricted: that was a foregone conclusion. What was at issue was how immigration would be restricted. Five major questions were debated in the Congress:

1. What census should be used as the basis for the quotas, and how large should the quotas be?
2. Should the New World remain outside of the quota system?
3. To what degree should family members be exempted from quotas?
4. Should the special diplomatic arrangements for Chinese "treaty merchants" and Japanese "family members" be allowed to continue?
5. What kind of a permanent system should be established?

Both extreme and moderate restrictionists won some victories, but overall the extremists appeared to have the upper hand. Albert Johnson, the chair of the House immigration committee, led the extreme restrictionist forces; if anyone can be called the father of the 1924 act, it is he. Johnson was an anti-Semite who used consular reports, many of which were fed to him by the similarly minded Wilbur J. Carr (1870–1942), who headed the Consular Service from 1909 to 1937. Carr wrote Johnson that "the great mass of aliens passing through Rotterdam . . . are Russian Poles or Polish Jews of the usual ghetto type. . . . They are filthy, un-American, and often dangerous in their habits." Johnson used such "data" to argue that the country was in danger of being swamped by "abnormally twisted" and "unassimilable" Jews, "filthy, un-American and often dangerous in their habits." The most influential voice in the Senate for moderate restriction had been silenced by the death of Senator Dillingham in July 1923; in his absence Republican Senator David A. Reed of Pennsylvania (1860–1953), a proponent of more rigorous restriction, became the dominant voice in the upper chamber.

The most visible battle, that over the size and basis for the quotas, was won by Johnson and his supporters. Dillingham would have supported a continuation of the 3 percent using the 1920 census; but agreement was soon reached to reduce it to 2 percent. Few wanted to use the latest census, and although many did favor continuing to use the 1910 figures, Congress eventually went back to the census of 1890. The extreme restrictions were frank about their motives: too many eastern and southern Europeans would be let in if the earlier censuses were used. Johnson told the House that, if the 1920 census were used, there would be 42,000 Italian and 31,000 Polish quota slots annually but that going back to the 1890 census (before the heaviest increments of Italians and Poles) would admit only 4,000 of the former and 6,000 of the latter annually, a reduction of 86 percent. Going back to 2 percent of the 1890 census also lowered the total number of spaces from about 270,000 annual quota immigrants to some 160,000, a two-fifths reduction from the figures generated by 2 percent of 1910, and less than half of the 350,000 quota spaces available under the 1921 law.

The moderate restrictionists prevailed on the question of keeping Western Hemisphere immigration outside of the quota system. This was largely because many southwestern and western legislators, who were generally extreme restrictionists, insisted that the need of their region for Mexican agricultural workers was more important than restriction. The exemption for Western Hemisphere natives of independent countries remained the same, but for nonnatives exemption from quotas occurred only after ten years' residence.

The question of family members was treated similarly. Wives and unmarried children (under age eighteen) of U.S. citizens came in as nonquota immigrants, but husbands of U.S. citizens received only preference status in the quota. This principle of the priority of family reunification—ironically first established in the "treaty merchant" provision of the 1882 Chinese Exclusion Act—would become one of the pillars of American immigration law later in the century.

The 1921 act had exempted from the law "aliens from countries immigration from which is regulated in accordance with treaties and agreements relating solely to immigration." This convoluted language described Chinese "treaty merchants and their families and Japanese family members." As noted previously, the adoption of the provision barring immigration of "aliens ineligible to citizenship" abolished those privileged exemptions from what was called "Oriental exclusion."

Other important innovations in the 1924 act set up what is called a "consular control system," which required visas obtained abroad from a U.S. consulate before admission, even for Western Hemisphere immigrants. A visa cost nine dollars and the head tax was then eight dollars, so fees of at least seventeen dollars a head were required for entry. This was not a major deterrent for those paying for a transatlantic passage, but for border immigrants, particularly Mexicans, it was a major obstacle. In addition, many Mexicans were involved in going back and forth and the law stipulated a three dollar reentry permit for each subsequent border crossing. Many Mexican workers and their employers ignored the new regulations and continued to cross and recross informally: what had been legal was now illegal without paying fees that amounted to several days' wages.

Finally, the law called for a "scientific" study of the origins of the American people as of 1920 to serve as a base for a new "national origins system," which would govern immigration after 1 July 1929. The total number of quota spaces from then on was to be reduced to about 150,000. On the basis of that study, the President was to promulgate national quotas by Executive Order.

What did Congress mean by "national origin"? One section of the statute seems reasonably straightforward. "National origin" was to be determined by calculating "the number of inhabitants in continental United States in 1920 whose origin by birth or ancestry" is attributable to each nation. However, the next section (which I have never seen described) excludes from "inhabitants in the United States in 1920" the following: any immigrants from the New World and their descendants; any Asians or their descendants; the descendants of "slave immigrants"; and the descendants of "American aborigines." If anyone requires evidence that Congress regarded the United States as a "white man's country," this clause—subdivision "d" of Section 11 of the Immigration Act of 1924—provides it. Persons descended from Africans, Native Americans, and Asians were simply defined as not members of the American nation.

The study was executed by a committee of scholars under the auspices of the American Council of Learned Societies. These experts, including the father of immigration history, Marcus Lee Hansen, complied with the racist prescriptions of the Congress and clearly shared their general biases. They "calculated" somehow the precise ethnic origins of the American people. The result was closer to mysticism than social science. The expert guesstimate was that persons whose ancestors were here before the first census constituted 43.4 percent of the American people (ignoring blacks, Native Americans, and Asians) and that later immigrants and their descendants constituted the rest. The practical results of this were significant: it raised the quota for the United Kingdom from 34,007 to 65,721, and cut all but the smallest national quotas. The quota for the Irish Free State was lowered from 28,567 to 17,853; Germany, from 51,227 to 25,957; and those from Sweden, Norway, and Denmark from a combined 18,803 to 6,872. All of this was approved by the secretaries of state, commerce, and labor and proclaimed by Herbert C. Hoover in the first month of his presidency. In an accompanying statement he stated his opposition to national origins—Hoover knew enough statistics to know how shaky its empirical base was—but noted that he was "strongly in favor of restricted and selected immigration."

The Immigration Act of 1924, in essence, placed the assumptions of the Immigration Restriction League and other nativists onto the statute books of the United States. The law's chief author, Albert Johnson, celebrated the law's presumed effects in 1927:

> Today, instead of a well-knit homogenous citizenry, we have a body politic made up of all and every diverse element. Today, instead of a nation descended from generations of freemen bred to a knowledge of the principles and practice of self-government, of liberty under law, we have a heterogenous population no small proportion of which is sprung from races that, throughout the centuries, have known no liberty at all. . . . In other words, our capacity to maintain our cherished institutions stands diluted by a stream of alien blood, with all its inherited misconceptions respecting the relationships of the governing power to the governed. It is out of appreciation of this fundamental fact . . . that the American people have come to sanction—indeed demand—reform of our immigration laws. They have seen, patent and plain, the encroachments of the foreign-born flood upon their own lives. They have come to realize that such a flood, affecting as it does every individual of whatever race or origin, can not fail likewise to affect the institutions which have made and preserved American liberties. It is no wonder, therefore, that the myth of the melting pot has been discredited. . . . The United States is our land. . . . We intend to maintain it so. The day of indiscriminate acceptance of all races has definitely ended.

Whether or not Johnson's views (which would not have been out of place in Hitler's Germany) were also the views of the majority in America in the 1920s, it is reasonably clear that the larger goal he sought—significant curtailment of immigration—was approved by a majority of the American people. It is difficult to argue with the general proposition that in a frontierless, urbanized, and industrialized democracy, some kind of restriction of immigration was both necessary and desirable. What is unfortunate, it seems to me, was that it was done in a narrow and bigoted way.

DECREASING IMMIGRATION, SEVERE RESTRICTION (1924–43)

The 1924 act is a wonderful example of the aforementioned "law" of unintended consequences. The majority in Congress and in the press expected immigration to fall to the level of the quotas or below. A contemporary cartoon, which has been widely reprinted in history textbooks, showed the 1924 act as a funnel reducing immigration to a mere trickle. That was not the case. In the last prequota year (fiscal 1921), 805,000 immigrants entered. In the three years under the 1921 act, an average of 513,000 entered annually, and in the first six years under the 1924 act immigration from all sources averaged 294,000. This was a substantial reduction, but the 1,762,000 persons admitted were far from a mere trickle.

Table 1.3 provides a breakdown of immigration in the period 1 July 1924–30 June 1930, that is, just before the effects of the Great Depression began to be felt. Note the following:

1. Quota immigration provided only slightly more than half (51 percent) of all legal immigration, and
2. sizable New World and family immigration were numerically more important than most in Congress imagined. New World immigration had run at about 10 percent in the five years immediately preceding World War I. This migration was greatly increased during the war and under the quota acts. For the period shown in table 1.3, about 45 percent of all immigration came from the New World. More than 60 percent of New World immigration came from Canada, and more than 30 percent from Mexico.

Not shown in table 1.3 is the ethnic distribution of European immigrants. Johnson told Congress that Polish and Italian immigration would be cut to 6,000 and 4,000, respectively, but members of these groups quickly learned how to use the law to their advantage. In 1930, for example, 9,000 Poles and 22,000 Italians immigrated to the United States, more than triple the number allowed under the quota. The two largest European groups were from the British Isles and Germany: nearly 50,000 a year came from the first and about 45,000 from the second, so the two groups amounted to 62 percent of quota immigration as opposed to 13 percent of European immigration in the decade 1901–10.

The truly drastic reduction in immigration was caused by the Great Depression of the 1930s. Many authorities, including the usually accurate *Harvard Encyclopedia of American Ethnic Groups,* report that more persons left the United States than entered it in the 1930s, but that is not the case. There was negative immigration in the four-year period 1 July 1931–30 June 1935, but for the entire decade recorded entries (528,431) exceeded recorded departures (459,738) by almost 69,000.

Under the impact of the depression, Herbert Hoover, who had come into office on a platform hailing immigration restriction but suggesting the need for some relaxing "modification," soon called for even stricter control, and by 1932 he was campaigning for "rigidly restricted immigration." In his December 1930 annual message he insisted that "under conditions of current unemployment" immigration ought to be made "more limited and more selective." No significant change in immigration law was enacted in Hoover's administration, but the Quaker president ordered immigration officials to reinterpret the "LPC clause" in such a way as to exclude all but the apparently affluent. As noted previously it had originally been used only to keep out those who were so aged, infirm, or otherwise handicapped that they seemed unlikely to be able to support themselves.

Actually, the innovative application of the LPC clause to Mexicans had originated in the last months of the Coolidge administration during a period of prosperity. The Hoover administration not only used the clause more systematically and to greater effect, but it also applied the new interpretation to prospective immigrants from Europe, a policy that would later have murderous consequences for many attempting to flee Nazi Germany. The real innovation of the Hoover administration was a program of supposedly voluntary "repatriation" of Mexican Americans, some of whom were native-born American citizens. Working in cooperation with state and local governments and some corporations, and with the acquiescence of the Mexican government, perhaps as many as 500,000 were sent to Mexico, many of them on special trains hired for that purpose. Most were from California, but some came from as far north as Gary, Indiana.

Although Hoover's successor, Franklin D. Roosevelt, was an innovator who changed almost every aspect of government policy, there was nothing even approaching a New Deal for immigration. No major immigration legislation was enacted during the New Deal. Although FDR's tone was quite different from Hoover's—it is impossible even to imagine the Iowa engineer telling the Daughters of the American Revolution to "remember, remember always that all of us, and you and I especially, are descended from immigrants and revolutionaries"—immigration policy was largely the same. The New Deal did treat resident aliens more generously. The informal repatriation policy was abandoned and formal deportations, which had risen steadily in the Republican era from 2,762 in fiscal 1920 to 19,865 in 1933, dropped below 9,000 in 1934 and stayed at that level throughout the 1930s. New Deal relief regulations insisted on the eligibility of resident aliens (and of persons of color), but local control of hiring meant that these groups were generally discriminated against. The great failure of Roosevelt's immigration policy was its inability to meet the challenge of the refugee crisis created by the rise of Adolf Hitler.

Before that issue became paramount the Roosevelt administration dealt effectively with the problem of the immigration of Filipinos, who, as "American nationals," could not be kept out. In 1932 Congress passed a Philippines independence bill, which barred Filipino immigrants as "aliens ineligible for citizenship" after independence; Hoover, a foe of independence, vetoed the bill during his last weeks in office but iterated his belief that "immigration [of Filipinos] should be restricted at once." The Roosevelt administration solved the problem in 1934 with the Tydings–McDuffie Act, which promised the Philippines independence in 1945 but immediately reduced Filipino immigration by a clause exempting Filipinos from "the aliens ineligible to citizenship clause of the 1924 act" and granting them a quota of fifty slots annually, although previously the smallest quota had been a hundred. This is the first example of a colonial power banning immigration by its former subjects, a policy that would be adopted by European colonial powers in the 1950s.

While New Deal immigration policy was largely a continuation of existing policy, the refugee question was a new issue. Much of the writing about the Roosevelt administration's now notorious relative inaction is written through the prism of the Holocaust, and, all too often, it is written with an assumption that the Holocaust was implicit in everything that happened after Hitler came to power at the end of January 1933. The historiography of the American reactions to what we now know as the Holocaust is broad and diverse. Judgments range from William Rubinstein's fatuous notion that "no Jew who perished during the Nazi Holocaust could have been saved by any action which the Allies could have taken" to Arthur Morse's phrase "while six million died," which created the equally false notion that the United States, merely by changing its immigration policies, could have saved all or most of the Jews of Europe, a palpable impossibility. By the time that Americans learned about what Walter Lacquer has called the "terrible secret" of the Holocaust, the fate of most of the Jews of Europe was sealed, but, to be sure, even at that late date more could have been done. If one wishes to make a judgment, it is hard to improve on the one made in 1979 by Vice President Walter F. Mondale: the United States and the other nations of asylum simply "failed the test of civilization."

Although refugees had come to the American colonies and the United States since the seventeenth century—the first group were Jews who fled from Portugal's conquest of the short-lived Dutch colony in Brazil—the 1924 immigration act had no category for refugees so any who wished to come had two American barriers to cross: they had to convince American consular officials that they were not "likely to become a public charge," and they had to find space within the cramped quota system. The latter was, until the Kristallnacht pogroms of November 1938 throughout Germany, not difficult. The generous German quota was undersubscribed during most of the 1930s. From 1 July 1932 through 30 June 1938, there were a total of 157,155 German quota spaces; only 45,952 were used. Getting a visa was another matter. The attitudes of American consular officials varied greatly: Raymond Geist, in Berlin, actually went into concentration camps in 1938 and 1939 to get visa holders out, while his colleague, John G. Erhardt, in Hamburg, seemed to do everything possible to grant as few visas to refugees as possible.

Franklin Roosevelt, who could have insisted on a change of policy, was largely passive. He was sympathetic to the plight of refugees from Germany but unwilling to risk his prestige by public actions. Two examples, both from the last months of peace, will suffice. In early 1939 the Wagner-Rogers bill proposed to bring 20,000 German children to the United States outside of the by then oversubscribed German quota, but it never even came up for a vote in either house. It had a great deal of support from prominent Americans (including Herbert Hoover) but was opposed by a sizable majority of Americans, according to the public opinion polls. We do not know what would have happened had the White House tried to lead public opinion and put pressure on reluctant Democrats. FDR was willing to allow Secretary of Labor Frances Perkins and Children's Bureau Chief Katherine Lenroot to testify in its favor. Other officials, such as Secretary of State Hull, took no stand but informed Congress about all the administrative difficulties the proposed law would create. Roosevelt even told his wife, in February 1939, that "it is all right for you to support the child refugee bill, but it is best for me to say nothing [now]." Now became never as he never said anything for the record. In June, as the bill was dying, the president annotated a memo asking for his support "File No Action, FDR." In addition, some of his personal and official family viciously opposed the bill: one of his favorite cousins, Laura Delano, wife of Commissioner of Immigration and Naturalization James Houghteling, told people at cocktail parties that the "20,000 charming children would all too soon grow up into 20,000 ugly adults."

In May 1939 the most flagrant example of American rejection of refugees occurred. The *St. Louis* was a Hamburg-Amerika line vessel bringing 933 passengers, most of them Jewish refugees, to Havana. Many of the refugees were on the American quota list but held numbers that had not yet come up. They and others came to Western Hemisphere ports to wait their turn. There were already some 2,500 refugees in Havana. A total of 743 of the passengers had applied for visas and had the necessary affidavits of support. For reasons that are not entirely clear, the Cuban government refused to let the refugees land. The *St. Louis* hoped to land those with visa applications in the United States, but the vessel was refused permission to dock. For a time it was so close to Miami Beach that the passengers could hear dance music being played at its luxury hotels. That was as close as the refugees on board came to what they regarded, mistakenly, as their promised land. The Treasury Department even assigned a Coast Guard cutter to shadow the *St. Louis* to make sure that no one tried to swim ashore. There being no New World port open to its passengers, the liner was forced to take them back to Europe. Some European governmental hearts were a little softer and Great Britain, France, Belgium, and the Netherlands each agreed to take about a fourth of the passengers. Some of the ship's refugee passengers survived to observe the fiftieth anniversary of their ordeal at a reunion in Miami, but others perished when their havens were overrun by German armies.

On the other hand, FDR made a number of nonpublic directives that greatly enhanced the ability of refugees who had arrived in the United States on tourist and other temporary visas to remain. In 1938, for example, he "suggested" to Frances Perkins that such visas be automatically renewed every six months. This enabled about 15,000 persons to remain in the United States. In a note to the 1938 volume of his *Public Papers,* written in late 1939, Roosevelt wrote an extended apologia for his relative inaction that seems to be evidence of a guilty conscience. In it he claimed that the United States had always been a "haven of refuge." Few passengers of the *St. Louis* or unsuccessful Jewish visa seekers in Germany would have agreed, and many of those who were turned away were murdered in the Holocaust.

Yet the record of the United States is not totally negative. It is important to note that perhaps 150,000 refugees, the overwhelming majority of them Jews, did manage to reach the United States before Pearl Harbor. Possibly another 100,000 came during and after the war, both as displaced persons and as immigrants from other nations of refuge. This quarter million was several times more than were admitted by any other nation, but many more could have been saved by a more resolute policy.

INCREASING IMMIGRATION, DECREASING RESTRICTION (1943–65)

THE WAR YEARS (1943–45)

It is now apparent that World War II marked a positive turning point in American immigration policy, because questions of ideology and international politics began to supersede questions of race, ethnicity, and narrow nationalism. There was no general change in either immigration law or policy, but specific wartime alterations in favor of three groups— refugees, Mexicans, and, above all, Chinese—do in fact represent change and are harbingers of further change.

The immediate effects of the war were largely negative, however. In June 1940 as Hitler's blitzkrieg was overrunning France amidst largely mythical stories about subversive "fifth column" activities, Roosevelt transferred the Immigration and Naturalization Service (INS) from the Department of Labor to the Department of Justice, from a department whose functions (at least under Secretary Perkins) were largely protective to one whose efforts were essentially prosecutorial. Later that month Congress passed and Roosevelt signed the Alien Registration Act, which required all aliens to register, be fingerprinted, and keep the government informed of their address. They were required to have, but not to carry, what amounted to an internal passport. Other parts of the act made deportation easier and created a peacetime sedition act, often referred to as the Smith Act, which was the statute under which officials of the American Communist Party were sent to jail in the 1950s. Four months later there was a major revision of nationality laws. A 1924 revision had made all Native Americans born in the United States, including those born on reservations, citizens. In 1940 the privilege of naturalization was extended to include "descendants of races indigenous to the Western Hemisphere" who had sometimes been barred as "non-white." Other provisions barred "persons opposed to government or law" from naturalization.

But the fall of France also spurred Roosevelt to take a small but positive secret step to rescue refugees. He instructed his Advisory Committee on Refugees to make lists of eminent refugees who were in Vichy, France or Iberia and then ordered the State Department to issue temporary visas in their names. The Department's records indicate that nearly 3,300 such visas were issued but that only about a third of them were used. To get as many of the visas as possible into the hands of refugees, the Advisory Committee sent an improbable secret agent to Marseilles, a thirty-two-year-old classicist named Varian Fry who had been an editor for the Foreign Policy Association in New York. Among the thousand plus thus rescued were such cultural superstars as Lion Feuchtwanger, Heinrich Mann, Franz Werfel, Anna Mahler Werfel, Marc Chagall, Jacques Lipchitz, Marcel Duchamp, and Wanda Landowska.

Two other unpublicized bureaucratic measures in late 1940 and early 1941 helped refugees. American consuls outside of Germany were allowed to issue visas chargeable to the German quota to refugees who had gotten to places like Portugal, French Africa, and China, and an agreement with Canada allowed refugees in the United States on temporary visas to make a pro forma entry into Canada so that they could seem to be applying for a permanent visa from there and then recross the border. This charade was necessary because American law forbade a visitor from changing status without leaving the United States.

No further significant action was taken until January 1944 when Roosevelt's closest friend in the cabinet, Treasury Secretary Henry Morgenthau, gave the president a report prepared by his staff: "Report to the Secretary on the Acquiescence of this Government in the Murder of the Jews." From its blunt first sentence ("One of the greatest crimes in history, the slaughter of the Jewish people in Europe, is continuing unabated") to the end it was a damning indictment of American policy in general and of the State Department in particular. Just six days later FDR issued an executive order to set up the War Refugee Board (WRB), whose bills were paid by a combination of the President's discretionary funds and money donated by Jewish organizations. The language of the executive order claimed the following:

> it is the policy of this Government to take all measures within its power to rescue the victims of enemy oppression who are in imminent danger of death and otherwise to afford such victims all possible relief and assistance consistent with the successful prosecution of the war.

In fact, however, the truth of the situation had been and continued to be otherwise. The WRB, with the exception noted below, was not authorized to bring refugees into the United States, although together with the U.S.-financed United Nations Relief and Rehabilitation Administration (1943–49) it did much to keep refugees and survivors of the Holocaust alive in camps in Europe, North Africa, and the Middle East.

The one exception occurred in June 1944 when Roosevelt, by executive order, ordered almost 1,000 refugees "paroled" into the United States and then informed Congress of what he had done. The refugees, mostly of Yugoslav and Polish nationality and almost all Jews, came from camps in Italy and were kept in a facility at Fort Oswego, New York, run by the War Relocation Authority, whose chief mission was to warehouse incarcerated Japanese Americans. The refugees were supposed to return to their native lands after the war, but almost all remained in the United States. Sharon Lowenstein, the historian of this episode, has rightly styled it a "token shipment." It is an example of the kind of effort which, applied earlier, might have saved more had Roosevelt been willing to risk congressional and popular displeasure. However it had more than a token impact on immigration policy: later presidents would use presidential parole authority to enable hundreds of thousands of other refugees to come to America.

As had been true during World War I, labor shortages on the American home front caused the government to take steps to bring what it supposed was temporary labor to the United States. Chief of these during

World War II were Mexicans, although a significant number of Caribbean people (particularly Jamaicans and Bahamians) were imported as well. Congress passed a series of laws, beginning with a 1943 law to import "temporary agricultural workers" and a 1944 law importing workers for industries and services essential to the war effort, and which lasted, with minor interruptions, until 1964. What is usually called the Bracero Program—from the Spanish *bracer,* meaning "arm," and thus a person who does manual labor—eventually brought hundreds of thousands of Mexicans and smaller numbers of other New World laborers to work in the United States. The peak year was 1959 when 450,000 Mexican workers entered. During this twenty-one-year period both workers and employers developed a symbiotic relationship that continued, without sanction of law, after 1964. The braceros were supposed to return to Mexico, and most did, but larger and larger numbers remained in the United States and others continued to come in a pattern that specialists describe as "circular migration": large numbers of Mexican workers continued to live in Mexico but returned, often annually, to the United States to work for extended periods, most usually a growing season. At the same time, legal immigration from Mexico, which had dropped to a trickle in the 1930s, began to grow again, as table 1.5 indicates.

The fluctuations in legal immigration from Mexico, as well as that of imported "temporary workers" not included in table 1.5, have been in response to changes in American immigration policy as well as to conditions in Mexico. The growth in the 1910s was due both to the Mexican Revolution and to World War I labor shortages, whereas that in the 1920s

Table 1.5
MEXICAN LEGAL IMMIGRATION TO THE U.S., 1901–70
(DOES NOT INCLUDE BRACEROS)

Years	Number
1901–10	49,642
1911–20	219,004
1921–30	459,287
1931–40	22,319
1941–50	60,589
1951–60	299,811
1961–70	453,937

Source: 1996 Statistical Yearbook of the Immigration and Naturalization Service (Washington, DC: Government Printing Office, 1997), Table 2, p. 27.

was largely a response to the "niches" in the U.S. labor market made available by the limitation of European immigration. The decline in the 1930s was because of a different enforcement of the immigration laws as well as a reaction to the forced repatriation program; the wartime and postwar surge was largely a response to the effects of the Bracero Program on both sides of the border.

Although unrecognized at the time, the real turning point in American immigration policy came in 1943 with the repeal of the fifteen separate statutes that had affected Chinese exclusion. FDR persuaded Congress to do this not because of the rights of the 80,000 Chinese Americans, about half of whom were aliens ineligible to citizenship, but as a kind of merit badge for the heroism of a wartime ally. The act, which passed easily, but without recorded vote, gave China an annual quota of 105 and made Chinese, but no other Asians, eligible for naturalization. Roosevelt's message to Congress urging passage stressed that "China is our ally" and tried to allay nativist fears by noting the small size of the annual quota and insisting that "there can be no reasonable apprehension that any such number of immigrants will cause unemployment or provide competition in the search for jobs."

There was, of course, much apprehension in nativist ranks. As John B. Trevor, one of the lobbyists who had worked for the 1924 act, put it in a private letter:

> This movement [to repeal the Chinese Exclusion Laws] is obviously a prelude to undoing the work of twenty years of immigration restrictions. It places in grave peril the provisions of the Act of 1924, which exclude persons ineligible for citizenship.

The nativist was a better prophet than the president. In 1946 a new law gave immigration and naturalization privileges to Filipinos and "natives of India," and, in 1952, as will be shown, all purely racial bars to immigration and naturalization were dropped although numerical limitations continued to discriminate. In 1946 Congress also enacted a law making Chinese wives of American citizens eligible to enter the United States on a nonquota basis, a provision that Congress had considered but rejected in repealing exclusion. In the six years after passage of the 1946 act, nearly 10,000 Chinese women, most of them in their childbearing years, came as nonquota immigrants to join husbands. This had a major demographic impact on the small Chinese American community, which had, in 1940, only 20,000 females of all ages. Similar impacts would be made by nonquota female immigrants from other parts of Asia once their eligibility for citizenship had been established. It is both ironic and fitting that, just as Chinese Exclusion Act of 1882 had been the hinge on which the golden door had begun to close, its repeal in 1943 marks the beginning of an opening swing of that same door.

THE POSTWAR YEARS: CONSCIENCE IMMIGRATION (1945–52)

The awareness of at least a fraction of the true horror of the Holocaust began to impinge on the consciousness of most Americans only in the spring of 1945 when the ghastly newsreel and still pictures of the liberated concentration camps began to appear in American theaters and newspapers. It was, in the final analysis, this impact which caused the United States, however belatedly, to institute a real legislative refugee program in 1948.

At the end of World War II the United States and its allies found that in their part of liberated Europe (as opposed to that part liberated by the Soviet Union) there were some 8 million refugees, now called "displaced persons." Perhaps 7 million of these were, fairly rapidly, repatriated to their former homelands. As the winter of 1945–46 began there were still about a million left in camps plus growing numbers of ethnic Germans expelled from Czechoslovakia, Poland, and other parts of Eastern Europe plus a growing number of refugees from Soviet occupied lands. Only a minor fraction of these were Jewish survivors of the Nazi Holocaust, and most of these wished to go to Palestine (Israel after 1948), not America.

FDR's successor, Harry Truman, expressed verbal sympathy for the plight of the refugees but initially offered nothing outside of the quota system. He first proposed allocating half of all existing quotas for displaced persons and estimated that 40,000 refugees could come in annually. In the first nine months of 1946, however, only some 5,000 were able to do so. Just before the November elections Truman began to talk about the possibility of bringing in refugees outside of the quota system, and in his January 1947 State of the Union message he urged Congress to find ways in which the United States could fulfill its "responsibilities to these homeless and suffering refugees of all faiths." This is the first presidential statement of an American responsibility for foreign refugees. Truman's proposal set off a three-year legislative struggle. In early 1947 an Illinois Republican,

William G. Stratton (b. 1914), introduced a bipartisan bill calling for the admission of 100,000 refugees over and above the quota for each of the subsequent four years. A year and a half later—just before the nominating conventions—Congress passed and Truman signed the Displaced Persons Act of 1948, the first piece of legislation that established refugee policy as opposed to immigration policy.

The law called for the admission of 250,000 displaced persons over the next two years. It pretended to maintain the quota system by the legal fiction of quota mortgaging: that is, most of the displaced persons admitted were charged to some quota and slots were borrowed from future years. By 1952, to cite an admittedly extreme case, the tiny Latvian quota had been mortgaged up to the year 2274. Predictably, as the act was expiring, in 1950, the same forces that passed it managed to get it extended for two more years, and the authorized total was raised to 415,000.

All told, slightly fewer than 400,000 displaced persons were actually admitted to the United States under the two statutes by the time that they expired on 30 June 1952. However, because of the increasing Cold War orientation of American government and society, a minority of those actually admitted were Hitler's victims. A larger number, perhaps a majority of all admitted, were members of groups that had supported or benefited from the Third Reich: ethnic Germans and former residents of the Baltic states who had fled to West Germany. The leading scholar of displaced persons in America, Leonard Dinnerstein, has calculated that nearly 140,000 Jews were admitted to the United States between the end of the war in Europe in May 1945 and the end of 1952. This works out to fewer than 20,000 persons per year. To put this number into perspective, total legal immigration in that period totaled 1.3 million, or about 200,000 per year, and births in the United States totaled between 3.4 and 3.9 million annually.

COLD WAR IMMIGRATION (1952–65)

Although Cold War concerns partially shaped the displaced persons legislation of 1948 and 1950, it was the Immigration Act of 1952, often called the McCarran–Walter Act, that put the stamp of the Cold War firmly on American immigration policy. Its "liberal" elements can be explained by understanding that, as a rule, immigration policy is a subset of foreign policy. In an era in which "isolation" was espoused, a policy that excluded much of the world's population seemed appropriate. In the Cold War era in which the United States aspired to be "the leader of the free world," however, a policy that blatantly excluded Asians was clearly inappropriate. The law's Cold War origins are especially clear in the severe ideological criteria applied to keep out not only members or former members of the various communist parties as immigrants, but also prevented many left-leaning intellectuals from even visiting the United States. For example, the important postwar French philosopher-playwright, Jean Paul Sartre (1905–80), was kept out, although his plays were performed widely.

The 1952 law, the first general revision of immigration law since 1924, was a bitterly divisive measure eventually passed over Harry Truman's veto. Although it was a conservative measure essentially continuing the national origins system, and still using the 1920 census as a base line, it had a number of innovations that Truman approved of despite his veto. The chief of these were as follows:

1. All racial bars to immigration and naturalization were removed;
2. family unification was expanded so that wives as well as husbands could bring in alien spouses: citizens could bring in spouses and certain other family members as nonquota immigrants without numerical limitation, whereas resident aliens gained privileged status under the quotas for such persons; and
3. the law recognized the parole power first used by Roosevelt for the "token shipment" of refugees in 1944 and made it a basic element of refugee policy (although the word "refugee" does not appear in the statute).

Truman's chief objection to the law was what he called the "greatest vice of the quota system," the continuation of most of the biases that were fundamental to the 1924 act: "it discriminates, deliberately and intentionally, against many of the peoples of the world. The purpose behind it was to cut down and virtually eliminate immigration to the country from Southern and Eastern Europe."

The message and the subsequent report of Truman's Commission on Immigration and Naturalization opened up a thirteen-year debate on the nature of American immigration policy, a debate that was capped by the passage of the Immigration Act of 1965, which is still the basic immigration law of the land. The commission's report, issued just before Truman left office in 1953, echoed many of the points made in the 1952 veto message. Its chief recommendations were as follows:

1. Abolition of the national origins system;
2. adoption of a unified quota system allocating visas, without regard to national origin, race, creed or color according to five principles: the right of asylum, reunion of families, needs in the United States, needs in the "Free World," and general immigration;
3. allocation, for three years, of 100,000 visas annually to refugees, including remaining displaced persons;
4. total amount of annual immigration to be based on one-sixth of 1 percent of the 1950 U.S. population instead of the same fraction of the 1920 population, as the 1952 act did. This would result in a base annual quota number of 251,162 as opposed to 154,657 under the 1952 act.

The 1952 law's coauthor, Nevada Democratic Senator Pat McCarran (1876–1954), attacked the commission's report as communist inspired, and insisted, falsely, that "the rock of truth is that the Act does not contain one iota of racial or religious discrimination." To buttress his claim he cited a number of groups associated with more recent immigration, including the National Catholic Welfare Council and the Japanese American Citizens League, which supported his law.

What neither the defenders nor the attackers understood was how the act would work, and it was yet another example of a law having unintended consequences. The seeming numerical cap was chimerical. In the years for which the law was in effect (1953–65), quota immigration accounted for only a minor fraction of those legally admitted. Of the nearly 3.5 million immigrants admitted in those years, just over a third were quota immigrants. As a writer in the *Annals* pointed out in 1966, it had been a matter of the tail "wagging the dog" insofar as the national origins system was concerned. Whereas much of the extra immigration came from Cold War refugees, many immigrants, Asians in particular, were able to use the 1952 law to their advantage in ways not imagined by its authors.

Japanese were, for a time, the prime Asian beneficiaries. Casual readers of the law, noting that Japan's quota was 185 per year, might assume that at most, a couple of thousand Japanese a decade might come to America. However, between 1952 and 1964 some 63,000 came, nearly 5,000 a year. Almost all were nonquota immigrants, spouses and other relatives of U.S. citizens. Thus, although many in Congress insisted on maintaining the quota system, it was more like a sieve that a real barrier (although to be sure, any restrictive system will keep some immigrants out).

In addition to the obvious loopholes in the 1952 act, both Congress and the executive continued to make large exceptions. In August 1953, a little over a year after the Displaced Persons Act expired, Congress passed the Refugee Act of 1953, which authorized the admission of 214,000 refugees in the subsequent two and a half years. Its Cold War orientation can be seen by comparing its beneficiaries with those of the displaced persons acts. The 1948–50 acts spoke of "refugees" and "displaced persons"; the 1953 act used the terms "escapee" for someone fleeing from communism and "German expellee" for ethnic Germans from anywhere in Eastern Europe. The 1953 act, for the first time, included Asians as potential beneficiaries: 2,000 spaces were allocated for Chinese and 3,000 for other "Far Eastern" refugees. A 1956 law expanded the eligible "refugees-escapees" to the "general area of the Middle East," which congressional geography defined as stretching from Libya to Pakistan and including Ethiopia.

In 1956 the first large-scale use was made of parole authority as the Eisenhower administration began accepting refugees from the attempted Hungarian revolution against Soviet domination: eventually almost 40,000 were admitted. Later large-scale parole authority was exercised for Cubans beginning in 1961, and later for Tibetans, Vietnamese, and other Southeast Asians. By 1962 refugee programs had become truly global. Between 1945 and 1980, as table 1.6 shows, more than 2,250,000 persons were admitted to the United States as refugees, nearly 20 percent of the total immigration of those years.

HIGH IMMIGRATION, LOW RESTRICTION (1965–80)

The dramatic shift in style from Eisenhower to Kennedy (Abbie Hoffman characterized it as "like spring after winter") changed the rhetoric about immigration policy, but not much else. Although candidate Kennedy had written or signed a publication praising immigration, and both Republican and Democratic platforms in 1960 had pro-immigration planks, nothing of substance occurred until after the election of Lyndon Johnson in 1964. The immigration committees in both the House and Senate were firmly in the hands of reactionary restrictionist Democrats—Frances E. Walter (1894–1963) of Pennsylvania in the House and James Eastland (1904–86) of Mississippi in the Senate—and all attempts at reform, in-

Table 1.6
REFUGEES ADMITTED, 1945–80

Years	Category	Number
	Admitted Under Special Statute or Parole Authority	
1948–52	Displaced Persons	ca. 450,000
1953–56	Refugee Relief Act	ca. 205,000
1956	East European orphans	925
1956–57	Hungarians	38,045
1958–62	Portuguese (Azorean earthquake victims)	4,811
1960–65	East Europeans (Fair Share Refugee Law)	19,745
1962	Chinese from Hong Kong and Macao	14,741
1962–79	Cubans	692,219
1963	Russian Old Believers from Turkey	200
1972–73	Ugandan Asians	1,500
1973–79	USSR	35,758
1975–79	"Indochinese" (10 programs)	ca. 400,000
1975–77	Chileans	1,400
1976–77	Chileans, Bolivians, Uruguayans	343
1978–79	Lebanese	1,000
1979	Cuban prisoners	15,000
1980	Refugees, all sources	110,000
	Admitted under 1965 Immigration Act	
1968–80	Cold war refugees	ca. 130,000
	Admitted without Authority	
1980	Cuban and Haitian "special entrants" (boat people)	140,000
Total		about 2,261,564[a]

Soure: My structuring of INS data, from *Statistical Abstract of the United States, 19XX,* and *Statistical Yearbook of the Immigration and Naturalization Service, 1997.*
[a]Total legal immigration for the period 1945–80 was 10,943,48, so these refugees were about a fifth of all immigrants (20.7 percent). To be sure, many additional persons who were actually refugees were admitted under other categories, for example, as family members.

cluding a complex proposal for a full revision of immigration policy from the Kennedy administration in July 1963, were stalemated.

Kennedy's assassination and the accession of Lyndon Johnson to the presidency seemed to cast a shadow on immigration reform; Johnson, unlike Kennedy, had voted to override Truman's 1952 veto of the McCarran–Walter Act. However, as Robert Dallek has shown, before and during World War II Congressman Lyndon Johnson had been instrumental, behind the scenes, in helping "hundreds" of European Jews get into the United States. Johnson made it clear in his initial State of the Union address in 1964 that he supported immigration reform, and the immigration plank in the 1964 Democratic platform was similar to the 1960 version. The GOP, conversely, receded from its 1960 stand and merely backed family reunification and a continuation of refugee policy. Despite these differences, immigration was not a significant campaign issue in 1964.

Early the next year Democratic Representative Michael A. Feighan of Ohio (1905–92), chairman of the key House subcommittee and long an opponent of immigration reform, succumbed to the potent combination of cajolery, favors, and threats that became known as the "Johnson treatment" and suddenly supported immigration reform. On the Senate side, James O. Eastland of Mississippi, the Democratic chair of the governing Senate committee and one of two members on the sixteen-person committee who opposed immigration reform, stepped aside and let fellow Democrat Edward Kennedy of Massachusetts (b. 1932) manage the Senate version of the bill.

The substance of the ensuing congressional debate was little different from that which had prevailed since early in the century, although the once naked prejudice of some adherents of restriction was muted. Nativist congressmen such as Albert Johnson, the father of the 1924 act, had openly espoused ethnic discrimination, but by 1965, in the midst of the Civil Rights Era, naked intolerance was out of fashion and most adherents of the status quo insisted that they were not prejudiced. In the Senate, for example, Sam Ervin, a Democrat from North Carolina (1896–1985), consistently opposed civil rights legislation on "constitutional" grounds and claimed that the existing McCarran–Walter Act was

> like a mirror reflecting the United States, allowing the admission of immigrants according to a national and uniform mathematical formula recognizing the obvious and natural fact that those immigrants can best be assimilated into our society who have relatives, friends, or others of similar background already here.

What opponents of change like Ervin never admitted was that the mirror was not at all an accurate reflection of the American people in the 1960s, but of that mythical "National Origins" population created by bigoted politicians and biased scholars in the 1920s.

The debates over what became the 1965 act were not over whether to change the law—change was a given—but over how and to what degree the old system would be revamped. A whole spectrum of proposals were considered, including a no-hoper by Democratic Senator Allen J. Ellender of Louisiana (1890–1972) for a five-year suspension of all immigration. The focus here will be on what became law. One old argument was settled in a new way: a cap was placed on Western Hemisphere immigrants, but because roughly half of the total number of slots were reserved for them, this was a liberalization rather than the restriction that it would have been in 1924.

The major provisions of the new system of immigration restriction (which in many ways resembled its predecessors, particularly the 1924 and 1952 acts) were as follows:

1. The new law abolished the quota system for individual nations and substituted for it hemispheric limits on visas issued. Originally there were to be 170,000 visas for the Eastern Hemisphere and 120,000 visas for the Western Hemisphere, with a cap of 20,000 visas per nation in the Eastern Hemisphere only. (A 1976 statute abandoned the hemispheric limits and applied the 20,000 visa per nation cap everywhere.)
2. This seemed to set up a 290,000 per year limit on visas with a preference system similar to that adopted in 1952. However, as had been the case during the life of the McCarran-Walter Act, there were parallel systems. The first, which went back to 1924, admitted certain close relatives of Americans without numerical limitation. The second system added refugees of all kinds, and set aside for them what turned out to be, as table 1.6 demonstrates, an utterly inadequate 6 percent of the preference visas (17,400 annually).
3. The 1965 law abandoned the "Asia-Pacific triangle" concept but retained almost all of the specific restrictions that Congress had been adding since the 1880s, including, most significantly, the LPC clause, requirements for physical and mental health, and various ideological and moral tests.

Table 1.7 makes specific comparisons between the 1952 and 1965 acts. The clearest difference between the two preference systems is the increased emphasis on family reunification. The 1965 act added parents of U.S. citizens to the "admitted without numerical restriction" category and allocated 74 percent of preference visas to family members, as opposed to 50 percent in the 1952 act.

Table 1.7
PREFERENCE SYSTEMS: 1952 AND 1965 IMMIGRATION ACTS

Preference	%
Immigration and Nationality Act, 1952[a]	
1. Highly skilled immigrants whose services are urgently needed in the U.S. and their spouses and children	50
2. Parents of U.S. citizens over age 21 and unmarried adult children of U.S. citizens	30
3. Spouses and unmarried adult children of permanent resident aliens	20
4. Any visas not allocated above distributed as follows:	
a. Brothers, sisters, and married children of U.S. citizens and accompanying spouses and children	50
b. Nonpreference applicants	Any remaining visas
Immigration Act of 1965[b]	
1. Unmarried adult children of U.S. citizens	20
2. Spouses and unmarried adult children of permanent resident aliens	20
3. Members of the professions and scientists and artists of exceptional ability[c]	10
4. Married children of U.S. citizens	10
5. Brothers and sisters of U.S. citizens over age 21	24
6. Skilled and unskilled workers in occupations for which labor is in short supply[c]	10
7. Refugees from communist or communist-dominated countries, or the Middle East	6
8. Nonpreference	any remaining visas[d]

[a]Spouses and unmarried minor children of U.S. citizens are exempt from preference requirements and numerical quotas.
[b]Spouses, unmarried minor children, and parents of U.S. citizens are exempt from preference and numerical requirements.
[c]Requires U.S. Department of Labor certification.
[d]Because there have been more preference applicants than can be accommodated, this provision has never been used].

The bill was signed in a telegenic ceremony at the foot of the Statue of Liberty in New York Harbor. In signing it Lyndon Johnson observed: "This bill that we sign today is not a revolutionary bill. It does not affect the lives of millions. It will not reshape the structure of our daily lives, or really add importantly to our wealth or our power." Although this statement seems like uncharacteristic modesty, it was not. It was what LBJ's experts had told him, and he would have been startled had it been revealed to him that later historians would declare that the Immigration Act, **along** with the Voting Rights Act and Medicare, marked the high watermark of late twentieth century American liberalism. LBJ did not even mention it in his memoirs! The conventional wisdom was that the new law redressed past wrongs done to peoples "from southern and eastern Europe," meeting goals set out by Truman's 1953 commission. Johnson expressed pride that the system abolished by "my signature" had "violated the basic principle of American democracy" and had "been untrue to the faith that brought thousands to these shores even before we were a country."

In fact, however, the new law facilitated first, the entrance of immigrants from Asia, and, later, immigrants from Mexico and Central America. This had not been foreseen by either experts or advocates. Administration officials had told Congress, in good faith, that the law would have little effect on Asian immigration, and the most active Asian American civil rights organization, the Japanese American Citizens League, which supported the new law as it had supported McCarran–Walter, nevertheless predicted that although the new law eliminated all overt discrimination against Asians "in actual operation immigration will still be controlled by the now discredited national origins system and the general pattern that exists today will continue for many years yet to come."

Clearly these and other "experts" did not know what they were talking about. Immigrants after 1965 increasingly practiced chain migration, as immigrants to America had done since the seventeenth century. That is, immigration in which immigrants from the same area or family follow one another, like links in a chain. The 1965 law, which privileged family unification, facilitated family chain migration. Immigration from Asia boomed as did the Asian American population. In 1940 the Asian American population stood at about 500,000. Twenty years later there were about 900,000, and most of the growth had come from natural increase. In the following twenty years (1960–80), the Asian American population nearly quadrupled, to 3.5 million, with the bulk of the growth coming from recent immigrants and their children. By 1979, immigration from Asia, once a matter of "grave consequences" between the United States and Asian nations, had become a subject for humor at the highest levels. Jimmy Carter reports in his memoirs that when Chinese leader Deng Xiaoping visited Washington in 1979 and noted the dispute between the United States and the USRR over Jewish emigration, he volunteered: "If you want me to release ten million Chinese to come to the United States, I'd be glad to do that."

As important as the 1965 act was, it was not, as textbooks allege, the sole cause of the increase in immigration to America. It can be shown that a long-term and continuing secular trend of increasing immigration has been in place since the end of World War II. As table 1.1 demonstrated, immigration has grown in every decade since the 1930s: there were 1 million in the 1940s, 2.5 million in the 1950s, 3.3 million in the 1960s, 4.5 million in the 1970s, 7.3 million in the 1980s, and perhaps 9 million in the 1990s, with a steeper rate of growth in the years before 1965 than in the years since then. On the other hand, it is obvious that the new law did sustain and foster the continuing increase in ways that a continuation of the 1952 act would not have done.

By 1980 it was becoming clear to most observers that the 1965 law was not working out in the expected way. Although there had been, in the congressional debates, the usual oratory about opening the floodgates, not even the harshest critic of immigration reform suggested that in the 1980s alone, nearly 6 million legal immigrants would enter the United States. Nor did anyone even imagine that Asians and Latin Americans would so completely dominate American immigration. In the 1980s more than 80 percent of all legal immigrants came from either Asia or Latin America: if we had a way of accurately including illegal immigrants in our calculations, the figure would undoubtedly exceed 90 percent. The 1965 act, intended to redress past grievances of European ethnic groups and to give more than token representation to Asians has, in one sense, turned traditional immigration patterns to the United States on their heads.

In another sense, however, the patterns of immigration have remained consistent. People have tended to immigrate to the United States when a clear economic or social advantage could be gained from doing so. In the years between 1965 and 2000 the average Briton, German, or Scandinavian could see no such advantage in emigration; neither could the average Japanese. Eastern Europeans might have come in greater numbers (as would be the case in the 1990s), but most were not free to do so. Many citizens of the Irish Republic wished to come, but because there was no large body of recent Irish immigrants in the United States, few could come in as family members. Large numbers of Irish came to the United States on tourist visas and remained (illegally) to work. By the end of the 1980s educated guesstimates posited that a quarter of a million or more Irish were illegal aliens, largely in the metropolitan areas between Boston and Baltimore.

The golden door had swung open much wider, but an entirely different mix of peoples was lining up to come in. To understand fully the impact of the 1965 law it is necessary to switch our focus from the law and its administration to the immigrants themselves, the categories under which they gained admission and the regions from which they came. Table 1.8 shows the growth of immigration from Asia and Latin America, whereas table 1.9 shows the kinds of admissions in 1977 and 1980, one a relatively low year, the other relatively high.

Note that even in the low year immigrants subject to numerical limitation were only 71 percent of legal immigration, a lower figure than the experts expected. In the high year they were only 36 percent. The number of those entering "subject to numerical limitation" was fixed at 290,000 and ran at a level slightly below the maximum. The numbers of those entering under other categories fluctuated widely, but at a generally ascending rate. Although the 1965 act devoted a fifth of its preference visas (preferences three and six) to persons with special skills, such preferences accounted for fewer than 4 percent of immigration in the years up to 1980. Most of the many professionals and other skilled persons who were admitted then entered under other provisions of the law. Part of the reason for the low utilization of the third and sixth preferences was the slow growth of the American economy; in addition, getting a visa in that category involves dealing with one additional layer of American bureaucracy and immigrants who have a choice generally choose the simpler way.

The "wild card" was, of course, refugees, under whatever name. No other category of immigrants were subject to such extreme fluctuation, 1.2 percent of all immigrants in 1977, 42.9 percent just three years later. Nothing better symbolizes the dual nature of American immigration regulation in this era than the fact that, on the very day he signed the 1965 Immigration Act (which, as noted above, allocated 6 percent of immigration

Table 1.8
ASIANS AND LATIN AMERICANS AS A PERCENTAGE
OF LEGAL IMMIGRANTS, 1931–79

Immigrant origin	1931–60	1960–69	1970–79
Asia	5	12	34
Latin America	15	38	41

Source: Gardner et al., *Asian Americans: Growth, Change, and Diversity.* Washington, DC: Population Reference Bureau, 1985, fig. 1, p. 2.

Table 1.9
NUMBERS AND CATEGORIES OF
IMMIGRANTS ADMITTED, 1977 AND 1980

Category	1977	1980
Subject to numerical limitation	275,531	289,479
Exempt from numerical limitation	117,857	165,325
Refugees	4,701	201,552
Cuban-Haitian entrants[a]	—	140,000
Total	389,089	796,356

Source: My structuring of INS data.
[a]Refugees in fact but not in law.

slots, or 17,400 spaces annually, for refugees), Lyndon Johnson also exercised his parole authority to authorize a resumed flow of Cuban refugees to
the United States, a flow that would bring nearly 400,000 Cubans to this
country in less than fourteen years.

The dichotomy between the theory of the seventh preference in the
law—6 percent for refugees—and the reality of American immigration
practice was made even more apparent by the aftermath of American participation in the misbegotten war in Vietnam. Starting in 1975 the Ford
and Carter administrations assembled a jerry-built collection of ten separate refugee programs that brought to this country some 400,000 Vietnamese and other Southeast Asians in a little over four years.

A Carter administration proposal to eliminate the distinction between
immigration theory and practice was enacted by Congress as the Refugee
Act of 1980, the last significant avowed liberalization of American immigration law in the twentieth century. The act eliminated the seventh
(refugee) preference established by the 1965 immigration act and created a
"normal" 50,000 annual slots for refugees and, in partial compensation, reduced, in stages, the allocated slots to 270,000 annually, making normal annual admissions 320,000 plus however many came in "without numerical
limitation." One note of realism was added: the President might, after consultation with Congress, raise that number at his discretion. This was, in
essence, providing structure to the parole practice begun by FDR in 1944.

One aspect of the 1980 law broke entirely new ground: for the first
time American law recognized the right of asylum and created a new (for
the United States) legal category of refugee, the asylee. Asylees are refugees
and must meet, eventually, the established criteria for refugees. Unlike

other refugees, however, an asylee is a person who has already reached the United States, whether legally, on a temporary visa, or illegally. The law, as interpreted by the courts, has come to mean that if a person merely gets to an American immigration facility and applies for asylum, the application must be considered and the applicant admitted until the matter has been adjudicated. Although this was a radical departure from previous American practice, it (and the rest of the 1980 act) was noncontroversial at the time of passage. It sailed through the Senate 85–0. Less than half a century after the United States had turned its back on many refugees from Hitler's Europe, a broad and relatively generous refugee policy had become part of the American consensus. To be sure, a putative lid of five thousand annual admissions was placed on asylees, but this was an illusion. By the beginning of fiscal 1996 the INS reported that 461,764 asylum cases—some of which involved more than one individual—were pending.

A little over a month after the passage of the Refugee Act of 1980 Fidel Castro set off what became the Mariel Crisis. It was triggered by a trilateral dispute between the United States, Cuba, and Peru about some 3,500 Cubans who had entered the Peruvian Embassy in Havana and refused to leave. The United States was willing to accept them as part of the ongoing Cuban parole program, but only if they came by way of Costa Rica. At that time Cubans could not come directly to the United States, only 90 miles away, and most of the parolees came by way of Madrid. Castro broke off the negotiations and declared that anyone who wanted to leave Cuba could do so, but only from the tiny port of Mariel on Cuba's northern coast west of Havana, and only if they went directly to the United States.

The Cuban community in South Florida quickly organized a "boatlift" and, contrary to American law, brought some 125,000 Cubans directly to the United States, making a shambles of normal immigration procedures. The Carter administration, determined to make human rights an integral part of foreign policy, was of two minds. On the one hand it wanted to embarrass Castro; on the other hand it wanted to preserve the structure of refugee admissions. In addition, there was an election coming up in November. Initially federal officials issued warnings and confiscated some, but not all, participating boats. Then, when massive TV coverage produced positive public reactions to the influx, Carter himself in early May gave the exodus his approval by offering "an open heart and open arms" to all who came. By the end of the month, however, amid reports that Castro was opening jails and mental institutions, public support was

replaced by public alarm. Federal officials again "got tough" and began fin-
ing boat captains and seized a few vessels and the movement ended. In a
bizarre example of bureaucratic newspeak, the Marielitos, as the Cuban
American community styled them, were categorized by the INS not as
refugees or asylees, but as "Cuban Entrants (Status Pending)." (Most of
these "entrants," and others who came before 1 January 1982, were adjusted to permanent immigrant status by the 1986 immigration act, which
meant that they could be eligible to become U.S. citizens by 1991.)

Public concern was aggravated by reports that the newly discovered
plague of AIDS existed in the refugee population. The Reagan administration, which took office in January 1981, dithered as badly but less publicly
than the Carter administration, but after the rhetoric about a mass return
and jail terms died down, it allowed all but about 2,500 of the boatlift
Cubans to regularize their status in 1985 and by 1990 those regularized
could bring in family members. Refugees and would-be entrants from a
neighboring Caribbean country, Haiti, met an entirely different reception
from a succession of American administrations. Although in 1980 the
Carter administration set up a Cuban-Haitian Entrant Program giving
Haitian refugees the same temporary status as Cubans while seeking political asylum and Congress gave the Cuban and Haitian entrants the same
rights as refugees, Haitians never received the welcome or level of support
the Cubans did. Because of the Cold War orientation of the American government, refugees from right-wing governments in the Americas, whether
from Guatemala and other Central American republics, Chile, or Haiti,
had a great deal of difficulty in gaining refugee status that was all but au-
tomatic for those fleeing from the Castro regime.

HIGH AND INCREASING IMMIGRATION;
INCREASING BUT ESSENTIALLY INEFFECTIVE
RESTRICTION (1980-PRESENT)

Precisely when "the turn against immigration" (David Reimers's phrase) took
place is a matter of debate, but the Mariel Crisis and the controversy that surrounded it serves as a useful marker. A case could also be made for using the
beginning of the Reagan presidency in January 1981 as the turning point. In
either case, however, by the mid-1980s the tide of public opinion clearly had
turned against the liberalism of the 1960s on immigration and many other

matters. To be sure, there has always been a note of nativism in American culture, sometimes faint, sometimes strident, and even when nativism has been dominant some past immigrants have been celebrated.

Public opinion polls throughout the second half of the twentieth century have shown a residual anti-immigration bias among a majority of Americans, but it is too little noticed, even by most specialists, that the questions are often loaded. In 1993, for example, a *New York Times-CBS News* poll posited a patently false opinion ("most of the people who have moved to the United States in the last few years are here illegally") and found that 68 percent of those who answered the question agreed. What such polls do not measure is the intensity of beliefs. When asked, de novo, to list their major concerns, most Americans, even in the anti-immigrant 1980s, listed immigration fairly low on their totem pole of fears.

The Mariel Crisis connected immigration intimately with two major fears of most Americans at that time: crime and AIDS. In addition the stringent economic conditions of the late Carter and early Reagan years created a climate in which many, particularly among the disadvantaged, sought scapegoats and found immigrants a convenient target. It has been traditional for trade unionists and labor economists to blame the economic problems of working people in general and trade unions in particular on immigrants. Other sources of anti-immigrant feeling have included the INS, which had an anti-immigrant bias from its inception and has persistently magnified the illegal immigration problem, partially from conviction and partially from a natural desire to increase its budget.

In the early 1980s, in part sparked by Ronald Reagan's inflammatory comments about the danger of our being overrun by "feet people" from Central America, old-style nativist rhetoric took on new life and was punctuated by a few well-publicized ugly incidents. These included physical attacks on Vietnamese fisher folk in Texas and elsewhere on the Gulf Coast; protests about the "unclean habits" of Cambodian and Laotian refugees resettled in central cities; the fatal attack in Detroit on the American-born Vincent Chin by an unemployed autoworker who thought that he was Japanese and, somehow, responsible for his job loss; the vile comments of auto executive Bennett E. Bidwell, a Chrysler vice president, who suggested that the best way to stem car imports would be for the industry to charter the *Enola Gay* and replicate Hiroshima; and the complaint by Democratic Representative John D. Dingell of Michigan about American jobs being taken by "little yellow men." All are in the older nativist style.

But much of the "new nativism" of recent years, including the bulk of the propaganda emanating from the most active anti-immigrant pressure group, the Federation for American Immigration Reform (FAIR), is of a very different character. The new restrictionist coalition stresses class, not race or ethnicity, and seems more concerned with the environment than with the nation's bloodstream. One of the more respected proponents of post-1965 restrictionism was the Select Commission on Immigration and Refugee Policy (1978–81), whose somewhat ambiguous proposals seemed to some observers to be a case of the "good cop-bad cop" routine; that is, being nice to some immigrants while harassing others. On the one hand, it urged that the policies laid down in the 1965 law be continued essentially unchanged and that a seemingly unprecedented amnesty proposal be instituted to allow some illegal immigrants who had managed to establish themselves in the United States to regularize their status and become U.S. citizens. On the other hand, it recommended tighter border controls to keep out future illegal immigrants, and, in a proposal the sent chills down some civil libertarian spines, urged the government to do the necessary research to create "forgery proof" I.D. cards to be carried by all Americans. (A "forgery proof I.D. card" is, perhaps, the philosopher's stone of the new nativist movement, indicating that some elements of the traditional American faith in technology remain.)

By 1986, the year that an immigration "reform" measure actually was enacted, the Select Commission's chair, Father Theodore M. Hesburgh, stressed the need for the United States to "regain control of [its] borders," a non-sequitur which had become a shibboleth among post-1965 restrictionists. His chief rationale was a concern for the domestic rather than foreign poor. Writing in 1986, he predicted:

> During the next 15 years, assuming a persistently strong economy, the United States will create about 30 million new jobs. Can we afford to set aside more than 20 percent of them for foreign workers? No. It would be a disservice to our own poor and unfortunate.

In the year Hesburgh wrote the civilian labor force was 90.5 million, the unemployment rate was 7.0 percent, and immigration was 601,708; twelve years later, in 1998, the labor force had mushroomed to 137.7 million, the unemployment rate had dropped to 4.5 percent, while immigration was 660,477. (Immigration had been significantly higher in most of the intervening years.) These figures indicate how obsolete the traditional economic arguments against immigration are; as of May 2000 the country has experienced an unprecedented 111-month continuous economic expansion. The creation of 30 million new jobs over fifteen years that Hesburgh foresaw had become almost 50 million in just twelve years.

Such views illustrate nicely John Kenneth Galbraith's comment that "on few matters are we so determinedly obscurantist as on attitudes toward immigration." What Father Hesburgh and others see as "job stealing," Galbraith sees as economic development. He also noted that "fortunately the power of government is small so the movement continues," which could serve as an obituary for the Hesburgh Commission's recommendations and much subsequent immigration reform.

Other representatives of the "new nativism" have been overtly hostile to foreigners. For example, columnist Carl Rowan, also pushing for immigration curtailment, wrote: "The United States is a nation without meaningful control of its borders. So many Mexicans are crossing U.S. borders illegally that Mexicans are reclaiming Texas, California, and other territories that they claim the Gringos stole from them." The heated debate over immigration in the 1980s initially focussed on clearly restrictive immigration proposals authored by two serious legislators, Romano L. Mazzoli (b. 1932), a Democratic representative from Louisville, Kentucky, and Alan K. Simpson (b. 1931), a Republican senator from Wyoming. Both were intelligent and articulate, and neither represented a constituency with many immigrants, although the Italian American Mazzoli understood well the prejudice that existed against persons whose "names ended in vowels." Despite what seemed like overwhelming support, none of the several restrictive measures that they sponsored focussing on illegal immigration became law.

Simpson, who had served on the Select Commission, was greatly concerned with cultural unity, and he worried not only about the cultural values of some immigrants but also about the ability of their children to conform to not fully specified standards. Shortly after the Commission report appeared he wrote:

> A substantial proportion of these new persons and their descendants do not assimilate satisfactorily into our society. . . . They may well create in America the same social, political, and economic problems that exist in the countries from which they have chosen to depart. Furthermore, if language and cultural separation rise above a certain level, the unity and political stability of our nation will—in time—be seriously eroded.

The bill that he and Mazzoli tried to push through Congress was in many ways similar to the Commission proposals. It would have raised slightly the numerical limits but by placing all relatives within the numerical limitation it would have decreased the actual number of immigrants admitted significantly. In addition, the bill would have abolished the fifth preference—adult brothers and sisters of U.S. citizens—which would have limited significantly the pattern of chain migration that has characterized post-1952 immigration. In justifying this change Simpson stressed, as was his wont, a desire for cultural homogeneity: "I do feel that family preference categories should be based on the U.S. concept of the nuclear family and not on the definition of such a family as expressed in other nations."

After five years of debate accompanied by a rising drumbeat of media attention largely hostile to immigration and focussed on illegal border crossers, a compromise immigration law went on the books. The measure, the Immigration Reform and Control Act of 1986 (IRCA), was sponsored by Simpson and Peter W. Rodino (b. 1909), a Democratic representative from New Jersey, best known as the Judiciary Committee chair who had managed the committee that moved for the impeachment of Richard Nixon and who had a long history of immigrant advocacy. The law was hailed by some of its backers, most of the media, and the INS as a solution to immigration "problems." In his signing statement, Ronald Reagan called it "the most comprehensive reform of our immigration laws since 1952," conveniently ignoring LBJ's 1965 act, and claimed that "Future generations of Americans will be thankful for our efforts to humanely regain control of our borders and thereby preserve the value of one of the most sacred possessions of our people: American citizenship."

Despite its anti-immigrant rhetoric, the IRCA actually expanded legal immigration to the United States significantly and did little or nothing that would limit future illegal immigration effectively. Its major provisions can be divided into two groups: those that expanded immigration and those that supposedly "cracked down on" or "got tough with" illegal immigrants, their procurers, and their employers. Two separate aspects of IRCA resulted in major expansions of immigration, a dual amnesty program and what evolved into a "diversity program." The amnesty program enabled some 3 million illegal immigrants to regularize their status. The diversity program—at least in its initial states—can be described as an affirmative action program chiefly for white European immigrants in general and Irish in particular (although its advocates never so described it), which has enabled hundreds of thousands of persons to immigrate. The beneficiaries of both programs can sponsor relatives once their status has been regularized, thereby setting off new migration chains.

Amnesty (a word the INS refuses to use) had been recommended by the Hesburgh Commission of 1981 and been widely debated and discussed. In the form finally adopted under IRCA it was a dual program: a general amnesty and one restricted to "Special Agricultural Workers" (SAW). Under the general amnesty program, only persons who could demonstrate that they had been continuously in the United States since 31 December 1981 were eligible to apply. For visa overstayers with a documented entry this was not too difficult. However, for many if not most illegal entrants other kinds of documents—rent or utility receipts, for example—could serve to document residence. It was, for a time, difficult to persuade illegal immigrants that it was safe to file for amnesty status even though they could do so without dealing directly with the INS by submitting paperwork through immigrant-friendly-private agencies. One INS official in Southern California even donned a mariachi hat and sang as part of a "Trio Amnestia" on Spanish-language radio and TV stations to publicize the advantages of the new law. Eventually some 1.7 million persons applied and were accepted into the program.

While the basic amnesty program had been worked out in detail, the SAW program was thrown into the law very late in the day and was subjected neither to hearings nor sophisticated analysis. In practical political terms it was the "reward" given to congressional spokespersons for agricultural interests, largely from California, Texas, and Florida, in exchange for their needed votes for the entire IRCA measure. That aspect of the bill was handled by Representative Charles E. Schumer (b. 1950), a Democrat whose Brooklyn district contained many immigrants but little agriculture. The SAW program had two major provisions. One enabled the importation of a new set of seasonal agricultural workers (in essence another Bracero Program), and the other provided an opportunity for illegal immigrants who had worked in agriculture for at least ninety days between May 1985 and May 1986 to be allowed to regularize their status and become permanent resident aliens. How many persons this might involve, no one knew. The often compliant Congressional Budget Office estimated a total of 250,000 potential applicants. When the period for amnesty application ran out in 1988 1.3 million had applied and been accepted under the SAW provisions. Thus, IRCA made it possible for 3 million illegal immigrants to begin a process that could lead to permanent residence and, eventually, American citizenship, 43 percent of them under the SAW program. By 1993 2.6 million (88 percent) had achieved permanent resident status and a few thousand have done so in each year since then. A large percentage—it is impossible to say how large—of amnestied immigrants have become American citizens.

Who received amnesty? Of the more than 3 million persons accepted into the program, nearly 70 percent were Mexicans and more than 20 percent of the rest were also from the New World. They were 68 percent male, young (59 percent under age thirty, fewer than 10 percent over age forty-four), and highly concentrated geographically: 54 percent applied from California and 14 percent applied from Texas.

One problem that quickly arose from amnesty was the fact that the cutoff date often split families whose members had crossed the border at different times. A parent who had come, say, in 1980 with one older child would be eligible for amnesty, but other children and perhaps a spouse who had come in 1983 would not be. In 1990 Congress, predictably, solved the problem by authorizing a stay of deportation for spouses and children of persons who had applied for amnesty and gave permission for them to remain and be employed until they could become legalized. Other amnesties followed. In 1995, for example, Congress authorized an "adjustment of status" (i.e., legalization) for any "national of Nicaragua or Cuba and who has been physically present in the United States for a continuous period, beginning not later than December 1, 1995," provided that he or she were otherwise eligible for admission, and there is every reason to believe that similar "adjustments of status" will continue to occur.

What became a full-fledged diversity program began modestly in IRCA under Section 314, cryptically entitled "Making Visas Available to Nonpreference Immigrants." It allocated 5,000 visas in each of the 1987 and 1988 fiscal years "to qualified immigrants who are natives of foreign states the immigration of whose natives to the United States was adversely affected by" the Immigration Act of 1965 as amended. In other words, no Asians or Latin Americans need apply. These visas were to be granted to applicants "strictly in the chronological order" in which they applied. The 5,000 visas per annum of IRCA became 40,000 immigrant visas in the 1990 immigration act in each of fiscal years 1992, 1993, and 1994 with the added provisos that no one from a foreign state "contiguous to the United States" was eligible and that "at least 40 percent of the number of such visas in each fiscal year shall be made available to natives of the foreign state the natives of which received the greatest number of visas issued" in the program set up under IRCA. The unnamed foreign states were Canada and Ireland. Thus, no Canadian could receive a diversity visa, and a minimum of 48,000 of the 120,000 diversity visas were earmarked for the Irish. The 1991 amendments decreed that, for the purpose of diversity visas, "natives of Northern Ireland shall be deemed to be natives of Ireland," dropped the ban against Canadians, and changed the method of selection from chronological order to "strictly in a random order," making the diversity program in fact a lottery (although the statute avoided using that word).

Under the "permanent" diversity program that began in fiscal 1995, the special treatment for Irish lapsed and the lottery has not been otherwise rigged. The State Department puts a notice describing the terms in the Federal Register annually. For the "DV 2000" program (1 October 1999–30 September 2000), fifteen nations, including Ireland but not Northern Ireland, were excluded from the lottery because of relatively high immigration in a previous year. From fiscal 1986 through fiscal 1997 the various "diversity" statutes allowed more than 300,000 otherwise ineligible persons to immigrate to the United States as well as an unspecified number of their dependents. In 1997 almost 50,000 diversity immigrants were admitted, amounting to 6.2 percent of legal immigration.

The evolution of the diversity formula illustrates how the immigration process often works. The earliest versions were simply a sop to attract legislators with large numbers of Irish American constituents, and it is no accident that Senator Ted Kennedy of Massachusetts was one of its engineers, although it must be admitted that he has been an effective advocate for all immigrants. Eventually, when the rawness of the favored treatment for the Irish became clear, the system was made fairer and roughly congruent to certain American ideals.

If the major liberalizing aspects of IRCA described above can be viewed as successful—they have enabled millions of immigrants to become legalized or enter the United States legally—the "get tough" provisions of IRCA, the ones Ronald Reagan described as the struggle to "regain control of our borders," can only be regarded as an utter failure and a major factor in producing the critic's perception that the United States had "a broken system" of immigration control. The major provisions of IRCA, according to the INS summary, are as follows:

1. Created sanctions prohibiting employers from knowingly hiring, recruiting, or referring for a fee aliens not authorized to work in the United States; and
2. increased enforcement at U.S. borders.

Since most illegal immigrants enter the United States seeking work, an effective system of employer sanctions would, in time, largely solve the problem. Even under optimum conditions such sanctions would be difficult to enforce, and the conditions Congress has set are far from optimum. Even in the INS summary, the word "knowingly" sticks out like a sore thumb. Criminal statutes are not usually so modified. Congress, obviously, wants to deport or jail illegal immigrants, but it does not want to send respectable constituents to jail. In addition, various provisions in the law prohibit effective enforcement in terms of agricultural employment.

Nothing better illustrates the dual standards embedded in the law than Section 116 of Title I of IRCA, entitled "Restricting Warrantless Entry in the Case of Outdoor Agricultural Operations." The crucial clause of that section reads as follows:

> . . . an officer or employee of the [INS] may not enter without the consent of the owner (or agent thereof) or a properly executed warrant onto the premises of a farm or other outdoor agricultural operation for the purpose of interrogating a person believed to be an alien as to the person's right to be or to remain in the United States.

When the selective enforcement policies of the INS are added to such statutory provisions, much of the enforcement of the immigration laws becomes a farce. In agricultural areas of the Southwest and Southeast, and in the cities surrounded by them, one regularly comes upon early morning gatherings of men, largely Hispanic and African American, standing around vacant lots, often on corners. Trucks and pickup trucks arrive regularly, and, after brief conversations, some men get in the vehicles and they drive away. This is done quite openly and without apparent fear of arrest or other interference. To be sure, many of the men for hire at such rendezvous may well be legal immigrants and even American citizens, but if the INS were truly interested in "cracking down" on illegal workers, close surveillance of such places would be routine rather than rare. After illegal immigrants get past the border zone, their chances of arrest and subsequent deportation are relatively slight, particularly if they are working in agriculture.

To be sure, the INS reports increasing numbers of immigrants apprehended. In almost every year since 1977 the INS has reported more than a million apprehensions of aliens, but relatively few are deported and even fewer are sent to jail. In 1996, for example, the INS apprehended 1,649,986 aliens but formally deported only 50,064, a mere three-tenths of 1 percent. The government resorted to formal prosecution for immigration and naturalization law violations in only 16,326 cases, and it secured 12,241 convictions in which $1,219,263 in fines were assessed and sentences totaling 7,277 years were handed down (i.e., an average fine of $99.60 and average jail term of less than seven months). No persons in their right minds want to put immigrants in jail: it costs more to keep people in jail for a year than to send them to Harvard. (Current estimates speak of an average cost of $35,000 per federal prisoner per year, and that does not include the cost of the massive number of new federal prisons being built annually.)

The more than 1.5 million others were "voluntary departures," many of which were arranged by the immigrants themselves. The following anecdote demonstrates one of the ways that voluntary departures occur.

Some years ago in October an informant arranged for me to visit with a group of about thirty illegal immigrant farmworkers. These men had come into the United States that February in the Rio Grande Valley and had worked their way north to Michigan. Their leader told me that he had been working along this route for thirty years, often working for the same employers year after year. It was October and the men were ready to go home. It was explained to me that the leader and one or two other experienced migrants had just sent almost all of the money the men had back to Mexico by Western Union. They were gathered in a cheap motel and were enjoying fast food and wine and generally relaxed as they knew that they were going home. After a time the leader told me that he was going to telephone the INS to report "a bunch of wetbacks." My informant suggested that it would be prudent for us to leave and we sat in his car across the street. After a time, INS agents arrived, and sometime after that a bus arrived and took the men away. What would happen next, I was assured, was this: the men would agree to "voluntary departure." The government would fly them to the border and they would walk into Mexico. If they had money, they would have been charged a fare, but since they sent it home, they went at government expense.

This not atypical scenario demonstrates several things. First of all it shows how illegal immigrants learn to adapt to the rules of the game, written and unwritten. Second, it shows the kind of symbiotic relationship that has developed between illegal workers, farmers, and government officials. In this particular scenario—there are others—all have "won." Workers have earned money to support their families, often at a standard higher than most of their nonmigrating neighbors, and have received a free trip back to Mexico. Farmers have had their crops harvested efficiently at a relatively low cost. The American public gets its food at a lower cost. And the INS has achieved more statistics to show Congress in its never-ending quest for a larger budget and more personnel and other resources.

Although the "system" (some would say nonsystem) works, the media, many officials, Congress, and a good part of the public continue to exhibit concern about immigration in general and illegal immigration in particular. As a result and partially in response to this heightened concern sixteen separate public immigration laws were passed in the ten years after the passage of IRCA in November 1986. Nine of them were devoted solely to increasing immigration or providing resident status to persons originally admitted as nonresidents. Some of the nine were responses to specific American needs or reactions to world situations, including the shortage of nurses, especially in public hospitals, the breakup of the Soviet Union, and the massacre at Tiananmen Square:

1. The Amerasian Homecoming Act (December 1987) admitted an unspecified number of children born in Vietnam to American fathers and their immediate relatives and made them eligible to receive refugee benefits.
2. Part of an act implementing a U.S.-Canada Free Trade Agreement (September 1988) facilitated temporary entry and employment of Canadians.
3. A November 1988 law provided for the extension of nurses previously admitted for a limited period.
4. The Foreign Operations Act of November 1989 provided for the adjustment to permanent resident status of Soviet and Indochinese [sic] nationals who had been paroled into the United States after having been denied refugee status.
5. The Immigration Nursing Relief Act of December 1989 adjusted from temporary to permanent resident status registered nurses who had been employed for at least three years and set up a new nonimmigrant category for admission of qualified registered nurses.

6. The Armed Forces Immigration Adjustment Act of October 1991 granted special immigrant status to aliens who served in the U.S. Armed Forces for at least twelve years.
7. The Chinese Student Protection Act of October 1992 provided for adjustment to permanent status nationals of the People's Republic of China who were in the United States between 4 June 1989 and 11 April 1990.
8. The Soviet Scientists Immigration Act of October 1992 conferred permanent resident status to a maximum of 750 scientists from the former USSR (the limit does not include spouses and children).
9. The NAFTA Implementation Act of December 1993 made it easier for an unlimited number of Canadian and 5,500 Mexican persons to enter annually for business and professional employment. Canadians may bring in spouses and minor children without visas. Mexican spouses and children require non-immigrant visas.

Although not one of these statutes admitted a massive number of persons, when taken together the potential number of resulting direct admissions was sizeable, and, in addition, each person granted regular status was in a position to start new migration chains by bringing in relatives and becoming a citizen. The accompanying table(s) describe, by category, the more than 3 million legal immigrants admitted in the fiscal years 1994–97.

The other seven statutes were direct responses to the anti-immigrant mood: some were directed at specific abuses, whereas others were meant to punish immigrants already here. None contributed significantly to a reduction of either legal or illegal immigration.

1. The Immigration Marriage Fraud Amendments of November 1986 required that aliens entering the United States or improving their legal status through marriage be put in a conditional status if the marriage was of less than two years. To remove conditional status, the alien must reapply within ninety days after two years of conditional status.
2. The Immigration Act of November 1990 was a major revision of immigration law, whose effects were clearly mixed.
   a. It set up a theoretical cap of 675,000 immigrants beginning in fiscal 1995: 480,000 family sponsored, 140,000 employment based, and 55,000 diversity immigrants. As the tables in the ap-

pendix show, actual numbers have been 720,000 (in 1995), 916,000 (in 1996), and 798,000 (in 1997).

b. It repealed most of the 1952 McCarran Act's ideological prohibitions against the admission of "subversive" immigrants and visitors in keeping with the general post-Cold War relaxation of tensions.

c. It widened the ability of the government to grant temporary protected status to illegal aliens whose homelands were involved in armed conflict or subject to natural disasters.

d. It revised the rules for existing temporary worker visas and created four new categories of temporary worker visas. It created theoretical caps for many of these programs, caps that were often raised or ignored.

e. It revised naturalization requirements by transferring all but ceremonial jurisdiction from the federal courts to the INS and (at a time when "English only" amendments were getting much discussion) actually widened the grounds for waiving the English language requirement for older, long-time resident immigrants.

f. It strengthened the provisions for deporting aliens with a criminal record in the United States and increased the size of the Border Patrol, which has become the largest and least professional federal law enforcement agency.

The question of immigrant crime and making the borders less permeable became a major motif of legislation affecting immigration in the 1990s. Bills with fierce titles, such as the Violent Crime Control and Law Enforcement Act of 1994 and the Antiterrorism and Effective Death Penalty Act of 1996, contained provisions aimed directly at immigrants. Much 1990s legislation was devoted to punishing legal immigrants who were poor. Two 1996 statutes, enacted during the heat of a presidential election, combined highly moral titles—"Personal Responsibility and Work Opportunity Reconciliation Act" (August) and "Illegal Immigration Reform and Immigrant Responsibility Act" (September)—with unethical provisions of dubious legality. The major thrust of these laws barred legal immigrants already in the country from participating in a variety of income maintenance programs as well as further "cracking down" on illegal immigrants. Some of these provisions have since been declared unconstitutional by lower courts, and others have been modified or repealed. (Congress has tried on a number of occasions, largely without success, to limit judicial review of various administrative provisions of immigration law.)

In its enthusiasm for "getting tough," Congress has not only placed extra burdens on legal immigrants but on the INS itself. Long regarded as perhaps the least efficient of all the major federal bureaucracies (a February 1999 study of fifteen major federal agencies by Syracuse's Maxwell School of Public Affairs gave the INS a C2, the only agency to score so low), the spate of often ill-considered legislation has not only made the INS the largest and least trained of all federal law enforcement agencies but has also made it incapable of exercising some of its most basic functions effectively. Congress has increased the cost of citizenship; the cost of filing an application for naturalization went up from $95 to $225 in January 1999 at a time when the estimated waiting period for the initial processing had grown to 24 months. Between January 1997 and January 1999 the number of pending applications for naturalization grew from 100,000 to 1.8 million. INS Commissioner Doris Meissner admitted, in July 1998, to a *Los Angeles Times* reporter that "the history of [the INS], despite the thousands of committed and hardworking employees, has never had a culture that truly emphasizes the importance of service and rewards it." Yet, despite this and other mea culpas, the INS has continued to fall behind.

This is an embarrassment to conscientious INS staff. In December 1998 I spoke at a naturalization ceremony in Dayton, Ohio federal court. The INS official in charge apologized to the judge for the small number of new citizens (twenty-four) and said that many others were waiting but that their paperwork, which was funneled through Kansas City, just wasn't coming through promptly. Congress has mandated relatively large additions to the Border Patrol: it grew from 5,878 to 7,800 between 1997 and 1999. Even though the agency's budget increased from $1.5 billion in 1993 to almost $4 billion in 1999, it has starved the INS's naturalization functions. This means that although the law says that an immigrant is eligible to become a citizen in five years, most have to wait seven years or more because of bureaucratic inefficiency.

In addition, Congress keeps placing more demands (some of them probably impossible) on the INS despite its protests. The most recent nonsense is a 1996 mandate, already twice postponed, that the INS verify the identity not only of each of the 400 million annual border crossers into the United States, but also of the 400 million who depart! Initially adopted without much fuss in the anti-immigrant pre-election enthusiasm of 1996, it quickly dawned on representatives of border communities that the result, in places like San Diego and Buffalo, would be absolute gridlock. The business community finds even the existing inspection delays costly. A representative of the Ford Motor Company recently claimed that these cost American businesses at least $2 billion annually and reported that his company had been forced to fly catalytic converters by chartered jet from a plant in Ciudad Juárez, Mexico to one in Georgia to avoid closing down an assembly line. Even though Meissner and other INS officials have testified that the government does not have the technology even to consider such inspections at every border crossing, hard-line opponents of most immigration, such as Texas Republican Lamar S. Smith (b. 1947), chair of the House subcommittee on immigration, oppose canceling the provision permanently. His spokesman insisted that the "technology is already being developed . . . the INS will never make it a priority unless they are under a deadline like this one." On the other hand, congressional advocates of increased immigration, such as Republican Senator Spencer Abraham of Michigan (b. 1953), chair of the Senate immigration subcommittee, insist:

> The idea of putting into the laws of the United States something that would have to come into effect when we don't even know what it costs, how it could be done, whether it would work and how effective it would be, is not the proper way for us to do the public's business.

This mini-debate is symbolic of the conflicting attitudes and ideologies existing within the contemporary Congress and a partial explanation of why, despite immigration "reform" laws, immigration has continued to grow.

CONCLUSION: IMMIGRATION IN THE EARLY TWENTY-FIRST CENTURY AS SEEN IN A CLOUDY CRYSTAL BALL

As the twenty-first century dawned students of American immigration were faced with a seeming paradox. On the one hand, beginning with the Reagan years of the 1980s, there had been a rising chorus, in and out of Congress, for further restriction of immigration apparently supported by public opinion. On the other hand, as we have seen, immigration has increased significantly since 1980 and efforts to legislate effectively against it have failed. What immigration historian David Reimers correctly described in those years as a "turn against immigration" seems to have become one of those turning points at which history simply refused to turn. Why have the restrictionist assumptions and expectations of the 1980s and mid-1990s proved such a faulty guide to the recent past? In attempting to answer this seeming paradox it is necessary first to understand the anxieties of the na- tivistic mind of the era and then to examine the social and economic changes that have taken place in recent years.

Anti-immigration arguments may be grouped under two broad head- ings, economic and cultural. They are often combined, but I deal with them separately here. The economic argument usually includes some or all of the following. Immigration, or too much immigration, is bad because immi- grants are already an economic burden, because they are exploited, because they take jobs away from native-born poor, and because, at some future date, when the economy turns sour, they will become an intolerable burden.

The notion that immigrants are an economic burden at present is sim- ply not the case. In a booming, job-producing economy, with a low rate of unemployment, immigrants with low levels of skills have been easily ab- sorbed. Immigrants who come with a high level of skills, for example com- puter technologists and nurses, have helped to keep the boom alive and pro- vide necessary public services. The claim that either group of immigrants—those with high levels of skills or those with low levels of skills—take jobs that native-born poor would fill cannot be demonstrated. The urban poor of modern America are not competitors for low-paying, stoop-labor jobs: if immigrants don't take them they will simply not get done and the United States will become less and less agriculturally sufficient. As for the top-end jobs in places like California's Silicon Valley and Seattle, any suggestions that significant numbers of the American poor are equipped to take those jobs, which have increasingly gone to immigrants, simply ignore the sad facts about most contemporary American public education.

The fear that immigrants are a present economic burden persistently ignores the benefits that immigrants bring. Perhaps the greatest long-range economic problem of first-world economic powerhouses like Germany and Japan is the rapid aging of their populations, the shortage of workers, and the increasing percentage of their population that is in retirement and drawing levels of retirement income sufficient for a decent lifestyle. These countries, seeing that immigration has helped to lessen such problems in the United States (immigrant workers are younger, less likely to suffer from illness), have in recent years tried to overcome their traditional reluctance to accept foreigners as an integral part of their society by changing—or in the case of Japan trying to change—their immigration and natural- ization laws.

As for the future, some scholars draw a grim picture. Harvard's George J. Borjas asks: "what will happen when the economy takes a bump?" and answers that the "fiscal consequences of our current levels of immigration will be severe."

If and when serious unemployment recurs and persists, almost surely several things will happen. There will be mass protests. Congress will respond by reducing legal immigration. Even without that, the immigrant flow will, at least to a degree, slow down and many recent immigrants will return home. (That is what my paternal grandparents did in the depression of the early 1890s, only to return, this time permanently, later in the decade when things had gotten better.) A constant companion of nativist, restrictionist economic fears has been a lack of faith in the post-New Deal American economic system's ability to provide jobs for a growing population. Most have also failed to realize that, because the search for economic security has been the major impetus for immigration, any long-term economic downturn would result in lessened or even negative immigration, as happened in the early 1930s.

So striking has this long-term economic growth been that, in February 2000 the Executive Council of the AFL-CIO adopted a sharp change in policy by calling for blanket amnesty for illegal immigrants and an end to most sanctions against employers who hire them. The council proclaimed that it "proudly stands on the side of immigrant workers" and falsely implied that it had always done so. In fact, the council was reversing an anti-immigrant tradition in the labor movement that was more than a century old. What the AFL-CIO was recognizing, however belatedly, was that low-skilled immigrant workers were going to continue to come and that the labor movement's greatest opportunities for growth would come from organizing such workers. Its pragmatic rationale was that illegal immigrant workers were more susceptible to exploitation by employers and that only if they had legal protections would they be free to organize. In addition, it understood that, at the other end of the immigrant labor scale, most of the high-tech immigrants in computer and computer-related industries were not likely candidates for union membership.

For very different reasons, the conservative chair of the Federal Reserve Board, Alan Greenspan, has maintained a pro-immigration approach. As he put it just weeks before the AFL-CIO statement: "Aggregative demand is putting very significant pressures on an ever-decreasing available supply of unemployed labor. The one obvious means that one can use to offset that is expanding the number of people we allow in."

To be sure, there have been significant numbers of immigrants, many of them older persons from Southeast Asia who came as refugees as a by-product of the Vietnam War and its neighbors, who have not been economic assets, but the overwhelming majority of immigrants, legal and illegal, have been and are contributors to continued economic growth. Admittedly, as the AFL-CIO noted, immigrants are often exploited even more than native-born workers, but this has been true throughout our history. Most immigrants have come here because of an informed choice, and, while most do not understand advanced mathematics, almost all of them are capable of calculating a reasonably accurate cost-benefit analysis, which tells them that the advantages of American life outweigh its disadvantages. Reflecting that view, Muzaffar Chishti, immigration director for the garment workers' union Unite, was quoted recently in the *Wall Street Journal* as saying "If not the immigrants themselves, then at least their children are going to do very well in America."

The cultural arguments against immigration are more complex. The main cultural argument against immigration has been largely the same since the mid-eighteenth century: Immigrants are a threat to American culture generally and to the predominance of the English language in particular. That was Benjamin Franklin's fear in 1751 when he asked:

> Why should the palatine Boors be suffered to swarm into our Settlements, and by herding together establish their Language and Manners to the Exclusion of ours? Why should Pennsylvania, founded by the English, become a Colony of *Aliens*, who will shortly be so numerous as to Germanize us instead of our Anglifying them, and will never adopt our Language or Customs, any more than they can acquire our Complexion?

Very little separates the essence of this 250-year-old argument from the arguments of those contemporaries who have campaigned, with some success at the state level, for laws declaring that English is the official language. Some of these laws have even forbidden public officials from using any foreign language while performing their duties. The campaign for a national statute declaring English as the official language has not been successful. There is an English language requirement for naturalization, but that requirement can be and often is waived in the case of persons over age sixty-five or persons with disabilities. Whether we are talking about the eighteenth century or the twenty-first, almost all of the children of immigrants have been able to function in English, and the vast majority of third generation immigrants in 2000 as well as earlier have no significant grasp of their grandparents' mother tongue.

The contemporary versions of Ben Franklin's fears often focus on the dangers of "multiculturalism," a relatively new term for an old phenomenon. Because the word "multicultural" has different meanings for different people I will define what I mean by it. I use the term as shorthand for the increasing recognition that life and culture in the United States are not for "whites only," or, for that matter, not just for persons with Judeo-Christian religious beliefs. Multiculturalism is also an attempt to come to grips with one of the primary facts of contemporary American life: that persons who are neither European nor the descendants of Europeans are comprising an ever greater proportion of the American people.

Others, ranging from an immigrant racist such as Peter Brimelow (b. 1947), author of *Alien Nation: Common Sense about America's Immigration Disaster* (1995), to a traditional liberal historian such as Arthur M. Schlesinger Jr. (b. 1917) in his *The Disuniting of America: Reflections on a Multicultural Society* (rev. ed, 1998), have defined multiculturalism differently. In *Alien Nation,* Brimelow insists:

> It is simply common sense that Americans have a legitimate interest in
> their country's racial balance. It is common sense that they have a right
> to insist that their government stop shifting it. Indeed it seems to me
> that they have a right to insist that it be shifted back [to a point when
> whites were 90 percent of the population]. (p. 264)

Of course, such a "90 percent white age" has never existed, but facts do not bother Brimelow.

Arthur Schlesinger would never countenance such views, but he joins Brimelow and others who fear that immigrant languages will further disunite America. Many of the fearful see multiculturalism and the acceptance of widespread use of immigrant languages as a threat to American culture in general and to English-language hegemony in particular.

The most-feared intruding language today, of course, is not German but Spanish. Those afflicted with "Hispanophobia" mistake the nature of the complex and growing "Hispanic" population in the United States, a population that will soon outnumber the African-American population. Most equate Hispanic with Spanish-speaking, but that is a serious misconception. Most native-born Hispanic Americans speak English well and few are truly fluent in Spanish. In addition, perhaps a third of young native-born Hispanic Americans are married to persons of other ethnicities.

I can illustrate the linguistic reality with an anecdote. A few years ago I was a consultant to the University of Texas at El Paso (UTEP). In studying the university's literature I learned that an estimated 59 percent of the students were Hispanic and that its academic offerings included a number of sections of beginning courses in several disciplines, including American history and some of the sciences, in the Spanish language. I commented on this in my initial interview with the dean there by saying that it was generous to provide this instruction to its Chicano students. The dean, an old friend from graduate school, quickly disabused me. He explained that the courses in question were designed for students from across the border in Ciudad Juárez who attended UTEP in fairly large numbers because there were no Mexican universities nearby. Few of the Chicano students, he explained, had the linguistic ability to take college courses in Spanish although they could talk to their mothers or grandmothers in "kitchen Spanish."

In addition, there are many positive aspects of contemporary multi-culturalism. An increasingly multicultural America will be better equipped to function in a global economy and better able to attract and retain large numbers of the highly skilled foreign technicians and venture capitalists that have made Silicon Valley in California and Seattle such vital centers of a computer-oriented economy. A recent University of California study pointed out that one-quarter of all Silicon Valley companies started over the past twenty years were created by recent immigrants, mostly people of Chinese and Indian origin, and calculated that these companies employed 60,000 people. Never before in American history have so many well-educated immigrants come.

Millions of other immigrants come as students who feel less alienated in a multicultural America. According to the International Institute of Education, a record number of 491,000 foreign students were enrolled at U.S. colleges and universities during the academic year 1998–99. The three highest sources of these students were China, Japan, and the Republic of Korea which, between them, provided 29 percent of the total.

To be sure there are still "huddled masses" in multicultural twenty-first century America, as there were in previous centuries. In parts of California large numbers of recent "Hispanic" immigrants from Mexico have various Indian languages (e.g., Zapotec) as their mother tongue and have only marginal use of the Spanish language. This, too, is an example of multicultural America, as are the proliferation of Islamic mosques and the temples that serve increasing numbers of immigrants and their children who practice Asian religions. It seems to me that this growing diversity is largely positive, but those who favor a more homogenous America feel increasingly threatened by it.

Anti-immigration forces have been bolstered since the late nineteenth century by support from many of those concerned about "overpopulation" and the environment. Although it is popular to think of "greens" as persons of the left, the fact is that many of those who have opposed immigration on population, eugenic, or environmental grounds, such as Henry Fairfield Osborn (1857–1935), have also been proponents of racist and elitist attitudes. Except for a few like Brimelow, few of the contemporary "greens" are overtly racist.

A good recent example of environmental opposition to immigration is the unanimous support by the City Council of Aspen, Colorado, in December 1999 for a resolution supporting a drastic limitation of immigration to 175,000 annually. Among the grounds cited was the dubious claim that "For each person added to the U.S. population, about one acre of open land is lost." Even if the statistic were true, the spectacle of the yuppies of Aspen, who use on a per capita basis a great deal more of the environment and natural resources than the typical immigrant, insisting that it is immigrants who are to blame for America's environmental problems is ludicrous. What we have here is a version of the "lifeboat is full" argument. One should contrast this essentially selfish argument with the idealistic notion of Pope John Paul II, who, in the same month denounced the "tunnel vision" of some in developed countries who sought to narrow existing immigration patterns and appealed, instead, for solidarity in favor of thousands of "desperate men and women, many of whom are young," who "every day face sometimes dramatic risks to escape from a life without a future." Although the number of such persons who can be absorbed by the United States and other first world nations is limited, it was this kind of humanitarian concern that inspired the Refugee Act of 1980, the last major "liberalizing" initiative in American immigration law. Most effective support for continuing immigration to the United States rests on the more pragmatic ground of national expediency.

This being the case, I believe that we can expect that, as long as basically favorable economic conditions continue to prevail, American immigration policy will continue to admit some 700,000 to 900,000 persons annually, although, if there were to be another mass amnesty, we could expect a temporary "spike" in the figures, as occurred after the passage of the IRCA in 1986. Another possible scenario for a truncation in immigrant admissions would be some kind of foreign policy crisis or a domestic event associated with a foreign group. (After all, a century ago, the assassination of President William McKinley by a native-born American with a "foreign" sounding name—Czolgosz—triggered the first of a series of statutes designed to stop the entry of immigrant radicals.)

This "prediction" is offered with some trepidation. As Niels Bohr (1885–1962), the great Danish physicist, noted, "prediction is very difficult, especially about the future." As admitted above, my own record has not always been good. Nevertheless I believe that those of us who study the past have some responsibility to speak about present and future policies, although readers certainly cannot be expected to treat prognostication with as much respect as our analyses of the past.

Documents

1

LEGAL IMMIGRATION IN THE 20TH CENTURY

By Decade and Region, 1901–1990			Percent
1901–10	-	8,795,386	
Europe	-	8,056,040	91.6
Asia	-	323,543	3.7
Americas	-	361,888	4.5
Africa	-	7,368	0.1
Oceania	-	13,024	0.2
Unknown	-	33,523	0.4
1911–20	-	5,735,811	
Europe	-	4,321,887	75.3
Asia	-	247,236	4.3
Americas	-	1,143,671	19.9
Africa	-	8,443	0.2
Oceania	-	13,427	0.2
Unknown	-	1,147	–
1921–30	-	4,107,209	
Europe	-	2,463,194	60.0
Asia	-	112,059	2.7
Americas	-	1,516,716	36.9
Africa	-	6,286	0.2
Oceania	-	8,726	0.2
Unknown	-	–	–
1931–40		528,431	
Europe	-	347,566	65.8
Asia	-	16,595	3.1
Americas	-	160,037	30.3
Africa	-	1,750	0.3
Oceania	-	2,483	0.5
Unknown	-	–	–
1941–1950	-	1,035,039	
Europe	-	621,147	60.0
Asia	-	37,028	3.6

LEGAL IMMIGRATION IN THE 20TH CENTURY *(continued)*

By Decade and Region, 1901–1990			Percent
Americas	-	354,804	34.3
Africa	-	7,367	0.7
Oceania	-	14,551	1.4
Unknown	-	142	–
1951–1960	-	2,515,479	
Europe	-	1,325,727	52.7
Asia	-	153,249	6.1
Americas	-	996,944	40.0
Africa	-	14,092	0.6
Oceania	-	12,976	0.5
Unknown	-	12,491	0.5
1961–1970	-	3,321,677	
Europe	-	1,123,492	33.8
Asia	-	427,642	12.9
Americas	-	1,716,374	51.7
Africa	-	28,954	0.9
Oceania	-	25,122	0.7
Unknown	-	93	–
1971–80	-	4,493,314	
Europe	-	800,368	17.8
Asia	-	1,588,178	35.3
Americas	-	1,982,735	44.1
Africa	-	80,779	1.8
Oceania	-	41,242	0.9
Unknown	-	12	–
1981–90	-	7,338,062	
Europe	-	761,550	10.4
Asia	-	2,738,157	37.3
Americas	-	3,615,225	49.2
Africa	-	176,893	2.4
Oceania	-	45,205	0.6
Unknown	-	1,032	–
1991–97	-	6,944,591	
Europe	-	1,039,091	15.0
Asia	-	2,133,952	30.7
Americas	-	3,479,125	50.1
Africa	-	242,736	3.5
Oceania	-	41,181	0.6
Unknown	-	8,506	0.1

Source: INS, *1997 Statistical Yearbook.* Table 2. This, and eventually, later editions, is available on the web at: *http://www.ins.usdoj.gov/graphics/aboutins/statistics/ index.htm.*

2

LEGAL IMMIGRANTS, TOP 20 NATIONS
FOR BIRTH, 1995–97

Nation of birth	1997 #	1997 %	1996 #	1996 %	1995 #	1995 %
All countries	798,378	100.0	915,900	100.0	720,461	100.0
1. Mexico	145,865	18.4	163,572	19.9	89,932	12.5
2. Philippines	49,117	6.2	55,876	6.1	50,984	7.1
3. China	41,147	5.2	41,728	4.6	35,463	4.9
4. Vietnam	38,519	4.8	42,067	4.6	41,752	5.8
5. India	38,071	4.8	44,859	4.9	34,748	4.8
6. Cuba	33,587	4.2	26,466	2.9	17,937	2.5
7. Dominican Rep.	27,053	3.4	39,604	4.3	38,512	5.3
8. El Salvador	17,969	2.3	17,903	2.0	11,744	1.6
9. Jamaica	17,804	2.2	19,089	2.1	16,398	2.3
10. Russia	16,632	2.1	18,668	2.1	14,560	2.0
11. Ukraine	15,696	2.0	21,073	2.3	17,432	2.4
12. Haiti	15,057	0.9	18,386	2.0	14,021	1.9
13. Korea	14,239	1.8	18,185	2.0	16,047	2.2
14. Colombia	13,004	1.6	14,283	1.6	10,838	1.5
15. Pakistan	12,967	1.6	12,519	1.4	9,774	1.4
16. Poland	12,038	1.5	15,772	1.7	13,824	1.9
17. Canada	11,609	1.5	15,825	1.7	12,932	1.8
18. Peru	10,853	1.4	12,871	1.4	8,066	1.1
19. United King.	10,708	1.4	13,624	1.5	12,427	1.7
20. Iran	9,642	1.2	11,084	1.2	9,201	1.3
Subtotal	552,613	69.2	624,460	68.2	476,592	66.2
Other	245,765	30.8	291,440	31.8	243,869	33.8

Source: INS, *1997 Statistical Yearbook*. Table C. This, and eventually, later editions, is available on the web at: *http://www.ins.usdoj.gov/graphics/aboutins/statistics/index.htm*.

3

MAJOR PROVISIONS OF SEVEN 20TH CENTURY IMMIGRATION STATUTES
(Adapted from INS Summary)

1. IMMIGRATION ACT OF FEBRUARY 5, 1917
(39 *Statutes-at-Large* 874)
Codified all previously enacted exclusion provisions. In addition:
   a. Excluded illiterate aliens.
   b. Expanded the list of aliens excluded for mental health and other reasons.
   c. Further restricted the immigration of Asian persons, creating the "barred zone" (known as the Asia-Pacific triangle), natives of which were declared inadmissible.
   d. Considerably broadened the classes of aliens deportable from the United States and introduced the requirement of deportation without the statute of limitation in certain more serious cases.

2. QUOTA LAW OF MAY 19, 1921
(43 *Statutes-at-Large* 5)
The first quantitative immigration law. Provisions:
   a. Limited the number of aliens of any nationality entering the United States to 3 percent of the foreign-born persons of that nationality who lived in the U.S. in 1910. Ca. 350,000 such aliens were permitted to enter each year as quota immigrants, mostly from Northern and Western Europe.
   b. Exempted from this limitation aliens who had resided continuously for at least one year immediately preceding their application in one of the independent countries of the Western Hemisphere; nonimmigrant aliens such as government officials and their households,

aliens in transit through the U.S., temporary visitors, and aliens whose immigration is regulated by immigration treaty.

   c. Actors, artists, lecturers, singers, nurses, professors, aliens belonging to any recognized learned profession, and aliens employed as domestic servants were placed on a nonquota basis.

3. IMMIGRATION ACT OF MAY 26, 1924
(43 *Statues-at-Large* 153)
The first permanent limitation on immigration, established the "National Origins Quota System." In conjunction with the Immigration Act of 1917 governed American immigration policy until 1952. Major provisions:

   a. Contained two quota provisions:

      i. Until July 1, 1929 set annual quota of any quota nationality at 2 percent of the number of foreign-born persons of such nationality resident in the continental U.S. in 1890 (total quota = 164,667).

      ii. From July 1, 1929 used the National Origins Quota System: the annual quota for any country or nationality had the same relation to 150,000 as the number of inhabitants in the U.S. in 1920 had to the total number of inhabitants in the continental United States in 1920.

      Preference quota status was established for: unmarried children under 21; parents and spouses of U.S. Citizens 21 and over; and for quota immigrants aged 21 or over skilled in agriculture, together with their wives and dependent children under age 16.

   b. Nonquota status was accorded to: wives and unmarried children under 18 of U.S. citizens; natives of Western Hemisphere countries, with their families. . . .

   c. Established the "consular control system" of immigration by mandating that no alien may be permitted entrance into the U.S. without an unexpired visa issued by an American consular official abroad. Thus the State Department and the INS shared control of immigration.

   d. Aliens ineligible to become citizens barred from entering the U.S. as immigrants.

4. IMMIGRATION AND NATIONALITY ACT OF JUNE 27, 1952
(66 *Statutes-at-Large* 163)
Brought immigration law into one comprehensive statute. . . . In general perpetuated the immigration policies from earlier statutes with the following significant modifications:

a. Eliminated race as a barrier to naturalization or immigration.
b. Eliminated gender discrimination with respect to immigration.
c. Revised the National Origins Quota System by changing the quota formula so that the annual quota for a country was one-sixth of 1 percent of the number of inhabitants in the continental U.S. in 1920 attributable to it. All countries had a minimum quota of 100; a maximum of 2,000 was placed on natives of most Asian countries.
d. Required resident aliens and some visitors to report addresses annually and established a central index of all aliens in the U.S. for use by security and enforcement agencies.

5. IMMIGRATION AND NATIONALITY ACT AMENDMENTS OF OCTOBER 3, 1965 (Usually referred to as 1965 immigration act)
(79 *Statutes-at-Large* 911)

a. Abolished the National Origins Quota System eliminating national origin, race, or ancestry as barriers to immigration.
b. Allocated visas on a first come, first served basis, subject to a seven category preference system based primarily on family reunification and secondarily on skills needed in U.S.
c. Established two categories of immigrants not subject to numerical restriction:
   i. Spouses, children, and parents of U.S. citizens.
   ii. Certain ministers of religion; former U.S. government employees; certain persons who had lost citizenship; and certain foreign medical graduates.
d. Set up hemispheric numerical limits for all except those in "c". Eastern Hemisphere, 170,000 annually, with 20,000 per country; Western Hemisphere, 120,000.

6. REFUGEE ACT OF MARCH 17, 1980
(94 *Statutes-at-Large* 102)
Provided first regular procedure for the admission of refugees which had been proceeding on an ad hoc basis since the Truman directive of 1945.

a. Eliminated refugees from preference system.
b. Set world ceiling of 270,000 immigrants annually exclusive of refugees.
c. Provided procedures for consultation with Congress about refugee slots annually and set up emergency procedures.
d. Created an asylee status and provided definitions of both refugees and asylees.

e. Established a domestic resettlement program for refugees.

f. Provided for adjustment to regular status for refugees after 1 year of U.S. residence and for asylees 1 year after status granted.

7. IMMIGRATION REFORM AND CONTROL ACT OF NOVEMBER 6, 1986 (IRCA)

(100 *Statues-at-Large* 3359)

a. Authorized an amnesty for persons illegally in U.S. since January 1, 1982.

b. Created sanctions against employers who *knowingly* hire illegal aliens.

c. Provided for increased enforcement at U.S. borders.

d. Created a new category of seasonal agricultural worker.

e. Extended the date from which aliens, who had resided in the U.S. continuously and illegally, qualified for permanent resident status from June 30, 1948 to January 1, 1972.

f. Authorized adjustment to permanent resident status for certain Cuban and Haitian boat people who had resided continuously in the U.S. since January 1, 1982.

4

EXCERPT FROM *WHOM WE SHALL WELCOME*

Whom We Shall Welcome—the phrase comes from George Washington in 1793[1]—was a report on immigration policy by a presidential commission appointed by President Harry S. Truman in the last year of his administration and issued less than three weeks before he left office. It laid down some broad principles of immigration policy, many of which were eventually written into American immigration law in 1965. The Commission was created, in large part, as the introduction below indicates, in reaction to the McCarran-Walter Act of 1952 which had been passed over Truman's veto.

INTRODUCTION

The President of the United States established the President's Commission on Immigration and Naturalization on September 4, 1952, and required it to make a final report not later than January 1, 1953. He directed the Commission "to study and evaluate the immigration and naturalization policies of the United States" and to make recommendations "for such legislative, administrative, or other action as in its opinion may be desirable in the interest of the economy, security, and responsibilities of this country."

This Report is the result of the Commission's study, and contains the recommendations for an immigration policy best suited, in its judgment, to the interests, needs, and security of the United States. The Commission's functions under the Executive Order are now completed, and it ceases to exist 30 days after this Report is submitted to the President.

---

[1]John C. Fitzpatrick, ed. *The Writings of George Washington,* Vol. XXVII, p. 254, Washington, DC: GPO, 1938. Source: "Whom We Shall Welcome: Report on the President's Commission on Immigration and Naturalization," Washington, D.C.: U.S. Government Printing Office, 1953.

It is noteworthy that all the major religious faiths of America urged the President to appoint a commission for this general purpose. The General Board of the National Council of the Churches of Christ in the United States of America issued a statement to this effect in March 1952. In August 1952, the American Council of Voluntary Agencies for Foreign Service, through its Committee on Displaced Persons and Refugees, urged the creation of a commission to study the basic assumptions of our immigration policy. Its statement was signed by representatives of the War Relief Services of the National Catholic Welfare Conference, the Church World Service of the National Council of the Churches of Christ, the United Service for New Americans, and the National Lutheran Council. And in September 1952, the General Convention of the Protestant Episcopal Church urged the appointment of a commission to study the need for emergency refugee legislation and "to review our permanent immigration policy and its basic assumptions."

It became evident during the debate in Congress and public discussions after the passage June 27, 1952, of the Immigration and Nationality Act of 1952 (generally known as the McCarran-Walter Act) over the President's veto, that the new legislation does not adequately solve immigration and naturalization problems, and that the codification it contains fails to embody principles worthy of this country.

Immigration and nationality law in the United States should perform two functions. First, it should regulate the admission and naturalization of aliens in the best interests of the United States. Second, it should properly reflect the traditions and fundamental ideals of the American people in determining **"whom we shall welcome to a participation of all our rights and privileges."**

This Report discusses the manner in which the law presently regulates the admission and naturalization of aliens, recommends revisions, and explains why the Commission believes these revisions better serve the welfare and security of the United States.

As a separate document, the Judiciary Committee of the House of Representatives has published the extensive record of the 30 sessions of hearings held by the Commission in 11 cities in various sections of the country. The record shows what a substantial and representative cross section of the American people believe to be the best immigration policy for this country.

It is appropriate to examine the second function of immigration policy, the reflection of American traditions and ideals. The Commission would state them as follows:

We Hold These Truths . . .

1. America was founded upon the principle that all men are created equal, that differences of race, color, religion, or national origin should not be used to deny equal treatment or equal opportunity.

Americans have regarded such doctrines as self-evident since the Declaration of Independence.

The immigration law is a key to whether Americans today believe in the essential worth and dignity of the individual human being. It is a clue to whether we really believe that all people are entitled to those "unalienable rights" for the preservation of which our nation was created. It indicates the degree of American humanitarianism. It is a gauge of our faithfulness to the high moral and spiritual principle of our founding fathers—to whom people, as the children of God, were the most important resources of a free nation.

2. America historically has been the haven for the oppressed of other lands.

The immigration law is an index of the extent of our acceptance of the principle that tyranny is forever abhorrent and that its victim should always find asylum in the land of the free. It tests whether we continue to believe that the home of the brave should offer a promise of opportunity to people courageous enough to leave their ancestry homelands, to search for liberty. It is a measure of our fidelity to the doctrine upon which this country was founded, the right of free men to freedom of movement. The immigration law discloses whether Americans still concur in George Washington's challenge: ". . . To bigotry no sanction, to persecution no assistance."

3. American national unity has been achieved without national uniformity.

The immigration law demonstrates whether we abide by the principle that the individual should be free of regimentation. It attests whether we still respect differences of opinion and the right to disagree with the prevailing ideas of the majority, and whether we still welcome new knowledge, new ideas, and new people. It reveals the strength or weakness of our convictions that democracy is the best philosophy and form of government.

4. Americans have believed in fair treatment for all.

The immigration law is a yardstick of our approval of fair play. It is a challenge to the tradition that American law and its administration must be reasonable, fair, and humane. It betokens the current status of the doctrine of equal justice for all, immigrant or native.

5. America's philosophy has always been one of faith in our future and belief in progress.

The immigration law indicates our outlook on the future of America. Those who have faith in a dynamic, expanding, and strong American economy see immigration not only as a part of our heritage but also as essential to our future. On the other hand, those who regard the future of America in terms of a static economy and a maximum population, view immigration with alarm.

6. American foreign policy seeks peace and freedom, mutual understanding and a high standard of living for ourselves and our world neighbors.

The immigration law is an image in which other nations see us. It tells them how we really feel about them and their problems, and not how we say we do. It is also an expression of the sincerity of our confidence in ourselves and our institutions. An immigration law which reflects fear and insecurity makes a hollow mockery of confident world leadership. Immigration policy is an important and revealing aspect of our foreign policy.

No doubt our ideals have not been honored in America at every moment and in every respect. But they have certainly governed our thought and actions over the 175 years of the nation's life. They will continue to do so. The Commission believes that these traditions and ideals should be basic to our immigration laws. Insofar as our immigration policy violates these American traditions and ideals, it weakens the foundations of our liberty and undermines our security and well being. It also damages our position of leadership and destroys the esteem and good reputation the United States has earned in the past.

Other considerations must also condition our immigration laws, such as the protection and preservation of our security against the dangerous and the diseased. The Commission emphasizes that one of its major concerns in applying these principles has been the necessity for the immigration law to safeguard the welfare and security of the United States. However, it is convinced that a full regard for protecting our national security does not require a hostile attitude toward immigration; on the contrary, it believes that full security can be achieved only with a positive immigration policy based not on fears but on faith in people and in the future of a democratic and free United States.

What We Believe

The Commission believes that immigration has given strength to this country not only in manpower, new industries, inventiveness, and prosperity, but also in new ideas and new culture. Immigrants have supplied a continuous flow of creative abilities and ideas that have enriched our nation.

The Commission believes that an outstanding characteristic of the United States is its great cultural diversity within an overriding national unity. The American story proves, if proof were needed, that such differences do not mean the existence of superior and inferior classes.

The Commission believes that it is contrary to the American spirit to view every alien with suspicion and hostility. The Commission is convinced that the American people will not knowingly tolerate immigration laws that reflect distrust, discrimination, and dangerous isolationism. The Commission believes that the American people are entitled to a positive, not a negative immigration policy, and that they desire a law geared to the forward-looking objectives of a great world power.

The Commission believes that although immigrants need the United States, it is also true that the United States needs immigrants, not only for its domestic or foreign benefit, but also to retain, reinvigorate and strengthen the American spirit.

The Commission believes that we cannot be true to the democratic faith of our own Declaration of Independence in the equality of all men, and at the same time pass immigration laws which discriminate among people because of national origin, race, color, or creed. We cannot continue to bask in the glory of an ancient and honorable tradition of providing haven to the oppressed, and belie that tradition by ignoble and ungenerous immigration laws. We cannot develop an effective foreign policy if our immigration laws negate our role of world leadership. We cannot defend civil rights in principle, and deny them in our immigration laws and practice. We cannot boast of our magnificent system of law, and enact immigration legislation which violates decent principles of legal protection.

Nor can we ourselves really believe, or persuade others to think that we believe, that the United States is a dynamic, expanding, and prosperous country if our immigration law is based upon a fear of catastrophe rather than a promise and hope for greater days ahead.

The Commission believes that our present immigration laws—

flout fundamental American traditions and ideals,
display a lack of faith in America's future,
damage American prestige and position among other nations,
ignore the lessons of the American way of life.

The Commission believes that laws which fail to reflect the American spirit must sooner or later disappear from the statute books.

The Commission believes that our present immigration law should be completely rewritten.

5

EXCERPTS FROM REMARKS AT THE SIGNING OF THE IMMIGRATION BILL, OCTOBER 3, 1965

To sign the Immigration Act of 1965 President Lyndon B. Johnson chose to go to Liberty Island in New York Harbor. (He had wanted to sign it on nearby Ellis Island, but it was in such disrepair that the Secret Service prevailed on him not to go there.) In his remarks Johnson made it clear that he regarded the bill as a kind of symbolic redress for past wrongs and that he did not feel that the bill would have important consequences. ("It does not affect the lives of millions.") Johnson—and those who advised him—were clearly wrong. The 1965 immigration act, along with the Civil Rights Act and the Voting Rights Act of the same year, is now regarded by many historians as denoting the high watermark of post-New Deal American liberalism.

Remarks at the Signing of the Immigration Bill, Liberty Island, New York. October 3, 1965

. . . .This bill that we will sign today is not a revolutionary bill. It does not affect the lives of millions. It will not reshape the structure of our daily lives, or really add importantly to either our wealth or our power.

Yet it is still one of the most important acts of this Congress and of this administration.

For it does repair a very deep and painful flaw in the fabric of American justice. It corrects a cruel and enduring wrong in the conduct of the American Nation. . . .

Source: *Public Papers of the Presidents of the United States, Lyndon B. Johnson.* United States Government Printing Office, Washington, 1966.

And this measure that we will sign today will really make us truer to ourselves both as a country and as a people. It will strengthen us in a hundred unseen ways.

I have come here to thank personally each Member of the Congress who labored so long and so valiantly to make this occasion come true today, and to make this bill a reality. I cannot mention all their names, for it would take much too long, but my gratitude—and that of this Nation—belongs to the 89th Congress. . . .

This bill says simply that from this day forth those wishing to immigrate to American shall be admitted on the basis of their skills and their close relationship to those already here.

This is a simple test, and it is a fair test. Those who can contribute most to this country—to its growth, to its strength, to its spirit—will be the first that are admitted to this land.

The fairness of this standard is so self-evident that we may well wonder that it has not always been applied. Yet the fact is that for over four decades the immigration policy of the United States has been twisted and has been distorted by the harsh injustice of the national origins quota system.

Under that system the ability of new immigrants to come to America depended upon the country of their birth. Only 3 countries were allowed to supply 70 percent of all the immigrants.

Families were kept apart because a husband or a wife or a child had been born in the wrong place.

Men of needed skill and talent were denied entrance because they came from southern or eastern Europe or from one of the developing continents.

This system violated the basic principle of American democracy—the principle that values and rewards each man on the basis of his merit as a man.

It has been un-American in the highest sense, because it has been untrue to the faith that brought thousands to these shores even before we were a country.

Today, with my signature, this system is abolished.

We can now believe that it will never again shadow the gate to the American Nation with the twin barriers of prejudice and privilege.

Our beautiful America was built by a nation of strangers. From a hundred different places or more they have poured forth into an empty land, joining and blending in one mighty and irresistible tide.

The land flourished because it was fed from so many sources—because it was nourished by so many cultures and traditions and peoples.

And from this experience, almost unique in the history of nations, has come America's attitude toward the rest of the world. We, because of what we are, feel safer and stronger in a world as varied as the people who make it up—a world where no country rules another and all countries can deal with the basic problems of human dignity and deal with those problems in their own way.

Now, under the monument which has welcomed so many to our shores, the American Nation returns to the finest of its traditions today.

The days of unlimited immigration are past.

But those who do come will come because of what they are, and not because of the land from which they sprung.

When the earliest settlers poured into a wild continent there was no one to ask them where they came from. The only question was: Were they sturdy enough to make the journey, were they strong enough to clear the land, were they enduring enough to make a home for freedom, and were they brave enough to die for liberty if it became necessary to do so?

And so it has been through all the great and testing moments of American history. Our history this year we see in Viet-Nam. Men there are dying—men named Fernandez and Zajac and Zelinko and Mariano and McCormick.

Neither the enemy who killed them nor the people whose independence they have fought to save ever asked them where they or their parents came from. They were all Americans. It was for free men and for America that they gave their all, they gave their lives and selves.

By eliminating that same question as a test for immigration the Congress proves ourselves worthy of those men and worthy of our own traditions as a Nation. . . .

And today we can all believe that the lamp of this grand old lady is brighter today—and the golden door that she guards gleams more brilliantly in the light of an increased liberty for the people from all the countries of the globe. . . .

THE UNFINISHED REFORM:
REGULATING IMMIGRATION IN
THE NATIONAL INTEREST

Otis L. Graham

We all know that the past shapes both the present and the future, but we rarely appreciate how much the present shapes our view of the past. Responding to changed circumstances, we ask different questions of the history that is behind us, rethink it, bring away different meanings.

What changes ahead of us will force us to rethink parts of our past? Our best guesses begin with large changes already under way. Let us consider two large trends that happen to be connected.

The first is global ecocrisis, a convergence of unprecedented population growth and industrialization, which is spreading pollution and degradation of natural ecosystems so severe that in 1992 a group of 1,500 scientists, including ninety-nine Nobel Laureates, issued a "Warning to Humanity" that "human beings and the natural world are on a collision course." They, and all informed environmentalists, foresee an intensifying encounter of mounting human numbers with famine, erratic climate change, species extinction, collapse of oceanic fisheries, and other stresses of a global ecosphere mauled by 10 billion people. This crisis will inevitably produce a more critical view of those parts of our history that led to, and shielded from criticism, the excessive population growth and the environmental abuse that unfold behind and ahead of all peoples—including Americans.

The second trend is also global but more elusive, at work not in the natural environment but in social fabrics, where measurement and prediction are soft at best. We saw it first abroad. The largest international event of recent years was surely the 1989–91 breakup of the former Soviet Union into fifteen republics, but there were kindred developments elsewhere. Czechoslovakia peacefully divided into two parts; Yugoslavia splintered into four or five parts, and bloody separatist struggles continue. Secessionist movements disturb Spain and Canada, there is endless religious conflict in Ireland, and the Chiapas region of Mexico surges with rebellion aimed not at overthrow of the central government but at autonomy. Nations that were smoothly functioning entities a few decades ago are rent by internal division, and many subdivide. Approximately 190 nations exist in the world now, and writer-futurologist John Naisbitt predicts that number to rise to 500 by 2020, as the centrifugal force of tribal loyalties dismantles former nations that turned out to be fragile confederations of nationalities cohering until the mysterious acids of the end of the twentieth century weakened the glue.

No nation-state seemed stronger or more successful than the United States in the 1990s. Was America immune to the viruses of tribalism and fragmentation that were spreading globally? Many observers of end-of-century America think not. As early as the 1970s, journalist Kevin Phillips wrote "The Balkanization of America" as a result of racial, ethnic, and class antagonisms fanned by the winds of the 1960s. In 1989, distinguished historian Arthur M. Schlesinger Jr. wrote the best-selling *The Disuniting of America,* an account of several centrifugal forces—multiculturalism, bilingual education, Afrocentric curricula—that emerged out of the turbulent 1960s to fragment the nation's heritage. Journalist Robert Kaplan, author of *An Empire Wilderness: Travels Into America's Future* (1998), found that the entire Southwest was becoming a separate region as Mexican immigration relentlessly shifted population balances and that Los Angeles was becoming a globalized city-state where "there is no agreement anymore on culture," in the words of a UCLA sociologist. Newspapers in 1993 carried a cartoon titled "The Divided State of America," with the country divided into thirteen regions organized around ethnicity, race, cause (environmentalists took over Alaska), or foreign ownership (Haiti and Cuba took parts of Florida, Japan took Hawaii).

Global ecocrisis and national fragmentation qualify as fundamental and transforming trends, if they persist. The first is certain to do so; the second is more speculative, but must be taken seriously. The result of one or both will be to change our history ahead—and thus also behind, causing us to rethink our past, to shift our questions and inevitably our answers. Our immigration history connects to both trends. This essay builds on a rethinking of that history that has already begun and consolidates and extends it.

EUROPE SENDS THE GREAT WAVE

It is not clear who invented the phrase, "America is a nation of immigrants," but this now hackneyed thought is not true for any of our national history and only applies in the British colonies for the first few decades of the seventeenth century. Thereafter, most Americans (by which we mean North Americans in the territory now the United States) were native-born, and that has remained true for the rest of our history to this date. America is a nation of the native-born. However, it is certainly true, as historian Victor Greene observed, that "the immigration stamp is upon us."

Whatever else this implies, our history tells us that immigration in the American story has always been controversial—associated always with both benefits and costs. This reality has been lost in the current romantic view that immigration is always a good thing, both for host society and immigrants. In fact, this was not the view of the first human residents of the Americas, the indigenous peoples in this hemisphere when European explorers and immigrants began to arrive. For native populations, European immigration meant death by disease, warfare, and social disorganization, a virtual genocide in which their populations fell by 90 percent by 1600. In North America, a Native American population estimated from 2 to 20 million (a range lately narrowed to 4 to 7 million) had dropped to perhaps 250,000 at the start of the twentieth century. This is the primal American experience with immigration—grotesquely negative, unique, and (we fervently hope) unrepeatable. Yet it should anchor our understanding that immigration is morally complicated, immensely powerful in charting human destiny, and always a shifting mixture of Goods and Bads. That is why nations have immigration policy—hoping to minimize the latter and maximize the former.

When these death-bringing European immigrants became Americans by birth, their own response to further immigration was mixed. Industrious immigrants were indispensable in expanding colonial populations, and they were welcomed in the abstract and upon arrival. However, the quality of immigrants from the Mother Country was a constant issue of concern. "Slums and alleys were raked for labor to stock the plantations," writes historian Marion Bennett; dependent kinfolk were sometimes dumped on ships headed for America, and the British government was notorious for shipping felons to the southern colonies especially. Colonial assemblies enacted restrictions against paupers and criminal immigrants as early as 1639, and health restrictions followed. Independence placed such decisions firmly in American hands, and the Founders both welcomed immigration in principle and had serious reservations about its capacity for harm to the fledgling nation. Jefferson, in his *Notes on Virginia,* raised fundamental questions about populating the country by immigration. Natural increase would provide Virginia with 4.5 million (which he thought in fact too large a number) in eighty-two years, so there seemed no need to accelerate that growth by "the importation of foreigners." There would be "inconveniences to be thrown into the scale" if immigration were the path chosen. "It is for the happiness of those united in society to harmonize as much as possible" in matters of civil government, but immigrants could be expected to come henceforth mostly from countries of absolute monarchy, bringing habits and outlooks rendering our polity "heterogeneous, incoherent, distracted." A few "useful artificers" might "teach us something we do not know," but the drafter of the Declaration of Independence specifically discouraged building the future nation out of immigration. Hamilton, this time, agreed with his political rival: "The opinion advanced in [Thomas Jefferson's] *Notes on Virginia* is undoubtedly correct . . . The influx of foreigners must . . . tend to produce a heterogeneous compound; to change and corrupt the national spirit . . . to introduce foreign propensities." These sentiments were widely shared. George Washington spoke of his hopes that "the poor, the needy and oppressed of the Earth" would "resort to the fertile plains of our western country" where of course he was a landowner. At other times, however, he seemed to agree with Jefferson about growing from the American population base as it came out of the Revolution: "I have no intention to invite immigrants, even if there are no restrictive acts against it. I am opposed to it altogether." He and the other Founders had continuing concerns about the habits, particularly the language, political principles, and morals, of those stepping off the boats. How to guarantee the immigration only of "foreigners of merit and republican principles" (James Madison) but not "the common class of vagrants, paupers and other outcasts of Europe" (Congressman James Jackson of Georgia)? Policy makers expressed such worries without devising an effective filter against bad immigration, and the country remained essentially open to settlers.

The Europeans (and, involuntarily, for a few years after the Revolution, Africans) continued to leave their homelands and come, although annual arrivals in the first three decades of the republic were estimated at less than 10,000 a year (no records were kept until 1820), well below 1 percent of the resident population in any given year. The United States was growing primarily by the natural increase of its population, as Jefferson preferred. These early decades were a lull before a larger demographic convulsion that would eventually force Americans to rethink their empty-continent optimism. Europe had entered an astonishing 150-year surge of population growth, generating a mass movement of peoples of which the settling of the British colonies was only the first ripple. In the words of historian Alfred Crosby, Europeans "swarmed and swarmed again" during the nineteenth century, driven by population pressures, starvation, and civil and religious unrest. A "Caucasian tsunami" of some 50–60 million immigrants came to colonize the rich soils and temperate zones of what Crosby calls the "Neo-Europes" of North America, Argentina, Australia, and New Zealand.

A heavy pulse of Germans began to reach the United States in the 1830s and Irish immigration began in the 1840s, boosting the annual average immigration to 120,000 a year between 1820 and 1860, averages that masked the erratic surges out of Europe that brought nearly 3 million in the 1850s alone. This was the first stage of the Great Wave, and the Civil War and economic depression of the 1870s brought a lull. Then in the 1880s the Europeans "swarmed again" in a second and last phase, as industrialization and farm mechanization moved south and eastward on a disruptive journey through European regions with rapidly growing populations and chronic unemployment. In the next fifty years nearly 30 million Europeans migrated to the United States, "new immigrants" from new places—Italians from the southern regions of their peninsula, the multiple ethnic subsets of the Russian Empire, Poles, Serbs, Croats, Bulgarians and Hungarians from the Austro-Hungarian Empire, Armenians, Greeks, Portuguese. Two million of the world's 7.5 million Jews relocated to America out of central and eastern Europe during these years. To the other American coast, to the "Golden Mountain" of California, came Chinese and Japanese.

This was the Great Wave, the most massive of all human migrations to date, provoking a protracted, soul-searching national debate, culminating in the 1920s in a decision to take control of the nation's demographic destiny and end the era of uncontrolled immigration to the United States.

THE GREAT WAVE AND THE AMERICAN FUTURE

The Great Wave washing out of Europe was generated by unprecedented population growth during the 200-year "demographic transition" from high to low birth and death rates. The transition was disastrously slow. Death rates came down first and fastest, the decline in birthrates lagging by decades. A stupendous surge of population growth was the result. This vast migration of millions of humans from their homelands was driven by the pull of industrial-urban expansion and the push of rural poverty and unemployment, political and civil wars, and (especially in the case of the eastern European Jews) religious persecution or the well-founded fear of it.

Remembering that Jefferson's America absorbed less than 10,000 immigrants a year, the size of the Caucasian tsunami when it hit in the 1880s was beyond historic experience. Some 27 million immigrants arrived in the United States between 1880 and 1930 when the wave was curbed by restrictive policies and worldwide depression. In the years after 1900, arrivals averaged close to or above 1 million a year. There was much re-immigration back to Europe, but still the permanent demographic impact was enormous. The foreign-born population in the early years of this century is now estimated at 13–15 percent of the total; the South was home to only 2 percent, and the rest of the country, especially the seaboards, had populations that were approximately 20 percent foreign-born. Economic historian Richard Easterlin estimates that at its peak, in the decade 1900-10, immigrants were contributing roughly 40 percent of U.S. population growth, and much more than that if their descendants are added.

The societies producing this surge of humanity toward America and the other Neo-Europes were not in the western tier of European nations, but the eastern and southern peripheries. Whatever their many shortcomings in practice, the western European societies peopling America in the seventeenth to nineteenth centuries had been early and advanced incubators of constitutional democracy; the beginnings of religious pluralism (within a Christian framework); and unprecedented progress in science, technology, and economic development. By contrast, Great Wave arrivals were from nations or regions within the Russian and Austro-Hungarian empires that by Western standards were profoundly backward. These mostly peasant peoples had "lived much closer to serfdom" (in historian John Higham's words) than earlier arrivals. To heighten the sense of a cultural gap between Americans and newcomers, much of the Great Wave was not Protestant but Roman or Orthodox Catholic, or not Christian at all but Jewish—or, on the West Coast, practitioners of Asian religions entirely foreign to Americans.

THE AMERICAN DESTINATION: A TROUBLED SOCIETY

This tide of new people from different homelands than had historically provisioned America also arrived at an inauspicious time for absorbing more people from anywhere, let alone from more alien traditions. The powerful energies of urbanizing industrialism within the United States were dislocating America's rural populations. Mechanization on the farm and the lure of industrial jobs siphoned millions into expanding cities unable to cope with crowding and pollution or to maintain basic social services. The United States had entered that phase of economic development referred to by economist Walt Rostow as the "take-off" into industrialization. In the long run, this meant rising living standards that doubled American per capita incomes between the 1860s and World War I. The bad news was that these early decades of industrialization were plagued with disorder. First was a savage business cycle, in which economic growth was interrupted between the Civil War and the beginning of the twentieth century by three grinding depressions, one arriving in the middle of each decade. Immigrants setting out for the United States in these years were voting their belief that America was and would continue to be the most wealth-producing economic machine in the world. In the short run, however, workers and businesses in America existed in conditions of economic depression for almost half the years from the Civil War to the new century, with high unemployment even in good years. Labor unrest and massive strikes plagued basic industries. The rise of agrarian radicalism, the growth of labor organization, and the stirrings of a socialist movement clouded the future. These economic strains merged with a set of political and social worries—political corruption, urban congestion and vice, child labor, alcohol and tobacco abuse, degradation of natural environments. A broad "progressive reform" movement began to build, and in the first two decades of the twentieth century a main theme of American history would be the multifaceted interventions (historian Robert Wiebe called it "a search for order") to address these problems through research, public education, formation of activist social institutions, and a resort to government power.

Into this America came the streams of Great Wave immigrants, igniting a sustained controversy that was inextricably a part of the broader social reform impulse. Great Wave immigration was seen by progressive-era reformers as another uncontrolled force threatening harm to political democracy, the aspirations of labor, social order in the cities, and American identity itself.

BEGINNINGS OF REFORM:
CLOSING THE DOORS TO THE GOLDEN MOUNTAIN

The long road to immigration reform began in an unlikely place—on the West Coast, with the question of the Chinese. Mine owners and railroad builders in the region, desperate for cheap and docile labor ready for back-breaking tasks, began importing Chinese coolie (the term was an English version of a Hindu phrase for unskilled laborers transported from the Orient) labor about 1850, along with a few females for prostitution. The reception of California citizens at first tended to be genial to the almost entirely male labor force, described by one citizen as "sober, industrious, and inoffensive." The reception turned hostile when at the end of the 1860s the gold rush boom had waned and the Union Pacific Railroad was completed (1869), but Asian immigration continued. Chinese numbers by the 1870s reached 10 percent of the state's population and one-quarter of its labor force, a low-wage labor pool beginning to compete with American labor. The specter of continuing and unlimited flows of Chinese peasant labor seemed to many to threaten more than a downward pressure on wages. "Transported and largely controlled by certain Chinese societies," John Higham writes, "they awakened fears of a new kind of slavery in a nation already convulsed by the struggle over African slavery."

Beyond posing a fundamental economic threat to American workers, the Chinese were almost universally thought entirely unassimilable for permanent settlement. They fled, or were sent into virtual slavery, from a once-respected ancient civilization, which by the mid-nineteenth century had fallen into the chaos of civil war and banditry of the Taiping Rebellion (1851–64) with its outward ripples of disorder. The American image of China, once favorable, veered toward the view that this disintegrating empire, and therefore its citizens, now had little to teach the civilized world in the arts of government or civil society. In America the Chinese kept strictly to themselves in their residential enclaves and to the American eye retained peculiar customs and questionable health standards, operating private courts of justice through their secret societies or "tongs," which were also said to control gambling and opium rings. The fact that Chinese migrating to Hawaii met with far less cultural resistance and showed less ethnic isolation suggests that their "unassimilability" on the West Coast was at least partially a result of their reception by white society. In any event, resistance to their growing numbers mounted and occasionally could become vicious.

There were taxes on and boycotts of Chinese laundries and other businesses, community expulsions, and even riots. Organized opposition to Chinese immigrants came from a coalition of workers, small farmers and shop owners, energized by the harsh depression of the mid-1870s. Denis Kearney of the California Workingmen's Party, composed substantially of immigrants, mostly Irish, provided passionate, even angry leadership behind the slogan "The Chinese must go!" Employers also came in for harsh criticism for using the Chinese as pawns. Anti-Chinese sentiment erupted also on the East Coast when significant numbers of Chinese laborers arrived, and some were used as strikebreakers in Massachusetts and New Jersey.

In response to a remarkable intensity of complaint on the West Coast that was increasingly shared nationwide (the platforms of both political parties endorsed restriction of Chinese immigration in 1876 and 1880), Congress moved rapidly toward an historic reversal of the tradition of laissez-faire in immigration matters. A Chinese Exclusion Act in 1879 was vetoed because it violated the Burlingame Treaty of 1868. The treaty was renegotiated, and Congress by wide margins passed the Chinese Exclusion Act of 1882, suspending the admission of Chinese "laborers" for ten years. (Chinese "other than laborers" could legally come to the United States with Chinese government certificates, an odd form of control; in any event, Chinese were declared ineligible for citizenship.) It was the first sharp curtailment of immigration to America—colonial, state, and federal bars to the insane and "persons likely to become a public charge" kept out very few—and was extended with minor adjustments for sixty years, until 1943, when Chinese "exclusion"(which had never been total) was eased.

A new tradition of restricting immigration through federal policy had begun. Unfortunately, it was a fumbling start on the road to national control over U.S. demographic destiny and the labor market. West Coast Americans' understandable concerns over an unlimited flow of cheap Asian labor had sometimes veered into panic or anger, leading on occasion to resorts to force against very peaceful invaders, with much racialist language harsh to the modern ear. In the public debate, the arguments for continuing the laissez-faire regime on national immigration were remarkably puny—a combination of sentimental invocations of the permanent and circumstances-ignoring claims of a heritage of "hospitality to all suppressed nationalities," along with the argument, candidly stated by the Reverend Henry Ward Beecher, that without the Chinese, we Americans would have "no race that will be willing to do what we call menial work."

Against this, restrictionists built a compelling argument that swung huge majorities behind immigration reform. "We do not object to the Chinese because of their race or their language or their religion," editorialized a labor union journal, whose readers surely agreed only in part: "But we do object to an organized effort to introduce cheap laborers into the Republic."

Even those who were initially hesitant to break with the nation's open door policy concluded that, in addition to the labor problem, Americans and Chinese were simply too different to permit large and sustained Oriental immigration with the resultant social conflict. "If they are brought rapidly, in large numbers, into any Western country, there will be unpleasant friction . . .", said University of Michigan President James Angell, who had led negotiations to rewrite the Burlingame Treaty. In the crisis, democratic government had a responsibility to respond to overwhelming majority opinion. "The public peace is disturbed," said respected Republican Senator George Edmunds of Vermont, "and if you can save it by giving time for reason to restore itself and passion to cool, is it not wise? . . . Then let us protect the Chinamen by having them hold up a little while . . . While all mankind are of one kin . . . one destiny," the Chinese were very different in culture and religion, and "no republic can succeed that has not a homogenous population." Edmunds was one of many, observes historian Andrew Gyory, who "did not condemn the Chinese or call them inferior; he simply stressed their differentness."

Thus, a beginning had been made in the emotionally difficult transition from traditional laissez-faire toward immigration limits. In retrospect, and even to moderates at the time, some of the terms of the debate needlessly offended another nationality and stigmatized those of Chinese origins remaining in America. A drastic reduction in Chinese immigration could have been amply justified in terms of labor market impacts and problems of assimilation of Asian immigration on a vast scale, without slurs on foreigners, and without denying citizenship to those already here. The restrictionist impulse activated many who never learned this lesson.

Another lesson was not fully grasped. Massive immigration of a surplus and thus low-wage population vastly different culturally from Americans generated severe social conflicts across the entire range of society (with the exception of large employers, always eager for cheap labor without concern for social repercussions). Those conflicts arose from real as well as perceived economic, social, and cultural threats to standards achieved and cherished by the native population. People will react to these forces, as they should in a self-governing republic, and the formula for turning those responses hostile and lengthy is unresponsive government. The Chinese Exclusion Act, with its stupid title and other flaws apparent to people living a century later (and to some at the time), prevented what had been building as a massive and sustained immigration of Chinese laborers to Jinshan—"the Golden Mountain"—with explosive potential. The U.S. government's first step toward controlling one of the uncontrolled forces tearing at the social fabric allowed the level of social conflict and accommodation between Caucasians and Chinese on the West Coast to slowly (too slowly for anyone's preference) drain away to be replaced by the Occidental-Oriental amity that generally prevailed on the West Coast in the latter half of the twentieth century.

The progressive reform impulse now moved on to a confrontation with the rest of the uncontrolled Great Wave, as reformers erratically searched for a national policy on immigration to replace the laissez-faire stance so inappropriate to the modern era.

THE DEBATE OVER THE NEW IMMIGRATION AND HOW TO EXERT CONTROL

The year 1882 also produced the first general federal immigration law, extending a colonial and state tradition of excluding those found on inspection to be convicts, lunatics, idiots, and paupers, followed in 1885 by a ban on immigrants brought in under the "contract labor system" in which employers or agents advanced sums to those without the means to finance the voyage. These were tiny steps, weakly enforced. Reformers pondered other grounds for exclusion, broad enough to cut the numbers in a way that barring paupers and lunatics would not. More positively, what were the criteria for choosing those most valuable to the country, providing a basis for excluding all others? How could the weak, minimalist government in Washington be given not just the legal mandate but the bureaucratic capacity to regulate immigration, now that the Supreme Court (in 1876) had ruled that this was a national and not a state function?

These questions arose in the 1880s, and pressure for acceptable answers began a forty-year buildup. The appeal for immigration control came from many quarters, "from society," in the words of one scholar, Keith Fitzgerald, who analyzed the lists of witnesses participating in key congressional hearings related to immigration from 1875 to 1891. The Knights of Labor were the principal sponsors of the 1885 Contract Labor Act, but by the time a House special committee to investigate the immigration problem began its work in 1888, hearings elicited calls for restriction from the new American Federation of Labor (AFL), local labor leaders, journalists, local public officials, some chambers of commerce, and governmental and private charities overwhelmed by the numbers of the indigent and ill. The social support for restriction was broad and diverse, and had black Americans been invited to testify before governmental bodies in these years, their representatives would certainly have added their appeals for stemming the tide of foreign labor, as Tuskegee Institute's Booker T. Washington had done in his Atlanta Exposition address in 1895.

Against a background of severe economic depressions in the mid-1880s and again in the mid-1890s, along with labor unrest, strikes, and spectacular episodes of violence (such as the 1886 Haymarket bomb explosion at a foreign-led anarchist political rally, which killed seven policemen), the political machinery began to respond. The Immigration Law of 1891 established the post of Commissioner of Immigration in the Treasury Department (a curious place to lodge immigration regulation), and by 1893 both houses of Congress for the first time had standing committees on immigration. The national government was taking the first halting steps toward equipping itself to make immigration policy.

Even so, it was lagging quite far behind public opinion. News media and magazines reflected a swelling discussion, and in 1892 the platforms of both major political parties recognized immigration as a problem. Acknowledging the need for some sort of filters or selection process, the Democrats "heartily approve[d] all legitimate efforts to prevent the U.S. from being used as the dumping ground for the known criminals and professional paupers of Europe" but "denounce[d] any and all attempts to restrict the immigration of the industrious and worthy." Again in 1896 both major parties endorsed restriction, although how the government would limit immigration was unclear. Organized labor held a lengthy debate on the issue beginning in the mid-1890s and shifted ground toward restriction. AFL head Samuel Gompers, himself the son of immigrants, wrote: "I have always felt that restricting opportunities for others is a grave responsibility. . . . America is the product of the daring, the genius, the idealism of those who left homes and kindred to settle in the new land." However, those sentiments steadily lost ground in the face of the numbers and character of the new immigration and its apparent impacts. In the 1880s, 5.2 million came, in the 1890s 3.7 million arrived, and in the first decade of the twentieth century 8.8 million arrived, a "long-term upward trend in immigration between 1880 and 1914 which was apparent to contemporaries and influenced public opinion," in the words of labor historian A. T. Lane. One-fifth of the work force in the country was foreign-born as the nineteenth century closed, and the foreign stock (foreign-born and their children) was 34 percent of the total white population in 1880, rising to 40 percent by 1910.

THE NEW CENTURY AND THE URBAN CRISIS

The American industrial city at the end of the nineteenth century was a vortex pulling in labor from wherever it was in surplus—the farms of New England and Midwest, but also the crowded rural villages of Poland, Russia, and Italy's Mezzogiorno. From 1880 to 1910 the American urban population tripled. Chicago grew on the average by 50,000 a year through the 1890s; New York counted 984 people per acre in the city's Sanitary District A, or 300,000 people in a six square-block area, a greater density than Bombay. More than a hundred American cities, most in the East and Midwest, doubled in size in the 1880s, growth rates that swamped social services. Economic dynamism drove the growth, but the price was high: "crowded tenement districts, chronic health problems, billowing smoke, polluted waterways, traffic congestion, unbearable noise, and mounds of putrefying garbage," in historian Martin Melosi's words. Although most of America's population growth derived from the high fertility of the native population, the problems of the cities were greatly intensified and shaped by the long, relentless tide of the Great Wave out of Europe.

These immigrants were mostly unskilled peasants, with the major exception of the Jews, classified by port officials as nearly 70 percent skilled workers. They clustered in ethnic neighborhoods and gave the turn-of-the-century city a memorable flavor of foreignness—an urban mosaic of non-English tongues and signage, exotic cuisine, dress, and holidays. Incredible density and unsanitary conditions became associated with the new immigrant—1,231 Italians counted living in 120 rooms in New York, chickens and goats fed and slaughtered in halls or alleyways, a single tenement where journalist Jacob Riis (in his *How the Other Half Lives*) found Jewish parents raising 58 babies and 38 children over five years of age. The nation's urban population was 41 percent foreign born by 1920, and because the South had never become a popular destination for immigrants, in most major northeastern cities the proportion was closer to two-thirds.

They had brought more than crowding. Chicago social worker Edith Abbott compiled a book of documents, *Historical Aspects of the Immigration Problem,* and in the section "Pauperism and Crime and Other Domestic Immigration Problems" reported a range of problems from insanity, pauperism, and criminality, to disease. None of these were new to America; all were copiously homegrown. How much was imported, and was there a remedy? Cholera, called the "disease of the poor" because the bacterium enters the intestine through human fecal contamination of the water supply, left the Indian subcontinent around 1820, spread into Europe to take root from Russia to Sweden, then crossed the Atlantic carried either by sailors, rats, and/or immigrants (medical authorities were not sure) to ignite epidemics in 1832, 1845, and 1866. An outbreak of the disease in Russia in 1892 came when immigration to the United States was at an all-time high and after an outbreak of typhus fever was contained by a ruthless quarantine of arriving Jews. "The 'cholera scare' . . . of 1893, which had its origin among the steerage passengers of the great Atlantic liners," wrote a respected journalist in *The Atlantic Monthly* in 1895, "brought the results of unlimited and uncontrolled immigration vividly before the American people."

MAKING THE CASE FOR REFORM

THE ECONOMIC IMPACT

Epidemics of infectious disease were intermittent, relatively rare, and by no means always brought on by arriving foreigners. The major immediate, daily impact of mass immigration is economic, chiefly felt in the labor market. By the 1890s the relentless augmentation of the labor force by foreign workers had shifted the attitudes of the American worker from solidarity to resentment. An early and forceful complaint at the New Immigration's scale and impacts came from the fast-growing AFL. At their annual convention in 1896, a depression year, President Samuel Gompers expressed disappointment at the results of earlier efforts "to close the floodgates for hordes of laborers . . . brought to this country like slaves under contract" and led his federation of unions toward a restrictionist position whose details were as yet unclear. Labor newspapers and meetings reflected mixed feelings, such was the hold of the ethic of worker solidarity, but increasingly the rank and file pushed labor leaders to face the realities that a mass infusion of foreign labor put downward pressure on wages and served employers' need for strikebreakers. A factory work force divided by language and nationality found class solidarity difficult, and management welcomed the disempowering diversity. Without restrictive legislation, the existing nonpolicy on immigration would produce, in a 1905 editorial in a labor magazine, "more rack rent for slum landlords . . . more rake-offs for contractors, *padroni* and foreign agents of transportation (companies), more voting cattle for our political stockyards . . . more non-unionists for manufacturing combines, more outlay for every charitable and penal institution in the country, and incalculably more misery for America's wage earners."

Labor leaders were surely thinking mostly of white labor, being white themselves. However, historians of black labor in urban places and industrial occupations find (in the words of historian David Hellwig) that "more than whites [they] suffered from competition by the largely unskilled migrants," as "struggles for jobs and housing bred deep-seated hostilities," especially among the Irish, staunch political allies of the Democratic Party. "Blacks in Steelton [Pa.] were pushed down and out . . . rather than upward by immigrants who followed them," writes John Bodnar; "The influx of Croats, Serbs, Slovenes, Bulgarians, and Italians into Steelton, especially after 1900, had a devastating impact upon the town's Black working force." Black leaders, too, expressed complaints about the economic impact of the Great Wave upon black workers and their futures, both north and south, although they were given precious little space in the forums of public discussion. "To those of the white race who look to the incoming of those of foreign birth and strange tongue and habit for the prosperity of the South," Booker T. Washington had urged an audience of mostly white business and industrial leaders at the Atlanta Exposition in 1895, "were I permitted I would repeat what I say to my own race, 'Cast down your bucket where you are.' 'Cast it down among the eight millions of Negroes whose habits you know . . . among these people who have, without strikes and labour wars, tilled your fields, cleared your forests, built your railroads and cities . . .' A trickle of northward migrating southern blacks had begun, but Washington knew that the ready availability of cheap foreign labor at the gates of northeastern industries left no incentive among employers to welcome or recruit black labor. The Great Wave was not only happening; it was preventing something else from happening in the nation's labor markets—a labor shortage that would have opened opportunities for American blacks, requiring only a short migration up the eastern seaboard.

THE CIVIC IMPACT

The turn-of-the-century conversion of the rank-and-file and leadership of the labor movement to a restrictionist stance (some of whom, like Samuel Gompers, were immigrants themselves) was mainly driven by economic harm, as they experienced it. Harvard economist Claudia Golden has documented "substantial and rising negative effects of immigration on both laborer and artisan wages from the late 1890s to the early 1920s" and tied the political strength of restrictionist sentiment to those impacts. However, another concern shared across class lines arose from the heart of nineteenth-century American political culture, from a cluster of ideas historians now identify as republicanism, a channel of thought and conviction running at full strength in the Founders' generation and persisting through the nineteenth and into the twentieth centuries. The core of republicanism was the unshakeable conviction among Americans that they occupied a unique place in history. They had sensed themselves as a people after a century and a half as colonial subjects of the Crown, demanded and won independence, established over a vast expanse of territory the only modern republic, one dedicated to freedom and (therefore) self-government. This was a rare, precious human experiment. Could Americans preserve, even expand it? The answer depended upon the constant cultivation and strengthening of civic virtue, best seen in active citizenship seeking the common good before any special interest. Republicanism began with the belief that a magnificent start had been made (an easy assumption to make among white males, since for them it was true). Moreover, the Republic's fortunate citizens must always be vigilant against decay and backsliding, ever realists about human nature and the possibility of losing the republican experiment through the erosion of civic virtue.

Self-rule thus demanded the active political participation of every voter, and the white male electorate of the mid- to late nineteenth century achieved astonishing levels of voter turnout. However, participation meant more: keen attention to issues as debated in meetings and in an intensely partisan press; participation in parades, conventions, meetings; and a nonstop and usually emotional engagement in the unending political struggle. If citizens slipped back from active involvement in public affairs, republicanism and history taught, corruption was always poised to capture the apparatus of government.

The political heritage and habits of the New Immigrants gave multiple cause for alarm. They migrated from the decaying autocratic empires of Russia or that "political tower of Babel" Austria-Hungary (in historian George M. Stephenson's phrase), their civic experience one of unrelieved subjugation. With such a background, it was no surprise that journalistic accounts and daily observations of life in the industrial cities in the East and Midwest piled up stories of a pliant and uninformed, non-English speaking and substantially illiterate immigrant public manipulated into voter fraud or bloc voting when voting at all. Political corruption has a long American history, but the exploding industrial cities of the late nineteenth century were by all reports in a class by themselves, and the Great Wave from Europe seemed a source of mounting misgovernment. The New Immigrants' central instinct about government seemed to be to distrust and avoid it. "They do not [unlike Americans]," Stephenson again, "conceive of government as part of themselves." If "to be American was to be free," Keith Fitzgerald summarizes the testimony before congressional committees in the 1890s, "to exercise that freedom politically, to be literate in the free art of republicanism," then "entire races were unfamiliar with [these qualities] . . . and probably mentally incapable of learning them."

THE QUESTION OF CULTURAL AND RACIAL DIFFERENCE: A GUIDE TO THE DEBATE

"Entire races . . . mentally incapable of learning them." Here was another aspect of the concern about Great Wave immigration, one that must be understood historically.

When Germans began to enter the United States in large numbers, they sounded and acted different, and the Irish even more so. Pre-Civil War objections to this surge of immigration focussed mainly on cultural differences that would impede assimilability and, if migration were uninterrupted, make Roman Catholicism ascendant. There was no resolution of this issue through the political system, which at that time was paralyzed by the slavery debate. The mass migration of Germans and Irish eased for reasons internal to those nations. The Civil War distracted attention from these immigration questions, and with time an answer slowly emerged in favor of confidence in assimilation even during periods of massive immigration. Germans and Irish, now Americans, fought bravely in the Union armies, erasing memories of the Boston Irish who had volunteered and fought with Mexico against the United States in 1848. Over a long period of time American Catholics proved, as successive Popes might be imagined as complaining, more American than Catholic. It helped in the absorption of this mass of foreigners that the flow of Germans and Irish abated. Round one in the debate over Great Wave immigration went (on points) to those confident of America's absorptive capacities. The election of Irish-Catholic John F. Kennedy as President of the United States in 1960 seemed a strong confirmation of that verdict. On the question whether to worry about the absorption of massive immigration of foreigners, experience by the Civil War seemed to show the optimists ahead, when they also had luck in their corner. Alien (though still Western European) nationalities could be Americanized, if the numbers were brought down.

When the Great Wave resumed after the 1880s, the immigrants were even more obviously and fundamentally different. Their numbers, poverty, low average educational levels, and tendency to cluster in industrializing cities compounded problems already festering in the United States. These generated a vast and rising volume of complaints that were, as we have seen, first economic and then civic: job competition, downward pressure on wages and standards, ethnic and linguistic fragmentation in the work force preventing class solidarity, augmentation of crowding, crime, pauperism, criminality. Added to all this was the worry, earlier discussed, over a cluster of civic maladies made worse as peoples from despotic societies settled as politically passive masses in an actively participatory Anglo-Saxon-based polity keenly atuned to the preservation of republican self-government.

These differences greatly concerned citizens and might be said to have opened (in the 1880s) round two of the debate between two groups: Americans who saw in mass immigration a multitude of current social costs as well as a long-term peril to the very nature of the republic and the identity of the American people, and those who were optimistic that uncontrolled immigration would again work out for the best this time as it had in the past.

To anyone recalling round one, round two would appear to be a new contest in a very different setting, even if the basic issue was familiar. Germans and Irish, coming as families, were one thing. Millions of displaced peasants from southern and eastern Europe, mostly male "birds of passage" with no apparent intent to take root in America, seemed another, both as to number and quality.

In the long debate over their assimilability, two very different levels of analysis were entwined and (in historical reconstruction) blurred. Were the new newcomers culturally so backward that not even the American environment could make of them promising citizen material in any reasonable length of time? Or were they "racially inferior" and thus beyond correction? Our generation, facing massive immigration from countries far behind the United States in most measures of civilization and influenced by postmodernist rejection of cultural judgments, steadfastly refuses to use the language of either cultural or racial hierarchy. Americans a century ago used both, robustly and with a confusing lack of precision.

Contemporary historians and their readers are especially offended by the racial judgments laced through the debates of that earlier time. Racism itself, as an ideology or set of beliefs, is imbedded in American history and is found in any historical account of this nation, whether of literature or politics or religion or sport. We would expect racism, whatever we mean by that travel-weary term, to make some mark within the story of immigration reform, as it does in every aspect of American life during the Progressive era.

The new element was scientific racism, an historically temporary enhancement of the power of racialist ideas long present in American history. Scientific racism refers to the new channels of intellectual energy opened to the idea of a racial hierarchy among humans by the immense influence of biology after Charles Darwin's *Origin of Species* (1859). Darwin wrote almost nothing about humans in that book (turning to human evolution in his *The Descent of Man* of 1871), but social scientists in Britain, Germany, and (especially) the United States were enormously influenced by the idea that biology had tipped the scales in the old nature/nurture or inheritance/environment debate decisively toward inheritance. After four centuries of discovery, exploration, and subjugation of non-European societies invariably unable to resist the accumulated prowess of the West, Darwinian biology led many intellectuals to varying degrees of conversion to the idea that racial hierarchy was scientifically established. Many of the most respected American natural scientists and the rising elite of social scientists gaining influence within policy debate in the United States developed in the decades around the start of this century a sense that science had confirmed a racial schema from Nordic supremacy down along a descending hierarchy of other races.

In this scheme, Africans occupied the bottom rung. Not until the 1920s did they begin to change their minds about this hierarchy of inherited traits (and indeed the very existence of discrete races).

Inevitably, the issue of the New Immigration, given its timing in the late nineteenth and early twentieth centuries, would to some degree bear the imprint here and there of the "findings" of scientific racism. The Reverend Josiah Strong, whose reputation as a writer was made by the success of his *Our Country* (1885), wrote in 1893 that "there is now being injected into the veins of the nation a large amount of inferior blood every day of every year." Francis A. Walker, variously Yale professor and president of Massachusetts Institute of Technology and chief of the Bureau of Statistics, provided a quotation that few historians have passed up, when he referred to the New Immigrants generally as "peasantry, degraded below our utmost conceptions. . . . They are beaten men from beaten races." Political science professor Thomas Woodrow Wilson, later two-term president of the United States, wrote in his *A History of the American People:*

> Throughout the century men of the sturdy stocks of the north of Europe had made up the main strain of foreign blood which was every year added to the vital force of the country, or else men of the Latin-Gallic stocks of France and northern Italy; but now there came men of the lowest class from the south of Italy and men of the meaner sort out of Hungary and Poland, men out of the ranks where there was neither skill nor energy nor any initiative of quick intelligence . . .

New York writer Madison Grant gave racial difference the dimensions of a global conflict in his *The Passing of the Great Race* (1916):

> The long-suppressed, conquered servile classes [are] rising against the master race. . . . The danger is from within and not from without. Neither the black nor the brown nor the yellow nor the red will conquer the white in battle. But if the valuable elements in the Nordic Race mix with inferior strains or die out through race suicide, then the citadel of civilization will fall for mere lack of defenders.

A generation later, Adolf Hitler would befoul and wound the world with language of that sort. This has created a temptation to find Hitler bedfellows wherever in earlier times and other countries the language of racial hierarchy and threat appears. This guilty association guarantees a misunderstanding of the American discourse of the early years of this century. Language exposing assumptions about superior and inferior racial endowments in that era did not mark off a unified category of retrograde people. Then, racialist terminology and assumptions were so widespread as to be virtually universal among whites (and some non-whites). In the relatively brief heyday of scientific racism, many of America's best-educated, progressive elite were led to race-based assessments of many contemporary social issues including immigration, guided by the best science of their day.

More important than recognizing its pervasiveness, the language of "race" did not mean they were talking about race in its biological sense. What is surprising is how often contemporaries selected a very different, nonbiological logic for explaining human difference. There was widespread acknowledgment that the incoming migrants from eastern and central Europe brought many negative social characteristics, but these were not attributed to "race" as often as contemporary terminology suggests. That generation of Americans used the word "race" carelessly, indeed, unscientifically. The word usually was used in immigration discourse to mean nationality. They spoke of the Polish or the Italian "race," or even subgroups within nations, as when northern Italians were sharply distinguished from Italians from the southern Mezzogiorno. What was being identified by such usage was not inherited biological traits, but deep historical and cultural deposits. Theodore Roosevelt, for example, spoke often and passionately about the "American race," but he knew very well that it was an interbred and mysterious amalgam, that is, a nation, a people.

Translating "race" into "nationality" or "culture" across vast areas of the debate over the New Immigration assists the modern mind in actually engaging the discussion. Those seeing in the New Immigrants from Europe (Asian immigration, a small part of the migratory surge at the end of the nineteenth century, was overwhelmingly seen in racial as well as cultural terms) a lower level of human capital than the first European settlers usually saw the strangeness and backwardness not as permanent (i.e., racial incapacities) but as a history-based cultural gap. In the view of many Americans, the issue posed by these central and eastern European migrants was whether their manifest social backwardness could in a reasonably short time and with no great cost be remedied in the American environment. Thus the language of "race" did not always mean they were talking about race. As the context requires, we should substitute "culture." The pervasive language of cultural difference and judgments about "inferiority" and generally "low" civic and educational standards, while they sound too often harsh and un-sympathetic, did not always imply contempt or hostility. Peter Roberts, au-thor of *The New Immigration* (1912), told his readers that "Foreigners do not bathe often," their women "are Drudges" with high fecundity, and "the evils Foreigners bring" include crime, filth, and voter fraud. Yet he more than balanced these generalizations by praising aspects of the incoming cul-tures making eastern seaboard cities so vivid, affirmed that "I believe in the immigrant," and "when agencies of amelioration are brought to bear upon these patches of backward Europe in America, they yield to treatment and appear clothed anew . . ."

THE AGE OF REFORM—IMMIGRATION'S TURN

So gathered end-of-century America's troubles: crowded, ill-governed, and vice-filled cities; menacing corporate monopolies; political corruption; la-bor-capital wars; the rapid and wasteful depletion of the nation's forest and mineral reserves; and the Great Wave, reaching a million a year. These and other maladies aroused the "muckraking" journalists and other bell-ringers who helped launch the Progressive Era, a national crusade to change the future rather than merely accept it. The pattern of reform was discovery and exposure of social maladies through journalism or other channels of communication, then organization for civic or political action, often as-signing government a larger role in societal regulation. In the 1890s one could see the national organizations forming for such action: the General Federation of Women's Clubs in 1890, The Sierra Club in 1892, the Anti-Saloon League in 1895, the Chicago forerunner of the Anti-Cigarette League in 1899, and the National Consumers League that same year, just to note a few.

Immigration reform followed a similar path. Before the 1890s, the im-pulse for restriction had been scattered geographically and among various labor leaders and unions, patriotic societies, and authors like Josiah Strong (*Our Country,* 1886). National organizations were the next stage. Some his-torians see immigration reform carried forward briefly by a fast growing (but short-lived) national organization, the American Protective Associa-tion (APA), a secret order that spread out of a base in Iowa in the late 1880s and held its first national convention in 1890. However, the APA deserves little space in the story. Its focus was on Americans—Catholic Americans and their campaigns, instigated by Church leadership, for separate schools; on the Irish domination of local politics in selected cities; on papal plots to control America, as described in lurid pamphlets. By 1900 the organization had collapsed without making any contribution to understanding or solving the immigration problem.

The Immigration Restriction League (IRL), founded in Boston in 1894, was another matter. It arose out of the Good Government movement in northeastern cities that contributed in a major way to the entire progressive campaign, and it mobilized the academic talent of New England's top universities and intellectuals, among them Massachusetts Institute of Technology President Francis A. Walker, historian John Fiske, and Senator Henry Cabot Lodge, with much of the work done by three Harvard-educated founders—Prescott Hall, Robert Ward, and Charles Warren. The IRL sent letters to governors of states asking if immigrants were desired and, if so, which races (meaning nationalities) were preferred. Twenty-six governors responded, eight saying no more immigrants were wanted, the rest happy to have Scandinavians, Germans, and other old immigration groups. The IRL would be active in immigration reform politics for more than two decades, its representatives often travelling from their New England base to Washington to influence the ongoing debate.

THE LABELING OF REFORMERS

Most IRL members shared Senator Lodge's disdain for the APA and its anti-Catholic, "nativist" cast. What did he and others mean by that clearly negative term? The *Random House College Dictionary* defines "nativism" as "the policy of protecting the interests of native inhabitants against those of immigrants," and *The Dictionary of American History* defines it as "the policy of favoring native inhabitants of a country as against immigrants." This does not take us very far. Most people would tend to feel closer affiliation with fellow countrymen than with foreigners. If the definition implies that these interests can sometimes conflict, then it is an odd citizen who is not a nativist. If it assumes, however, that there is and can be no inherent conflict of interests in which the natives' interests actually require defense, then nativism can only mean xenophobia, irrational dislike of foreigners and discrimination against them to the (unfair) benefit of natives. For clarification, we turn to history.

The word "nativist" derives from a particular era in American history, the 1830s to the mid-1850s, when American Protestants became deeply alarmed by the large numbers of arriving German and Irish Catholic immigrants and their manipulation (it was feared) by the Pope and the Roman Church to fundamentally change American society. The concern that Catholics, mobilized and instructed by their Church leadership in the Vatican, were becoming a force undermining republican principles and institutions "eventually proved mistaken, but it was not wildly implausible at the time," in the words of historian Stephan Thernstrom. The Roman Church was a conservative, authoritarian institution, and under Pope Pius IX, Thernstrom maintains, it "was a major supporter of reactionary European monarchs and a staunch foe of republican revolutionaries like Louis Kossuth who were heroes in America." Protestants, convinced (like many historians) that republican principles arose out of protestant thought and struggles, feared that immigrant-augmented Catholic communities as they became majorities would threaten American political institutions and public schools. There was confirming evidence, but it was scattered and augmented by much rumor. That American Catholics would in time prove highly independent of the political views of their Roman hierarchy was of course not known when the Irish and German Catholics surged into the United States. They did tend to cluster together, and, especially in the case of the Irish, voted as a bloc for ethnic comrades, legally or illegally. Urban political machines in the northeast made sure that "Irish immigrants landing in the morning might be voters by nightfall," wrote Carl Wittke in *We Who Built America*. Catholics both as voters and elected officials opposed tax-supported public education, which Protestants saw as the key institution in building national solidarity.

These can be called religious tensions, but not in the sense that mere religious affiliation was the only ground for hostility. Social values and institutions about which people felt deeply were challenged by newcomers. Large-scale immigration brought these conflicting values together, and social conflict was a natural result. There was some spontaneous violence, a good deal of anti-Catholic (and also anti-Protestant) pamphleteering of immoderate and angry tone, and then political organization. In the 1830s came the formation of the Native American Party, the growth of secret societies such as the Order of the Star Spangled Banner, then in the 1850s the American Party, its members soon called "Know-Nothings" for their habit of refusing comment on their plans to journalists and others. Their core belief was that one of the nation's greatest problems was Catholic hierarchy-guided political activity, made more potent every year by German and Irish immigration. They proposed little in the way of immigration restriction, never even mentioning immigration curbs in the party's 1856 platform. Instead they focussed on keeping Catholic immigrants already in the country from gaining political power. Lengthened naturalization requirements were their chief policy goal. Thus, they wound up advocating a sort of provisional status for Catholic immigrants here and neglected the supply side of the problem by failing to demand that the national government gain control of immigration. "Your movement is bigoted nativism," they were told, apparently the first use of that new negative word in American politics. Not so, came the reply: "Our movement is plain Americanism."

The unsavory definition of "nativist" stuck, as Senator Lodge's comment on the APA reveals. The Senator and his IRL colleagues wanted to limit immigration, not monitor American Catholic political activity, which was the nativist agenda. The nativists were cast in a bad light by the 1890s, because they had been immigrant reformers rather than immigration reformers, and even on the first mission, history had not confirmed their fears. If masses of Catholic voters had destroyed the public school system and shifted American voting patterns sharply to the right, hostility to their arrival would not be called nativism, but either "plain Americanism" (their term) or simply "patriotism." As American Catholics settled into the political mainstream, however, the Native American Party's worries from those pre-Civil War days increasingly appeared groundless. Forgotten were the seriousness of the ethno-cultural conflicts, the sudden and community-transforming scale of the pre-Civil War immigration, and the ebb of German and Irish immigration prior to the Civil War. The problem had subsided, if not at the level of community abrasiveness then at least as a national threat.

Therefore Know-Nothingism was remembered as mere xenophobia, groundless and irrational dislike of The Other, mobilizing itself in secret societies preparatory to political action directed against the political influence of recent-immigrant Americans, or as nativism, a marginal political flourish of the middle-nineteenth century. Early historians of the immigration reform debate that eventually led to curbs on Asian immigration between 1882 and 1906 and on European immigration between 1921 and 1929—writers such as Roy Garis, Marion T. Bennett, Edward P. Hutchinson, and George M. Stephenson—made sparing use of the term nativism.

To them, those actively seeking restrictions on immigration were simply re-formers. They were moved by real social problems—wage and job compe-tition, high costs of poor relief, disease, neighborhood crowding, and de-teriorating civic standards—as well as some very serious worries for which the evidence was not so clear-cut, such as the impression that the New Im-migrants were not assimilating to national norms, leading to questions about national cohesion and conflicting loyalties in foreign affairs.

This spectrum of worries was brought about by a massive new demo-graphic and cultural force in American life, the incoming millions of New Immigrants. It should be no surprise that massive immigration, and a wide-ranging discussion of its impacts, generated not only restrictionist reform but in places flushed out the marks of nativism as history had fifty years earlier revealed it—the exaggeration of negative evidence, political organi-zation to monitor the immigrants among us rather than go to the root and establish some control over the flow. This constituted immigration reform's irrational, unhelpful fringe in the nineteenth and early twentieth centuries.

Historian John Higham's *Strangers in the Land: Patterns of American Nativism 1860–1925* (1955), one of the brilliant and enduring volumes in American historiography of the past half century, traced a nativist tradition through three outbursts of especially intense and organized anti-alien po-litical activity: the 1790s, the Know-Nothing era before the Civil War, and the period of his main focus, the four decades prior to immigration re-striction in the 1920s. Thus, Higham cast the entire forty-year history of the New Immigration debate as in part a story of nativism ("intense oppo-sition to an internal minority on the ground of its foreign connection").

Were immigration reform and nativism, then, the same thing? Lodge emphatically had not thought so, but historians writing after Higham, and journalists following their lead, began to collapse the distinction, which im-plied that the entire immigration reform enterprise was, as the nativism of the 1830s through the 1850s now appeared, irrational and a bad thing. In the Index to Leonard Dinnerstein and David Reimers, *Ethnic Americans* (1988), for example, cross-references under nativism include bigotry, dis-crimination, and prejudice.

No one can deny the presence (to varying degrees) and harmful po-tential of such emotions in American (and every other nation's) life. How-ever, after Higham, and appearing to take his lead, historians and others developed a tendency to dismiss as nativism the entire impulse to see harm in unregulated immigration and to press for restrictions. Nativism, one way of reacting to mass immigration in the decades before the Civil War, came to be spread as a label over all subsequent criticisms of unlimited entry of foreigners into the United States.

The first dissenter from this was Higham. Shortly after the publication of *Strangers in the Land*, he published an article (1958) confessing "that nativism now looks less adequate as a vehicle for studying the struggles of nationalities in America than my earlier report of it . . . the nativist theme, as defined and developed to date, is imaginatively exhausted." As a concept it directs our attention too much to "subjective, irrational motives" and neglects and even screens out "the objective realities of ethnic relations" and "the structure of society." By this he surely meant the institutional rivalries of established Protestant and immigrant-fed Catholic churches, as well as immigrant impacts on wages, living standards, communities, and political systems. It was, Higham reflected, a "bad habit" to label "as nativist any kind of unfriendliness toward immigrants," leading to a neglect of "the less spectacular but more steadily sustained contentions imbedded in the fabric of our social organizations," or immigrant-driven challenges to or changes in ethnic, racial, or religious relations and economic and political structures. "Status rivalries have not arisen from irrational myths but rather from objective conditions," he went on, which "have not usually reached the point of hatred and hysteria." In the second edition of *Strangers in the Land* (1955), he stated that if he were writing the book again he would "take more account of aspects of the immigration restriction movement that cannot be sufficiently explained in terms of nativism."

Higham's continuing second thoughts on the role of nativism in the story of ethnic relations and immigration policy making in America have not been sufficiently heeded or explored. Nativism is the wrong framework for understanding immigration reform politics even in that era when there was apparently some of it about. The larger framework is mass immigration and the real social strains and thus policy issues that it invariably generates. "The absorption of numbers rather than ethnic or national origins," concluded Harvard economic historians Timothy Hatton and Jeffrey Williamson in their exhaustive 1998 study of immigration's impacts, "really lay at the heart of the immigration debate."

The term "nativism" should thus be returned from its current totalizing, dismissive, and prejudiced (in the sense that its use prejudges the life situations and motives of American citizens) usage to its historical roots. The term applies to organized efforts, often in secret fraternal societies and eventually in politics, to identify one or more foreign influences within America as dire threats to the American republic, when in fact the threat is nonexistent, greatly exaggerated, or misconceived. We need a word for this when it crops up. A litmus test is the tendency to devote energies to the unjustified (by "objective conditions") attacks upon immigrants within reach rather than to energetic efforts within political channels to change national policy governing immigrant admission. The short-lived APA of the 1890s was an example of nativism, as were the turn-of-the-century alien land laws and school segregation for Asians in California, as was the fitful attention given to immigrants by the Ku Klux Klan of the 1920s. These were on the margins of immigration reform at the front end of the twentieth century, troublesome fellow travelers.

THE LONG ROAD TO NATIONAL IMMIGRATION POLICY

What was to be done? The high unemployment and social tensions of the 1890s had gathered a powerful coalition for immigration restriction—organized labor, intellectuals and social reformers, virtually all Republicans, with the southern wing of the Democratic Party beginning to swing toward curbs. The national Democratic Party could be counted on to resist restriction because of its voting base in northeastern cities and its historic opposition to federal activism. Also favoring the status quo was tradition—a history of openness to immigrants and a record of successful assimilation of diverse European peoples.

On balance, restrictionist sentiment was politically ascendant in the 1890s. The problem was the lack of clear ideas, based on experience, about what to do to bring under national control something that had never been controlled by public policy: mass migration. The New York State Federation of Labor in 1896 recommended suspension of all immigration for five years until the demand for labor caught up with the supply, certainly no viable idea for the long term. The idea of a literacy test came forward, and it seemed well designed to curb the New Immigration with its high illiteracy rates. Senator Henry Cabot Lodge sponsored such a test, estimated to bar some 25 percent of the immigration from southern and eastern Europe. It passed in 1896 and was vetoed by President Grover Cleveland as he left office in 1897, the Senate failing by two votes to overturn the veto. A similar measure failed by two votes in the House in 1898, and if it had passed President McKinley almost certainly would have signed it, because the party platform endorsed a literacy test in 1896. The rest of McKinley's term was taken up with Spain, Cuba, war, and empire.

As the new century arrived, the Fifty-seventh Congress received 5,082 petitions in favor of restriction of immigration, some from every state. After Leon Czolgosz, son of recent Polish immigrants and a convert to European anarchist ideas, assassinated President McKinley in 1901, President Theodore Roosevelt in his annual message of 1 December 1901 found "our present immigration laws . . . unsatisfactory. . . . There should be a comprehensive law enacted" to achieve three goals: exclusion of anarchists, an educational test of "some intelligent capacity to appreciate American institutions," and exclusion of those "who are below a certain standard of economic fitness" which would "stop the influx of cheap labor." Roosevelt had lined up at the head of the immigration reformers, but his ideas were half-baked, part of the ongoing conversation and thinking out loud of those who were attempting to be the architects of something very new—an immigration policy that limited the numbers and selected those who would enter rather than let America be built as it had formerly been, by the choices of foreigners. It would require three more decades of thought, fact-finding, emotional debates, and legislative maneuvers, all in a context of a relentless human movement across the Atlantic, to devise a system that would finally control the Great Wave and allow this emotional issue to subside and move to the margins of the national agenda.

GATHERING FACTS AND KNOWLEDGE:
THE ROLE OF SOCIAL INVESTIGATION

A hallmark of progressive thinking was the conviction that facts must decide important public questions and that gathering them was the precondition for sound action. A string of official investigations added information and opinion on the immigration problem. The Immigration Investigating Commission reported to the Secretary of the Treasury in 1895, and the U.S. Industrial Commission (formed to shed light on the fierce conflicts between labor and capital) published in 1901 a 957-page report on the whole immigration question. This led in 1903 to the transfer of the Immigration Bureau from the Department of the Treasury to the Department of Commerce and Labor, and eventually to the Labor Department when it attained separate status in 1913.

When it came to Asian immigration, there seemed no need for further fact-finding. In Teddy Roosevelt's second term, Americans on the West Coast began to respond to the rapid increase in Japanese (and to a lesser extent Korean) immigration with denunciations by politicians, newspaper stories on the Japanese influx, and scattered anti-Asian riots in 1906–7. The Japanese were "a competent race," reported a study of broadly based American attitudes toward Japan, but their overpopulated island nation was colonizing along the West Coast of the Americas, sending high-fertility settlers who were nonassimilable into Western culture and "present impossible economic competition to the Caucasian race."

The Japanese government, which itself enforced national immigration bans on Chinese and Korean entry into Japan, protested sharply. President Roosevelt, irritated with all involved but eager to end the abrasive issue, arranged a so-called "Gentleman's Agreement" with Japan in 1908, in which Japan agreed to end the emigration of its laborers to the United States. (Australia, New Zealand, Canada, and South Africa all put in place arrangements to exclude Japanese immigrants during this era.) Japanese immigration continued, but at a declining level (83,000 in 1911–20; 33,000 in 1921–30; 2,000 in 1931–40), mostly in the form of brides. Curtailment of an immigration wave that had seemed spiraling upward again deflated the social tension on the West Coast. Here was a lesson to be learned several times, but was often forgotten: to reduce social conflict over immigration, lower the numbers.

There is a Gilbert and Sullivan ditty that runs:

> If you're pestered by critics and hounded by faction
> To take some precipitate, positive action
> The proper procedure, to take my advice, is
> Appoint a commission and stave off the crisis.

In 1906, Senator Lodge again maneuvered through the Senate legislation carrying a literacy test, touted by one supportive senator as a way to "separate the ignorant, vicious and the lazy from the intelligent and industrious." This sounded to friend and foe like a major curb on immigration numbers, and it attracted a large majority in the House, but Republican Speaker Joseph Cannon stubbornly deadlocked the legislation, which included authorization for the President's negotiations with Japan. Roosevelt convinced Lodge to drop the literacy test from what became the Immigration Act of 1907 (which made a few additions to excluded classes, such as persons with physical and mental defects) in return for the appointment of a commission to study immigration and come up with a plan for "a definite solution of this immigration business," as Cannon put it.

The Dillingham Commission (named after its chairman, Republican Senator William K. Dillingham of Vermont) labored for three years to produce a forty-two-volume report that was neither a plan nor "a definite solution" but had "enormous influence on the future course of immigration policy," in the assessment of historian Lawrence Fuchs. Mountains of data were gathered on the economic and social characteristics and impacts of the New Immigrants, out of which commission staff and members constructed a picture confirmed by later research—that the New Immigrants from southern and eastern Europe tended to be less skilled, less literate (35 percent illiterate in any language) male "birds of passage" whose attachment to America was questionable. Affirming that "further general legislation concerning the admission of aliens should be based primarily upon economic or business considerations," the commission found an "oversupply of unskilled labor in the industries of the country as a whole, a condition which demands legislation restricting the further admission of such unskilled labor." In making such economic or labor-force judgments, preference should be shown to those who "by reason of their personal qualities or habits" would be assimilated and "desirable citizens." How to select? The commission recommended a literacy test and a ban on unskilled workers entering without families, while suggesting another method for consideration: "the limitation of the number of each race arriving each year to a certain percentage of the average of that race arriving during a given period of years," a murky statement tying immigration to the demographic aspects of the American past. This latter idea would prove formidably difficult to turn into policy, but it exerted a strong appeal, and the laws of the 1920s would be built around it.

IMMIGRATION REFORM: THE BEGINNINGS OF A SYSTEM OF RESTRICTION

The administration of President William Howard Taft (1909–13) disappointed Progressives across the reform agenda, including those wanting some system of selecting and limiting immigration. Legislation embodying many of the Dillingham Commission's recommendations, chiefly the literacy test, passed in 1913 but was vetoed by Taft as he prepared to leave office. His argument was that he had "an abiding faith" that the American environment, particularly the school, would prove "an instrument for self-elevation," that it "has always contributed to the strength of our people, and will continue to do so." The Senate overrode the veto, but the House vote fell five short. This was the sixteenth recorded vote on the measure since 1896 in either House or Senate; it had never lost in Congress and never survived into law. The literacy test passed again in 1915 and 1917, when Congress overrode the second veto by Woodrow Wilson. The literacy test was finally in place, in a year in which few European immigrants crossed.

Restriction of immigration had already arrived. World War I divided Europe behind the bloody trenches and sealed the Atlantic with a naval blockade and deadly submarine warfare. The Great Wave suddenly stopped, at least temporarily.

REFORM'S PARALLEL TRACK: INTERVENING TO ASSIST ASSIMILATION

In the context of concern over "hyphenate" loyalties and wartime unity, both the government and citizens took a redoubled interest in an aspect of the larger immigration reform movement we have not yet addressed—Americanization, an organized effort to assist and accelerate the process of immigrant assimilation to American norms. This impulse long preceded the war. An Americanization movement could be discerned by the beginning of the twentieth century, a form of social intervention that identified it as a component of the larger Progressive Era. It was never a single enterprise but flowered in many forms under many sponsors. As early as the 1890s immigrant groups already established in America (most prominently German Jews, well-established and concerned about the unassimilable impression made by arriving Russian Jews) took the lead in programs to aid new arrivals to learn English, understand American laws, and disperse out of Eastern ghettos. New York's Educational Alliance, a Jewish social work organization, began Americanization programs in 1889, and the Finnish-American women in Calumet, Michigan organized an "Americanization Club" to learn American songs, history, civics, and English, all to "eliminate the hyphen" and become Americans.

This immigrant-generated enterprise was soon adopted by main-stream citizen groups concerned to move recent immigrants as quickly as possible away from inherited and toward "American" norms—settlement houses, churches, the YMCA, patriotic societies, employers and business leaders, unions, the General Federation of Women's Clubs. The first historian of the movement, Edward Hartmann (*The Movement to Americanize the Immigrant,* 1948), found two faces—a generous and welcoming visage, and an anxiety-driven, coercive one. John Higham called these "liberal" as opposed to "100 percent" types of Americanization. The first, born in settlement houses and among immigrant groups, preached the doctrine of "immigrant gifts," conveyed a sense of welcome, and combined an acceptance of foreign cultural inheritances with assistance to accelerate the transition to the American norms that were the gateways to economic and social success. The second face or style of Americanization typically launched programs to school the immigrants in the importance of abandoning their old ways at once and offering classes in English, citizenship, hygiene, and celebrations of American national holidays and heroes.

When war came, the issue of national unity naturally came to overshadow all else, and it was a matter of widespread anxiety that the population of the United States was substantially composed of people from Germany and the regions of the Austro-Hungarian Empire with whom the United States was now at war. "Hyphenate" American voices had made the debate over American neutrality policy divisive, and many feared wartime disloyalty, especially in those of German and Irish origin, anarchists, socialists, or pacifists. Patriotic societies and governments at all levels turned toward programs of the "100 percent American" style, and soon state and local governments were going beyond mandatory civics and English classes to laws declaring English the sole language of instruction (fifteen states by 1919) or requiring that schoolteachers be citizens. "The conformist tendency," one historian wrote, "became paramount and the permissive, humanitarian side almost vanished" (but even in war, not entirely: "Don't Preach. Don't Patronize" were the two rules laid down in 1917 by the Americanization Committee of the National Woman Suffrage Association). This wartime injection of anxiety, impatience, and Anglo conformity not only made Americanization efforts less effective, as immigrants resisted forced marches along the path leading away from the ways of the mother country toward an unsettling new cultural pattern. It also gave Americanization a bad name ("Americanization is an ugly word," wrote an Italian-American intellectual in 1919) that only one style of it deserved.

The history of Americanization tells two stories. The encouraging one is that both private sector and government efforts to aid immigrants in the assimilation and naturalization process have been and can be positive complements for the natural processes—participation in the economy, influences of media and community life—promoting assimilation. During the long Progressive Era it was discovered that a nation experiencing substantial immigration (i.e., any successful country in this crowded, troubled world) requires both an immigration policy combining limitation with selection, as well as what might be called an immigrant assimilation policy. The first decides who shall and shall not enter as prospective citizens, and it is the senior partner. The second has to do with facilitating the naturalization and assimilation of those admitted. One thing is clear: in the absence of an immigration policy during the Great Wave, immigrant assimilation policy swam against strong currents.

REFORM COMES:
CONSTRUCTING A SYSTEM OF RESTRICTION

Restriction had been surging through the American political system for years, but with only a literacy test in 1917 to show for it, an instrument that soon proved a puny screen of dubious merit. European literacy rates were improving, reading a 30–40 word passage was no rigorous test, and the law allowed illiterate relatives of admitted immigrants. Immigration remained essentially unregulated, beyond the cases of visible disease. The outbreak of war in Europe brought a temporary lull, but America's entry in 1917 vastly strengthened the immigration reform impulse in the United States, not always for the right reasons. Concerned that the war effort could be sabotaged by the spread of radical doctrines or political activities undermining the legitimacy of the U.S. government or our form of capitalist economy, Congress in 1918 authorized the President to control the entry of persons whose presence was deemed contrary to "public safety" and to deport anarchists and other radical aliens. Deportation for radical beliefs was expedited by a 1920 law at the peak of the "Red Scare" that was sparked by the success of the Bolshevik Revolution in Russia, terrorist bombings in the United States traced to anarchist groups, widespread labor unrest and strikes in major industries, and a general anxiety about global unsettlement in the wake of a war of unprecedented scope and destructiveness.

These war measures did not supply the systematic reform of immigration debated for so long, but the war itself, in destroying European economic systems, generated immense out-migration pressures and forced American policy makers to act. Although the war had checked the flow of European immigration, half a million immigrants came in 1920; the immigration commissioner at the port of New York, relying as much on instinct as evidence, reported that "more than ten million are now waiting in various parts of war-stricken Europe to swarm to the U.S. as soon as they can obtain transportation." A commissioner of the Hebrew Sheltering and Aid Society of America made a published statement that "if there were in existence a ship that could hold 3,000,000 human beings, the 3,000,000 Jews of Poland would board it to escape to America." "A deluge of immigration was impending such as the country had never known," limited only by the carrying capacity of ocean liners, wrote sociologist Henry Pratt Fairchild.

The congressional response was energetic if scattered. Many bills were introduced in the Sixty-fifth Congress (1918–19), and the House Committee on Immigration reported out a bill embodying the AFL appeal for a prohibition on all immigration for four years, a good indication of widespread sentiment as well as a confession that an overall immigration policy concept had not come forward. In the next Congress the House continued to think of an absolute moratorium (this time for two years), but Senate drafters produced a bill under which annual immigration would be restricted to 3 percent of the foreign-born population in the United States in 1910. It passed both houses by huge margins (62–2 in the Senate, 295–41 in the House), but President Wilson killed it with a pocket veto in his last days in office, sending no veto message and leaving not so much as a memo on his thoughts. The occasion seemed symbolic. The argument for continuing the open door nonpolicy had become a mechanical invocation of tradition or had gone silent. The moment for creativity and new ideas belonged to the reformers.

The presidential election of 1920 returned the Republicans, and Warren Harding of Ohio, to the White House, and the GOP platform contained the strongest endorsement of immigration restriction in the party's history. The time for immigration reform had finally arrived, although it would take the entire decade to work out the details. "There is a limit to our power of assimilation," declared the House Committee on Immigration in 1921, a year in which an economic recession pushed unemployment to 5 million. The committee reported out a "temporary measure" to "check the stream" until a long-term policy could be devised. This became the Quota Law of 1921, limiting the number of any nationality entering the United States to 3 percent of foreign-born persons of that nationality who resided in the country in 1910. This puzzling rationale, hatched by the Dillingham Commission, was predicted to produce totals of 200,000 for northern and western Europe and 155,000 for southern and eastern Europe, cutting immigration to approximately 360,000 "quota" immigrants, but exceptions were numerous. The measure was temporary, extended in 1922 for two more years, as Congress wrangled over its long-term intentions. When the law expired, warned the House Immigration Committee, "the largest migration of peoples in the history of the world may be expected to begin on July 1, 1924."

The totals did decline under the interim measure of 1921, but irregularly. The 800,000 immigrants admitted in 1921 were followed by 310,000 in 1922, then 523,000 in 1923, and 707,000 in 1924, much of the increase coming from Mexico, Canada, and other nonquota countries. However, the numbers were large and the non-English speaking migrants from southern and eastern Europe still predominated, which was not the result Congress had intended. Sentiment quickly shifted toward tinkering with the formula—3 percent could be made 2 percent, and the base year shifted from 1910 to 1890, before the Great Wave had reached full tide. A majority favored this change, although some commentators (and especially ethnic leaders claiming to speak for New Immigrant groups) complained that the change to the Census of 1890 was wholly arbitrary and intended to greatly reduce quotas from their homelands.

Charges of discrimination stung, even in that era in which the Jim Crow system of legally enforced racial segregation prevailed across the South. Supporters of a system of selection that would result in fewer immigrants from the "New" source countries and more from the Old responded with several arguments: all nations conceded to each other the right to decide who could make a home within their boundaries; it was wrong to think of group rights when the national interest was foremost and plainly argued for tests of assimilability of which nationality was the core; we do not imply "superior" or "inferior" by favoring certain nationalities, but properly give great weight to "like-mindedness." This latter term was the central part of the argument of Chicago lawyer Edward R. Lewis, who in *America: Nation or Confusion?* (1928) contended:

> Nations come of slow growth and long travail, that they depend on
> like-mindedness and . . . if the United States becomes a hodge-podge
> of a score of races, no one of which is dominant, it will lose its unity
> and become like Metternich's idea of Italy, a geographical expression.

Lewis was a voice of nonracial, cultural reasoning, and there were others
who used the "like-mindedness" logic that what was at stake in a regime of
unlimited mass immigration was the eventual destruction of a working
American nationality. Unfortunately, writers such as Lothrop Stoddard
and Madison Grant were free with terms like "unfit" and "mongrelization"
that implied a fixed racial hierarchy and mobilized contempt. Restrictionist Henry Pratt Fairchild regretted such arguments that were "furnishing
ammunition to the opposition, when it was possible to make out an amply convincing case on the basis simply of race differences, without any im-
putation whatever of respective superiority and inferiority."

Choosing what it hoped would be taken as positive language, the
House Immigration Committee in 1924 reported out a bill with the statement: "If . . . the principle of individual liberty . . . is to endure, the basic
strain of our population must be maintained and our economic standards
preserved." They moved the base year to 1890 and lowered the numbers
to 150,000, by cutting the proportion of immigration to base population
to 2 percent. The committee argued:

> With full recognition of the material progress which we owe to the races
> from southern and eastern Europe, we are conscious that the continued
> arrival of great numbers tends to upset our balance of population, to de-
> press our standard of living. . . . Late arrivals are in all fairness not enti-
> tled to special privilege over those who have arrived at an earlier date and
> thereby contributed more to the advancement of the nation.

Then a new idea emerged, apparently first (there are other claimants)
from Henry Curran, commissioner of immigration at Ellis Island, according to historian Stephen T. Wagner. "It has always seemed to me," Curran
testified before the Senate Immigration Committee, "that the most assimil-
able and the best kind of immigration we could get would be that which is
most nearly like the 100 million Americans who are now here." Why not design "each annual installment" as "a replica according to the different constituents of stock who are now here?" This concept won over Senator David
Reed of Pennsylvania on the spot, who inquired about possible charges of

discrimination. Curran: "I think there is not one iota of discrimination. If we let in every year the percentage that is already here of any nationality, nobody can object to that." So instead of basing immigration on some percentage of the foreign-born in some arbitrary year, as in the 1921 law, the basis would become the national origins of the current nation (whites only).

Reed, convinced that the "artificiality" of the selection of the 1890 census would place restriction on a shaky basis, took control of the legislation and enthusiastically endorsed the new concept. It proved a magnet drawing supporters. "If one were to imagine all the immigrants from other countries in a given year congregated on board a single vessel," said another senator, "the ship's company . . . would be in microcosm the United States of America in its racial distribution." It would take some time to make the calculations about the national origins of Americans in 1920, Senator Lodge commented, but after that "there can be no question then of discrimination, because it will treat all races alike on the basis of their actual proportion of the existing population." In this way, argued Reed, the discrimination built into the 1921 law and the House's Johnson Bill (in that they disregarded the American-born in calculating quotas) would be eliminated. To some senators, the important point was to lower the numbers, and Reed's bill did this in the most acceptable way. "If we will only check the tide of immigration and give freeplay to all the assimilative forces of our national life," said the senator from Maryland, the Italians, Poles and Russian Jews of Baltimore would surely contribute in time to the nation's welfare, just as had the British.

The House held to the 1890 census of foreign-born formula, but Reed's Senate version rested on a stronger argument and was chosen by the conference committee and then, overwhelmingly, by both houses. "The national-origins basis for immigration gives every national group as many immigrants to this country as that national-origins group has contributed to the population of the U.S.," stated the Senate Judiciary Committee, "and . . . it is founded, not on a foreign-born basis or on a native-born basis, but on an all-American basis" and "without discrimination against either foreigners or Americans." Some criticisms were heard, including the astute prediction that the national origins of the people of the U.S. in 1920 (the base year) were impossible to accurately determine. All objections were overridden by huge votes: 323–71 in the House, 62–6 in the Senate. The Johnson-Reed Act was adopted on 26 May 1924 and signed by President Coolidge.

It was a milestone, and it was both simple and complex. A new system of immigration policy had replaced no real policy at all, something the progressive generation had also done in the areas of monetary policy (with the Federal Reserve Act of 1913), monopoly (the Sherman Act of 1890, the Clayton Act of 1914), and in many other areas. The number of immigrants to America was to be sharply restricted, national quotas to be capped at a total of 155,000, plus several categories of "nonquota" slots that proved more expansive than intended. The selection of immigrants was determined by nationality (actually, country of birth, sometimes not the same thing), but inside national quotas, certain skills useful to the United States were given preference. The goal was a small amount of annual immigration that would basically replicate the nation, rather than transform its ethno-cultural or "nationality" base into something else. "America must be kept American," President Calvin Coolidge had put the sentiment, in his message to Congress on 6 December 1923.

If the goal was clear, however, the means to the end were not yet in place. The stopgap measure of 2 percent of the foreign-born recorded in the 1890 census would govern until a Cabinet committee determined the "national origins" of the American people in 1920, when a recent census offered the best and latest data available. A panel of experts reported in 1927 and stirred up an unexpected storm among the older immigrant groups (the "Nordics"). The English quota was too high, the Scandinavian and German too low, came the angry complaints. Decades of heavy immigration had indeed given the country and its politics a tribal cast. A confused period of ethnic antagonism ensued, both political parties and their 1928 presidential nominees wobbled about between the 1920 national origins idea and the 1890 foreign-born quota idea, and the skillful lobbying of John Trevor's Immigration Conference Committee combining the effort of thirty-three patriotic societies made the difference. President Hoover announced that the new quotas would go into effect on 1 July. "For a decade or more," John Higham observed of the restrictionists' victory, "the country had needed an effective numerical restriction to protect the living standards and the bargaining power of the American working class." The last progressive reform was in place.

RESTRICTION: RESULTS AND REFLECTIONS

From the early nineteenth century to 1930, the United States absorbed 60 percent of the huge surge of Great Wave immigration. As the United States finally decided in the 1920s to limit its intake, the other four major immigrant-receiving countries of the Neo-Europes—Canada, Argentina, Brazil, and Australia—were taking similar measures. Canada discontinued all immigration but from the United Kingdom and France (with skilled worker exceptions); Argentina and Brazil established preference systems for the nationalities of the early settlers, chiefly Portuguese, Italian, Spanish (and with Argentina, German, and Swiss); and Australia established a "white Australia" goal with preferences for those of British or American stock. Thus, all five, Anglo-Saxon and Latin-dominated alike, opted for selection systems (of varying degrees of effectiveness) designed, in different ways, to replicate the nation's structure of nationalities as historically understood.

Restriction brought the numbers entering the United States down sharply, although powerful forces were working in the same direction—the collapse of the American (and global) economy into the Great Depression lasting from 1929 to 1940 and the hazards of international travel during World War II. Recorded immigration to the United States averaged 305,000 from 1925 to 1929, under the interim quotas, then dropped sharply in the 1930s to an average of 53,000 a year that hides a virtual negative immigration in 1932. In the 1940s, immigration averaged about 100,000 a year, but with an upward trend after the war. Writing after the 1924 system had been in place for nearly 25 years, William S. Bernard estimated that, subtracting emigration, only 1.7 million people had migrated to the United States during that period, the equivalent of two years' arrivals prior to restriction.

The demographic consequences of ending the open door cannot be known with certainty, because no one can be sure what immigration would have been in the absence of restriction. Demographer Leon Bouvier has estimated that, assuming no restriction and prewar levels of 1 million a year for the rest of the century, the American population would have reached 400 million by 2000. This would mean 120 million more American high-consumption lifestyles piled upon the roughly 280 million expected in the census of 2000, making far worse the dismal figures on species extinction, wetland loss, soil erosion, and the accumulation of climate-changing and health-impairing pollutants that are being tallied up as the century closes.

Thus, restriction was a demographic blessing, slowing American population growth. The chief goal of policy reform, to tilt the sources of the immigration stream back toward northern Europe, was less decisively achieved, because numbers entering legally but outside the quotas ("nonquota immigrants," mostly relatives of those recently arrived and Europeans entering through Latin American and Caribbean countries) surprised policy makers by matching and in time exceeding those governed by quotas. With numbers so low, however, ethnic composition did not agitate the public. International economic maladies, war, and the new American system of restriction had thus combined to reduced immigration numbers to levels more in line with the long course of American history and to some observers seemed to have ended the role of immigration as a major force in American life. Apparently the nation would henceforth grow and develop, as Thomas Jefferson had preferred, from natural increase and the cultural assets of its people.

The Great Wave, like all immigration, had both benefits and costs. The arduous, unskilled work of our industrial expansion found willing hands. New ethnic communities brought many "immigrant gifts" beyond enumeration. Cuisine was diversified; the American wine industry based in California established an international reputation from the contributions of Italian and Hungarian immigrants' skills and tastes. The Great Wave brought America the creative talents of Fiorello LaGuardia and Robert Wagner, Frank Sinatra and Maria Callas, Irving Berlin and Jerome Kern and George and Ira Gershwin and Leonard Bernstein, Saul Bellow and Lionel Trilling. No one can fully enumerate these positive contributions.

However, a sentimentalist view of immigration is our era's clouded lens. Mass immigration from Europe's fringes brought costs—wage depression, urban crowding, disease, illiterates to be taught, international crime syndicates—and a cadre of violent criminals—McKinley's assassin Czolgoz; the Italian mobsters Charles "Lucky" Luciano, Frank Costello, and Al Capone; their counterparts, the "tough Jews" Bugsy Goldstein, Phil Strauss, and Rich Cohen; two of the plotters of the deadly East Coast bombings of 1919, Sacco and Vanzetti; the kidnapper and murderer of the Lindbergh baby, Bruno Richard Hauptmann; and Robert Kennedy's assassin, Sirhan Sirhan. Immigrants are like the rest of humanity, made, in Thomas Jefferson's phrase, in equal parts of poetry and mud.

Some of the costs of an era of unrestricted immigration were much clearer when it was curbed. In local and national politics the virtual disappearance of immigration from the agenda of American politics removed (with the regional exception of Mexican agricultural labor in the Southwest) a contentious and divisive issue from the center of American life.

Many employers in both manufacturing and agriculture had predicted economic hardship as a result of labor shortages, but as restriction shrank the incoming foreign labor pool in the 1920s and after, the economic results appear to have been beneficial in all directions. Tight labor markets in industry stimulated capital investments and operating efficiencies that raised productivity 40 percent across the decade of the 1920s, and economic historians detect the role of immigration restriction as one of the factors producing the wage gains of industrial labor and the reduction in income inequality that occurred in the interwar decades. Economist Paul Douglas found that annual manufacturing wage growth in the United States was 0.32 percent from 1890 to 1914 but an astonishing 3.3 percent from 1919 to 1926, a clear sign of immigration's wage-depressing effect. Reviewing the data from before and after restriction, Harvard economist Claudia Golden has much company in her conclusion that the perceived injury to American wages posed by the Great Wave had been a real one. The impact on native workers' wages was "generally negative and often substantial." "The [immigration] laws are on the books and are very advantageous to labor," wrote the author of a text on labor relations in 1947.

This was especially so for unskilled American workers with rural backgrounds, and chiefly for blacks. "The decline of European migration, coupled with the increased labor demands brought on by World War I, opened the doors of Pittsburgh's mills to incoming blacks," concluded historians of the effect of tight labor markets on black labor in a city typical of the industrial centers of the East and Midwest. Commenting in 1960 on evidence of the accelerating absorption of wage earners "into what was commonly called the middle class," labor historian Foster Dulles concluded: "This process was aided by the curtailment of immigration."

Ironically, one benefit of restriction—the successful and surprisingly rapid assimilation of the New Immigrants—was in time and with much irony interpreted to mean that the reformers had been wrong to fear national fragmentation. The curbing of the Great Wave created a forty-year breathing space of relatively low immigration, with two effects favorable to assimilation. The pressures toward joining the American mainstream did not have to contend with continual massive replenishment of foreigners, and immigrant communities realized that the "sojourn and return" pattern followed by the non-Jewish elements of the Wave was untenable. Writing of Italian-Americans, sociologist Richard Alba concludes that "the shutting off of the immigrant flow made clear to the second and third generations that their future lay in the new society." The result, to condense a complicated story, was that the squalid ghettos of the turn of the century thinned out, and the New Immigrants and their children moved rapidly toward the mainstream of American society—presenting Adolf Hitler, not even a generation after the Johnson-Reed Act, with an American nation far more united and formidable than the motley, mongrelized, and splintered America he confidently expected to meet in the great test of nations he launched in 1939. Without restriction, this story would plausibly have been one of high levels of social segmentation and conflict, rather than of successful and swift consolidation.

A policy that had such beneficial economic, social, and demographic impacts, especially upon the American working class, immigrants in America, and blacks, might expect favorable treatment in the history textbooks. This was so for a brief time, but modern histories are harsh. Why so? The restrictionist reform impulse was composed of two interwoven strands, a defensive sense of cultural-racial superiority, paired with a realistic calculation that the common good of the people already here required curbs on an unregulated mass flow. The second impulse was sound and produced beneficial policy reform. However, it has been entirely eclipsed in memory by a caustic denunciation of the first. Americans in the second half of the twentieth century have (laudably) repudiated the nation's historic operating racial assumptions, and now all we can or will hear in the earlier restrictionism are the discordant distinctions between preferred and, by implication or assertion, undesirable nationalities. The wiser of the immigration reformers anticipated this complaint and pleaded for a restrictionism justified only by the desire for like-mindedness, without invidious distinctions. They could not prevent some people from doing the right thing—curbing the numbers according to some rationale supported by public opinion—while expressing the wrong reasons.

There were blunders and misjudgments—as always—in the legislation. The 1908 Gentlemen's Agreement limiting Japanese immigration was unwisely repudiated and replaced by the explicit bar to "aliens inadmissible to citizenship" in the law of 1924, despite abundant testimony before Congress that Japanese-Americans and Japan saw this as insulting on several levels. The words were code for "Japanese," because Chinese and Asian Indians had been excluded earlier. They implied that Japan was not carrying out her part of the earlier arrangement, and Congress must step in to exclude the Japanese also. Because Japanese immigration continued but at a low level under both the Gentleman's Agreement and the 1924 act, nothing was gained by the legislative rebuff. Indeed, a central flaw of Progressive Era thinking and policy on immigration, judging it not just from our own era but within their own context, was the refusal, despite strong counterarguments, to expand citizenship to all those allowed to reside in the country, whatever their nationality. Limitation of foreign population flows was a proper goal. Barring from citizenship any group legally and permanently in residence, long after citizenship was extended to blacks by the Fourteenth Amendment (1867), was a sad error of most reformers (and the courts), headed otherwise in the right general direction.

Legislation, like sausage, has unsavory ingredients. Immigration restriction, with its flaws, was one of the many positive measures of the progressive reform era, which sought—with considerable success—to bring costly and disruptive social forces under democratic control.

REFORM OF THE REFORM? THE COUNTERATTACK QUIETLY BEGINS

The new immigration system was widely popular, and the immigration committees of Congress quickly became backwaters of minor tinkering or inactivity. The 1930s arrived with vast and chronic unemployment, and the American people wanted nothing from immigration. War in Europe would bring unprecedented refugee issues, but dealing with these—or avoiding them—did not require any rethinking of the basic system for deciding on the few thousand people who would be given immigration papers.

However, American immigration policy had a small but dedicated body of opponents, composed of elements of the religious and political leadership of ethnic communities associated with the New Immigration, especially Jews from central and eastern Europe who were deeply concerned with the rise of fascism and anti-Semitism on the continent and eternally interested in haven. Unable to interest politicians or the media in this settled issue of America's immigration law, these groups hoped for new circumstances in which the old regime of open doors might be restored.

One campaign of immense importance in this direction had already been well launched. In 1886 a gift to America from the French people and a symbol of friendship between two republics, in the form of the gigantic

Statue of Liberty sculpted by Frederic Auguste Bartholdi, was shipped to New York (Philadelphia narrowly missed out) and erected in the harbor. She was called "Liberty Enlightening the World," and beyond Franco-American friendship her meaning was as a symbol of America as a model to inspire other lovers of freedom. An accidental link to immigration had, ironically, been rebuffed. The Secretary of the Treasury, searching for a site for a federal immigration inspection depot in 1891, proposed locating it near the statue on Bedloe's Island and retreated in the face of spirited objections. "The Goddess of Liberty would gather up her skirts in disdain"; it would be "contaminated" by the flow of immigrants off the boats. The depot went to Ellis Island, and Liberty Enlightening the World was not defiled.

That was not the end of the matter, however. A temporary art and literary exhibition had earlier been organized to raise money for the pedestal that France was not supplying. Emma Lazarus, a Jewish young lady from a well-assimilated New York family who was shocked by news of pogroms in Russia, submitted a poem entitled "The New Colossus." It included the following lines:

> Give me your tired, your poor,
> Your huddled masses yearning to breathe free,
> The wretched refuse of your teeming shore.
> Send these, the homeless, tempest-tost to me,
> I lift my lamp beside the golden door.

It was read (along with other entries) at the opening of the exhibition in 1883, and then both poem and Miss Lazarus were largely forgotten.

In 1903 a friend of Lazarus gained permission to place a bronze tablet containing the poem on an inside wall of the pedestal. This went unnoticed. The arrival of millions of immigrants whose first view of America included that statue in the harbor generated among them a certain mythology of welcome and asylum around the upheld torch (the Lazarus interpretation of the monument), but to most Americans the statue was a local curiosity, or a proud acknowledgment that Liberty did indeed Enlighten the World.

This would change beginning in the 1930s, as journalists and history textbook writers began to link the statue not with liberty but with immigration, and Franklin Roosevelt made the first presidential link between the statue and immigration in a 1936 birthday celebration on the island. Tourists began to crowd the ferries running from Manhattan to Bedloe's Island, and the language of Park Service interpreters and the national media began a long-term shift of the meaning of "Lady Liberty"—and thus, America—from spreading freedom by example to offering unconditional asylum. It is not clear why this happened, but it happened without commentary or complaint. There were groups dedicated to reversing the immigration reforms of the 1920s who liked the Lazarus poem when they learned of it (wincing, of course, at the "wretched refuse" part). Talented writers such as the Yugoslav-born journalist Louis Adamic devoted his prolific writings to the importance of the poem. However, the transformation of the mythology of the statue from Liberty Enlightening the World to Mother of Exiles had legs of its own and probably reflected a desire among the intellectual elite to signal to the millions who had come during the New Immigration that they were now welcome and an essential part of America.

If America's symbol was Bartholdi's statue, and if the meaning of the statue was now to be unconditional asylum rather than an exemplar of liberty, the restrictions on the books were at odds with the country's core identity. Thus, the popular, politically unassailable reform system of 1924–29 had developed by mid-century a formidable potential adversary—a new myth about national purpose and identity embodied by a statue in New York harbor, no longer Liberty Enlightening the World by example, but now increasingly interpreted as the beacon guiding the world's huddled masses to a place of eternal asylum.

THE 1930S: A DECADE OF EMIGRANTS, NOT IMMIGRANTS

The collapse of the American economy that began in 1929 was severe and relentless, darkening every year of the 1930s and generating a considerable internal migration of forlorn, desperate Americans in search of work. Every job was precious and every worker shadowed by the unemployed. In those circumstances, observed one scholar of American immigration patterns, "we might say that for all practical purposes we have become opposed to immigration on a selective or any other basis." "I concluded," wrote President Herbert Hoover in his memoirs, recalling 1930, that in view of the large amount of unemployment at the time . . . directly or indirectly all immigrants were a public charge at the moment—either they themselves went on relief as soon as they landed, or, if they did get jobs, they forced others onto relief. I, therefore, stopped all immigration with some minor exceptions as to tourists, students, and professional men and women, and I made the order apply even to non-quota countries.

This combination of administrative sternness and, more important, bad news travelling along the immigrant kinship networks about America's dismal employment prospects cut overall legal immigration virtually to the vanishing point in the first half of the 1930s. The Great Wave subsided in a tiny ripple; an era had ended.

From another direction, an estimated 500,000 Mexicans (no one knows exactly how many) crossed the border into "El Norte" in the 1920s to work in the expanding irrigation-driven agricultural economies from Texas to California as well as the industries of the Midwest. This partially back-and-forth human movement in the arid Southwest was not seen as what it was, the Mexican harbinger of a new chapter in U.S. immigration history, the Second Great Wave.

THE 1930S AND 1940S: ON THE LEARNING CURVE WITH THE NEW IMMIGRATION POLICY

After a decade the new American immigration policy system (assisted by a collapsed economy) was achieving its goals of much lower numbers, and selection tilted more toward nationalities of familiar cultural heritage. But the system was not prepared for two sorts of immigration events the future would produce—"temporary" or "guest workers," and refugees seeking asylum from real or anticipated persecution.

War mobilization produced a domestic agricultural labor shortage, but in no region so severe and so close to a remedy as in the Southwest. Public Law 45 of 1942 inaugurated the Bracero Program of temporary admission of Mexican agricultural laborers, not intended or expected to have anything to do with immigration. Upon the discovery after the war that American labor did not seem abundantly available to perform seasonal, transitory farm labor at Third World wages, a new program was concluded with the Mexican government in 1948 and extended periodically until

1964. Criticism mounted over the years, and the Kennedy administration allowed the Bracero Program to end in view of resistance from the AFL-CIO and various Mexican-American community groups who had long been concerned about the impact of contract migratory workers. At the program's peak, almost 500,000 Mexican braceros were employed in the Southwest, and the fantasy of field armies of "temporary" male workers who would disappear after harvest and never bring families or put down roots (i.e., become immigrants) was at once exposed. The Mexican workers came again in the spring 1965, now a stream of illegal aliens constituting a new front in the coming wars over immigration. Policy makers who legislated this twenty-one-year subsidy to growers in the Southwest were producing a history lesson in the dynamics of guest worker programs—they drive out domestic labor, develop momentum, and become immigration streams.

A European refugee problem developed over this same mid-century period, a very different issue but equally stretching the boundaries and agitating the politics of national immigration policy. The trickles of immigration characteristic of the 1930s broadened as Germany's Nazi dictatorship under Adolf Hitler displayed a relentless hostility to Jews and other minorities, annexed Austria and Czechoslovakia, ignited another European war by invading Poland, and by 1940 established fascist control over all the Continent. Hitlerian Germany was giving the world, among other agonies, a grim new experience with unprecedented population expulsion, followed by the supreme horror of an organized effort to exterminate entire peoples, the Holocaust. Sensing ruthless repression (although not the unimaginable disaster that lay ahead), opponents of Nazism of all faiths and sectors of society, but especially Jews, began to leave Germany in mounting numbers, generating at the end of the 1930s refugee pressures that caught all countries of potential refuge unprepared, reluctant, and to some degree incredulous.

U.S. immigration law contained no specific provisions for refugees, despite a vague heritage of asylum for the politically and religiously oppressed. Ten million Americans were unemployed in 1939, and in the United States there was no sympathy for and much resistance to the idea of America becoming again the destination of millions of Europeans. President Franklin Roosevelt ordered the State Department to ease the rules for screening applicants for immigration visas, and in fact one-quarter of a million refugees from Europe entered the United States between 1932 and 1944, 100,000 of them Jews (they included physicists Albert Einstein, Enrico Fermi, and Edward Teller; philosophers Paul Tillich and Hannah Arendt; writer Thomas Mann; and other talented people who could have continued to enrich German life in saner times).

The ghastly discoveries of the death camps by advancing Allied armies in 1945 led some in retrospect to suggest that the United States should have accepted every boatload of fleeing Europeans in the late 1930s, or have organized some sort of international sharing, thus preventing the Holocaust. This is a retrospective wish, not an historical option. Close to 75 percent of Germany's Jews did relocate to other countries before the war, and after Hitler's stunning conquests made another 7 million Jews his wartime prisoners, there was no practical prospect for rescuing them (and others) from whatever the dictator had in mind (itself not clear until late in the war, and hard to believe even then). Even in the 1930s, an immediate open door for millions of Jewish refugees in a decade of massive unemployment, long before the Holocaust was more than a faint and unbelievable rumor, was not even proposed by American Jewish leadership at the time and was flatly a political impossibility in the United States and every other "country of refuge." However, even if such a policy course had been somehow constructed on a multinational basis, such a response would have encouraged Adolf Hitler and all other "ethnic cleansing" leaders in the future to expel undesirable populations as a matter of international routine. It is a hard truth that countries that generously accept refugees encourage the production of more refugees, creating a problem as they attempt to solve one. The core problem was the behavior of the German regime, and the absence of international sanctions on absolutely impermissible actions such as mass population expulsion or extermination. The terrible events of the 1930s and 1940s revealed the necessity of resolute and early international measures against regimes guilty of the barbarisms that launch massive flight from homelands.

The troubling refugee question emerged again as the war ended with millions of Europeans either displaced by wartime forced labor assignments or finding themselves living inside the war-expanded boundaries of a Russian Communist empire with the choice of either submission or flight in the direction that history had taught Europeans to flee—to the West, to the neo-Europes. Counting potential refugees is impossible, but official estimates ran from 8 to 20 million displaced persons in Europe in 1945, with 1.9 million living in Allied camps. The Congress of the United States would not normally have focussed upon this distant problem, but the White House and foreign policy establishment, energized by Franklin Roosevelt's activist style, was keenly aware of the new role as the managers of America's leadership in world affairs. Concerned with European stability and America's "world image" and not unaware that liberalized immigration rules translated into voter expansion in the Democratic Party's northeastern urban base, President Harry Truman began a pattern that holds to this day, the President wresting the lead in immigration policy away from (an often resentful) Congress. The Cold War was emerging as the new challenge to American security, and the executive branch realized that expanded immigration visas to the United States could become a foreign policy tool with no visible budgetary consequences. Truman ordered that refugees be given priority within quotas in 1945, and he pressed Congress to pass the first refugee policy measure in U. S. history (Displaced Persons Act) in 1948, allowing 205,000 visas over two years. Federal funds were appropriated for refugee relocation within the United States, disbursed to religious and civic voluntary agencies (Volags) that became an increasingly potent lobby for expanded refugee programs. Extended in 1950, the Displaced Persons Act eventually settled in the U.S. 410,000 or 40 percent of the 1 million Europeans relocated to 113 countries; most of them would have been ineligible under the laws of the 1920s.

These postwar refugee decisions began to open a major breach in the quota system enacted in the 1920s, although it was argued that they were a one-time adjustment to an unprecedented world war. However, one-time exceptions kept repeating themselves in an unstable world in which communism was expanding. The pro-Western government of China fell to revolutionary forces in 1949 and 1,600 Chinese students and professors were given visas; 30,000 Hungarians were admitted after the Russian military repression of the Hungarian Revolution of 1956; 215,000 Cubans crossed to Florida in 1959 and were admitted under the Attorney General's dubious new "parole authority." President Dwight Eisenhower persuaded Congress to pass refugee acts in 1953 and 1957, enlarging the stream of refugees and shifting their points of origin from Europe to Asia, the Middle East, and Africa. Charging refugee numbers to future quotas had long since been abandoned as a fiction. Human traffic around the national origins system was increasing as the executive branch reshaped immigration policy piecemeal toward larger numbers from more parts of the world, to the consternation of some congressional leaders.

One of these, Senator Patrick McCarran, son of Irish immigrants, sponsored an extensive study and review of immigration issues in 1950. Explicitly disavowing "any theory of Nordic superiority," the report forthrightly endorsed the National Origins System, affirming that Americans at the time of its adoption "were fully justified in determining that the country was no longer a field for further colonization." The report was notable in all the literature on American immigration policy discussion for its demographic focus and insight, apparently owing to the presence on staff of a talented American demographer, Dudley Kirk. Senate Report 1515 surveyed the history of immigration and immigration policy and found at mid-century signs of a "rising tide of immigration" that because of population growth in Latin America and Asia "might well again attain the proportion of the early years of the 20th century," and it came at a time when "certain nations of the world have already exceeded their optimum population" in relation to resources. The report implied, but lacked the data or analysis to assert, that the United States was one of these overcrowded countries and thus had an interest in curbing immigration-induced population growth.

Thus key congressional policy makers were in a mood to reaffirm the restrictive tilt of the National Origins System, whereas the executive branch now saw immigration expansion as a foreign policy tool in the cold war, especially in the Third World. Senator McCarran, joining forces with Representative Francis Walter, submitted legislation in 1952 to clarify American immigration and naturalization laws, an effort to re-establish congressional control of policy that had slipped away toward the White House. The McCarran-Walter bill retained the same totals as the 1924 law and affirmed the national origins quota system as "a rational method . . . to best preserve the sociological and cultural balance" of the American population. However, it continued an easing of the bars against Asians that had started during the war, when, under pressure from religious and business groups, Congress in 1943 had repealed the Chinese Exclusion Act ("We can correct an historic mistake," President Roosevelt said in his message endorsing repeal) and established an annual quota of 105 for China, repeating this action in the case of India and the Philippines in 1946. McCarran-Walter went farther, allowing immigration (usually at a minimal level of 100) from twenty-one countries or areas in what had once been called the "Asian Barred Zone," a phrase mercifully retired but replaced by another ghetto characterization, the "Asia-Pacific triangle." Racial discrimination in immigration policy was ended, advocates claimed, clearly stung by what was becoming the central theme of critics of the 1924 system. The proposed reform bill still favored applicants from northwestern Europe but excluded no race or people entirely.

Critics did not attack the popular national origins idea directly, although some witnesses complained that preferring some nationalities to others was "gratuitously offending most of the countries of the earth," in the words of a spokesman for the American Jewish Congress. Some proposed to shift the base year for quotas to 1950, which would increase allocations for eastern and central Europe. The McCarran-Walter legislation passed overwhelmingly, then was vetoed by President Truman with the stern words that "the basis of this quota system was false and unworthy in 1924" and is "a slur on the patriotism, the capacity, and the decency of a large part of our citizenry."

The veto was overridden, but the wording and tone of Truman's objections indicated that immigration politics was slowly taking on a new alignment. Mass immigration pressures at the turn of the century had given rise to restrictionist reformers in both parties, right and left of center. The ensuing reforms that curbed mass immigration grew in part out of progressive and socialist concerns about threats to American wage levels, urban disorder, and political corruption, although the legislation also was a response to anxieties about national cohesion and identity that are conventionally thought of as conservative issues. Immigration reform was bipartisan and drew strength across the political spectrum. By the time Harry Truman vetoed McCarran-Walter, New Deal liberals were increasingly lining up as their progressive predecessors had not, as strong critics of the reforms that had curbed the Great Wave. Liberals were the dominant intellectual and political force in American politics at mid-century, despite losing the White House to General Eisenhower in the 1952 election. Mc-Carran-Walter reaffirmed the reform system of the 1920s, but was another reform cycle somewhere in the wings?

THE ASSAULT ON THE NATIONAL ORIGINS SYSTEM

As they revised and refined the basic National Origins System for the long haul, McCarran, Walter, and the huge majorities that endorsed their work could not know how the tides were turning against them. They were intimately familiar with the ethnic, religious, and professional lobbies who had always testified against restriction in general and national origins as a formula—the Common Council on American Unity, the Association of Immigration and Nationality Lawyers, the National Catholic Welfare Conference, and the American Jewish Congress ("professional Jews," Representative Walter had angrily called the latter group, and the rest were "professional immigrant handlers"). These lobbies did not know exactly what they wanted in replacement of national origins restriction, and their cause had no resonance in public opinion, but far-reaching political changes were at work. The new immigrants and their children had moved into the Democratic Party in the 1920s because of its "ethnic outsider" image and its historic resistance to the moral reform agenda of Yankee Republicans. The presidential nomination of Catholic Governor Al Smith of New York in 1928 accelerated this alignment, and both the liberal social policies and the inclusive ethnic style of Franklin Roosevelt's New Deal pulled the urban ethnic vote into a New Deal coalition that would dominate American politics through the 1960s. Harry Truman understood the political potential, in northeastern cities pivotal to carrying the most populous states, of an attack on the existing immigration policy for being somehow unfair to Poles, Jews, and Italians (i.e., the New Immigrants, now voters). There seemed to be no political costs to be paid for offending the broad public, who were passively in favor of the system in place and unaware that it was under attack.

More important than ethnic coalition building, Truman and younger liberal Democrats such as Minnesota's Hubert Humphrey realized that their party had an historic rendezvous with racial discrimination, especially as entrenched in the (Democratic) South in the Jim Crow system. An assault on racial discrimination began to make sense to farsighted Democrats for several reasons—out of self-interest given the growing black vote in urban precincts, out of concern for Third World opinion in the Cold War, and out of common decency. Truman was a cautious friend of the gathering civil rights movement, and his support was enough to cause a southern Dixiecrat third party revolt in 1948. He was an even more vigorous denouncer of discrimination against foreigners: "The greatest vice of our present quota system," he had written in his veto message, "is that it discriminates . . . against many peoples of the world." This was 1952, a year in which he had nothing at stake in view of his decision not to run and could explore the potential of the language that would power the future: antidiscrimination. Immediately after his veto was overturned, Truman appointed a Commission on Immigration and Naturalization, whose report (*Whom We Shall Welcome*) proposed abolishing the national origins system, replacing it with a larger number (250,000, with an added 100,000 political asylees each year for three years) chosen by an independent commission on the basis of asylum, family reunification, and "needs in the U.S." McCarran and Walter were angrily negative, and Truman dropped the issue, having staked out the new liberal position.

It began to concern friends of the restriction regime, however, when the new Republican president, Dwight Eisenhower, no active opponent of racial discrimination but keenly interested in America's image in Third World countries who were pawns in the Cold War, referred in the 1952 campaign to "unfair provisions" of the basic immigration law. He also sponsored enlarged refugee exceptions, recommended immigration reforms in his 1956 State of the Union Address, and sent down legislative proposals to move the census basis from 1920 to 1950 and distribute the larger numbers on other than national origin grounds. In a Memorial Day speech in 1956, Francis Walter defended the "nondiscriminatory" policy in place and warned that reformers were bent upon trebling the number of allowable immigrants at a time when world population growth was accelerating, most importantly in non-quota-controlled Latin America. He and others sensed a fundamental challenge to U.S. immigration policy from liberal reformers.

What do the opponents of our national origins quota system want, asked former State Department Visa Office head Robert C. Alexander in an article in the *American Legion Magazine* in 1956? "When they glibly advocate action which would result in a change in the ethnological composition of our people . . . perhaps they should tell us, what is wrong with our national origins?" In a memo to colleagues in the American Jewish Committee, Sidney Liskofsky candidly remarked that the question was "a tough one to answer." Is there a justification for "a cultural-ethnic criterion for the admission of immigrants to the U.S." or not? In Liskofsky's view, open-immigration reformers think not, but the American people apparently thought otherwise. Alexander's question shifted the burden of proof from defenders of national origins to those who would end it. Do we propose to go back to free immigration? He called attention to a recent article by sociologist Nathan Glazer, who pointed out that those who want to go back to free immigration "write as if immigration had no effect on America except to make it bigger, better . . . more of the same." However, a "sense of history" tells us that "the greatest migration in history" has also made America "different." Do we

> want to become even more different, or are satisfied with what we are? In 1921, the American people decided they wanted to stop. . . . Nations have rarely been faced with deciding their ethnic makeup, but the

United States was. I think the racist thinking that accompanied that decision was reprehensible. The decision itself, however, one can understand. America had decided to stop the kaleidoscope and find out what it had become.

This brief volley of ideas was a remarkably candid and perceptive statement of the issues involved in overturning the national origins regime. The earlier free immigration system had been changing the country, and the American people had clearly decided to curb immigration so that it annually supplied a small mirror of America, giving time "to find out what it had become." Reformers of that policy decision were developing a strong critical argument but might also need a persuasive answer to the question, What is wrong with America that you would fix with a new (or restoration of the old) immigration system?

Publicly, the discussion of immigration policy was still a very minor, indeed, usually nonexistent theme in national politics. Both parties in the 1956 election adopted platform statements decrying "discrimination" in the immigration system, but neither Eisenhower nor Adlai Stevenson injected the issue into the campaign. Nor did immigration surface in the 1960 presidential campaign. It would be, however, one of the agenda items for the liberal reformers who took over in 1961, and the ground was prepared in the 1950s. The civil rights movement surged into national news and consciousness in 1955–56 with the Montgomery, Alabama bus boycott and the emergence of Reverend Martin Luther King Jr. For the next decade the discriminatory Jim Crow legal regime of the South came under a furious assault in Southern streets and schools, in national channels of news and opinion. The moral fervor of this crusade was so intense that it fanned into new life similar antidiscrimination movements among feminist, Native American, and gay communities. The enemy everywhere at the bottom of virtually every national blemish seemed to be discrimination, the historic, now intolerable subordinating classification of groups on the basis of inherited characteristics. The nation's national origin-grounded immigration laws could never have escaped an assault by these reformist passions. In retrospect, at least, the only question was: Who would lead, and formulate what alternatives?

Massachusetts Senator John F. Kennedy cautiously stepped out on immigration in the 1950s, sensing that a liberalization stance would gather vital ethnic voting blocs for his long-planned run for the presidency. His

work on a refugee bill caught the attention of officials of the Anti-Defama-
tion League (ADL) of B'nai B'rith, who convinced Kennedy to become an
author of a pamphlet on immigration, with the help of an ADL-supplied
historian, Arthur Mann, and Kennedy's staff. The result was *A Nation of
Immigrants,* a 1958 bouquet of praise for the contributions of immigrants
and a call for an end to the National Origins System. The ADL, part of a
Jewish coalition whose agenda included opening wider the American gates,
had made a golden alliance. John F. Kennedy was no crusader on immigration (or anything else), but he was an activist young president by 1961,
comfortable with immigration reform as part of his agenda, elected on a
party platform that pledged elimination of the national origins system.

IMMIGRATION REFORM AGAIN: ROAD TO THE 1965 ACT

House immigration hearings first took up the global population prospect
and its implications in 1962–63 and should have provided a valuable foundation for reform, especially with respect to immigration pressures from
Mexico and Central America; however, they were ignored in the press and
later. Real action waited on the President's agenda. Kennedy's victory had
been narrow, and he moved very slowly on sensitive issues, especially those
where he expected formidable resistance. That would come from, among
others, Francis Walter, but his death in May 1963 came just as Kennedy
was finally moving on civil rights legislation, and it seemed natural to link
the two causes whose joint target, by long agreement among liberals, was
"discrimination." Kennedy sent a special message on immigration to Congress in July, asking for repeal of a policy that "discriminates among applicants for admission into the U.S on the basis of the accident of birth." The
Asia-Pacific triangle limits should be abolished at once, national origins
quotas in five years, to be replaced by a selection system based on individual skills and family reunification, "first-come, first-served." There would
be a minimal increase in total numbers (from 157,000 quota immigrants
to 165,000). Reform never meant larger numbers, as the reformers constantly assured the public.

This initiative, along with the rest of the Kennedy program, was in-
herited by Lyndon Johnson after the assassination. He also inherited
Kennedy's determined reformist advisers on immigration, among them
Myer Feldman, Norbert Schlei, and Abba Schwarz. The latter convinced

the new President to endorse reform in his 1964 State of the Union Address and to hold a meeting with ethnic leaders where Johnson repeated the key slogan of the attack on the National Origins System: "We ought to never ask, 'In what country were you born.'" Still, reformers privately were pessimistic. In the words of the American Jewish Committee's lobbyist in Washington, "there is no great public demand for immigration reform" which "is a very minor issue."

It was indeed a minor issue to the public, not on the radar screen in a decade overheating with social movements and an escalating war in southeast Asia. However, liberal reformers discovered after John Kennedy's assassination that legislating social change could be accomplished even when only the policy elite, but not the larger public, recognized a problem needing a solution. There was emerging on the immigration question a pattern in public opinion and discussion that would be found on many issues: elite opinion makers selected a problem and a liberal policy solution, while grassroots opinion, unfocussed and marginalized, ran strongly the other way. Editorials in newspapers like the *New York Times* and the *Washington Post,* or in national magazines such as the *Saturday Evening Post* denounced the national origins system as the equivalent of Jim Crow and endorsed a repeal of it, saying little about an alternative. However, historian Betty Koed observes in her history of the 1965 act that editorials and letters to the editor "in smaller cities and towns" revealed "widespread condemnation of the new immigration bill" and of the idea of "liberalizing" immigration policy.

Legislative hearings began in the House in the summer of 1964, while the Senate was engaged in something more pressing but closely related: passage of the 1964 Civil Rights Act, which barred discrimination on the basis of race, creed, religion, sex, and "national origin." This language attracted frowning attention to the immigration status quo. How could the United States exert world leadership, Congressman Emmanuel Celler asked, if our current immigration system was "a gratuitous insult to many nations" because of its race-conscious basis? National origin had become race, suddenly an impermissible factor in decision making. We need "an immigration policy reflecting America's ideal of the equality of all men without regard to race, color, creed, or national origin," said Senator Hiram Fong of Hawaii when the Senate opened hearings in 1965. Against such sentiments, an American Legion spokesman countered that "it is in the best interest of our country to maintain the present makeup of our cultural and social structure." In the context of the Cold War and the civil rights struggle, there seemed considerably more energy and pertinence in the reformers' arguments. The National Origins System was on the defensive now, joined at the hip with Jim Crow.

Yet how could immigration reformers change a policy regime that was widely popular? A Harris poll released in May 1965 showed the public "strongly opposed to easing of immigration laws" by a 2 to 1 margin (58 percent to 24 percent). This must have discouraged immigration liberalizers, but they knew that a burst of Great Society legislation was beginning to pour through Congress in the mid-1960s, most of it not generated out of public demand or even understanding but out of the unique circumstances created by Kennedy's death, Johnson's legislative skills, and the intellectual and political collapse of American conservatism.

The defenders of the National Origins System—those who understood its complexities—conceded some of its flaws. Up to 2/3 of the immigration flows after World War II had come outside the quotas, from the Western Hemisphere, and refugees. The system was a Swiss cheese of loopholes, with the result that annual numbers had been rising and the cultural background of immigrants was not what the system was designed to produce. Complex maneuvering produced a House version of the administration's legislation that ended national origins quotas and shifted to a system of preferences based on family reunification and skills.

In the Senate, Senator Sam Ervin of North Carolina, a member of the Subcommittee on Immigration, was the only member defending the National Origins System. Ervin met every administration witness with the argument that you could not draft any immigration law in which you did not "discriminate," in that you favor some over others. Why not then discriminate, as the McCarran-Walter Act did (Ervin always defended the system as revised in 1952; liberal reformers, who might be called expansionists, always attacked the laws and lawmakers of the 1920s) in favor of national groups who historically had the greatest influence in building the nation? To put all the earth's peoples on the same basis as prospective immigrants to the United States, Ervin argued, was to discriminate against the "people from England . . . France . . . Germany . . . Holland" who had first settled and shaped the country.

The political problem with this argument was that the huge American population who would have approved of it were mostly dead, and those living had little interest in immigration issues or knowledge of what was being proposed. The ethnic groups associated with the New Immigration were represented by organizations mobilized behind immigration reform and were strategically placed politically in northeastern and midwestern urban states. It was also evident that the restrictions of the 1920s had lost important parts of their core support. A chief sponsor of limiting immigration had been organized labor, but the AFL-CIO leadership in the 1950s (although not, apparently, the rank and file) had shifted its ground on immigration, and by the 1960s it expressed none of the concerns about job and wage competition of an earlier era. As for another component of the restrictionist coalition, black leaders were beginning a move toward solidarity with all the world's "people of color" and could not be counted on to take the restrictionist positions staked out by Frederick Douglass and Booker Washington.

Even leaders of patriotic societies, reported the floor manager of the bill, Senator Edward Kennedy, "expressed little overt defense of the national-origins system" and indicated their willingness to consider a new framework so long as the numbers were not enlarged. Kennedy assured them that this was not the reformers' intention, and it is clear from the legislative record that "the reformers consistently denied that they were seeking to increase immigration significantly," in the summary of Steven Wagner. Both historians of the legislative background of the 1965 act, Wagner and Betty Koed, decline to call this outright deception, preferring to believe that the reformers had not given much thought to the system they were putting in place, for they "were looking backwards more than forwards." Their "main impetus . . . was not practical, but ideological." They were expunging what they took to be a legislative blot on America's internationally scrutinized record, more intent on dismantling than in the careful design of a substitute.

Ervin attempted to get the best bargain possible under the circumstances. "Congressmen don't want to look like racists," a *New York Times* reporter said, recording the intellectual victory of the reformers. Ervin asked pointed questions of administration witnesses about the legislation's impact on overall numbers and their composition, and he was given reassuring and (as it turned out) shockingly wrong estimates. Administration witnesses predicted that the bulk of new immigrants would come from large backlogs in Italy, Greece, and Poland and that annual numbers would increase only a modest 50–75,000. On the question of Latin American immigration, Attorney General Nicholas Katzenbach, obviously ignorant of the testimony in the population hearings of 1963 that Mexico's population had nearly doubled from 1940 to 1960 and that in the last decade 400,000 Mexicans had migrated to the United States as 3 million braceros crossed the border seasonally, stated that "there is not much pressure to come to the United States from those countries." Senator Ervin dug in here, and the administration had to accept a 120,000 "ceiling" (a porous ceiling; immediate family and refugee admissions were uncapped) on Western Hemisphere immigration.

It now is apparent that reformers were putting in place a new system under which total numbers would triple and the source countries of immigration would radically shift from Europe to Latin America and Asia—exactly the two demographic results that the entire restrictionist campaign from the 1870s to 1929 was designed to prevent. However, the two core ideas of the restrictionists, that modern America was better off without large-scale immigration and that the existing ethno-racial makeup of the American people should be preserved, were not directly challenged. Indeed, they were explicitly reaffirmed. Attorney General Robert Kennedy said in Senate hearings in 1964 that abolishing the restrictions on the Asia-Pacific triangle would result "in approximately 5,000 [immigrants] . . . after which immigration from that source would virtually disappear," and testified in 1965 (when he was a senator from New York) that placing emphasis on family reunification would maintain the status quo as to nations of origin. No one openly recommended either the desirability of moving America back to 1 million a year immigration levels or the idea that it was time for the nation aspiring to lead the world to be demographically altered so as to replicate that world.

The Senate bill passed by a vote of 76 to 18, and the nation had a radically new immigration regime. The Hart-Cellar Immigration Act of 1965 ended the National Origins System, which had served the nation well in some respects but whose principles of selection had increasingly embarrassed the nation as world politics and domestic attitudes toward race relations changed profoundly. In the new system, an inherited factor, nationality, still functioned as an element in selection (your nationality could keep you out in any year that your nation's quota exceeded 20,000), but "discrimination" was supposed to be thankfully gone, since all nations could send some migrants and no country or region was supposed to be favored. (This did not work out in practice; the new system surprisingly "discriminated" in favor of Latin Americans and Asians, as Senator Ervin had predicted.) The Eastern Hemisphere could send 170,000 a year, and for the first time (Senator Ervin's lone victory) Western Hemisphere immigration was placed under a "cap" of 120,000, which did not include refugees or spouses, minor children, and parents of U.S. citizens. The law established a new set of preference categories that represented a major retreat from the historic emphasis in American immigration policy on labor market/skills criteria (only two of the seven in the new system) and toward kinship relations said to promote "family reunification" (four of the seven).

The new system, like the old, was flawed by its rigidity. Congress wrote immigration law as if its judgments should endure for decades. However, immigration is a labor flow that should be meshed with the changing needs of the national economy, and a demographic nation shaper that should be harnessed to national population goals. Recognizing at least the former, one of the architects of the 1965 reform, Emmanuel Celler, pressed for an immigration board to recommend annual readjustments of skills-related preference categories. This was lost in the shuffle. The system was not open to administrative realignment in response to economic cycles or demographic trends. Even if it had been, family ties abroad, not skills needed in the United States, were the heart of the new selection process.

"The bill that we will sign today," said President Johnson, "is not a revolutionary bill" and "does not affect the lives of millions." What it did, he thought, was essentially moral and symbolic. It ends "the harsh injustice of the national origins quota system" which was "a cruel and enduring wrong." Journalist Theodore White offered a better interpretation, when, years later and with hindsight, he called the new immigration law "noble, revolutionary—and probably the most thoughtless of the many acts of the Great Society."

THE SECOND GREAT WAVE UPON A FRAGILE SHORE

Revolutionary? The Immigration Act of 1965 was not given much contemporary attention in a decade of social upheaval and a war in Vietnam, and it is routinely allotted one or two sentences in history textbooks.

This emphasis will change, and attention to the 1965 act will grow, because it represents a demographic turning point, as suggested by White's choice of the word "revolutionary" to describe the act. With all due respect to the epochal and invaluable changes made in the American South when the Jim Crow system was killed by the Civil Rights Act of 1964, the passage of time may position the 1965 immigration law as the Great Society's most nation-changing single act, especially if seen as the first of a series of ongoing liberalizations of U.S. immigration and border policy extending through the end of the century and facilitating four decades (so far) of mass immigration. For the 1965 law, and subsequent policy, shifted the nation from a population-stabilization to a population-growth path, with far-reaching consequences, all of them negative. The fundamental alteration of the streams of cultural replenishment in American life brings changes so complex and long-range that Americans living in the early stages of this transformation might see it as merely cosmetic, or enriching through a much-needed diversification, or nation-ending. The 1965 act bids to be seen as the largest, if most slow-moving, of the reforms of that liberal era. Demography is destiny.

Like many of history's cascading events, the revolutionary impact of the immigration reform launched in the 1960s (White's word "thoughtless" was meant in the sense of unintended, at least at the beginning) is evident in hindsight but was missed by intelligent policy makers at the time. Despite (poorly attended) hearings in the House in 1962–63 on world demography past and future, they ignored the implications of a world in the latter phases of what economic historian Walt Rostow called *The Great Population Spike* (1998). An unprecedented and ultimately tragic event in human and planetary life, the surge in the number of Homo sapiens from 1 billion in 1830 to 6 billion by the end of the twentieth century to the expected 9–11 billion sometime in the twenty-first century, came within 250 years, a mere instant in humanity's 100,000 years on the globe. This upward spike in human populations is a combination of a success story—economic and social modernization, which lowered death rates as it improved standards of living—with a disastrous inability of humans to understand the need to lower their birthrates as quickly. The results of this stupendous failure of culture and intelligence has been and will be exploding populations becoming too large for the carrying capacity of environments and socioeconomic systems—hence billions of humans fated to live with malnutrition, starvation, disease, and wars for resources. Rostow, optimistic about human ingenuity in the long run, sees the period from the 1990s to about 2025 as "a period of maximum strain on resources and environment when global population is still expanding . . . a global crisis of Malthusian consequences" made worse by the unknown strains of global warming. Another sophisticated observer, Hamish MacRae, in *The World in 2020* (1994), sees a turbulent era of water and oil shortages, relentless habitat destruction, and international conflict over transborder pollution and basic resources.

Mass migrations toward earth's successful, more moderately populated societies continued. The first massive and concerted flow generated by this upward spike of human numbers was the Great Wave, washing in the eighteenth and nineteenth centuries from that part of the world (Europe) that first experienced the modernization-driven explosion of human numbers. That European wave headed west to the Neo-Europes, dragging millions of enslaved Africans with them for a short time.

In the United States, the 1965 Immigration Act came just as the population spike was sending a Second Great Wave of human migration surging out of overcrowded, environmentally damaged impoverished nations which were the next-in-line modernizers. In the second half of the twentieth entury this meant Latin America and parts of Asia, with secondary eddies out of the Middle East, Russia, and North Africa. This second vast human migration continues as this book is written and will extend deep into the twenty-first century. As it gained momentum, policy reformers gave the United States a new, more porous immigration system and "asylum as the meaning of America" ethos which absorbed and even encouraged rather than limited the volume of the Second Wave, inaugurating a long era of large-scale and nation-changing immigration to the United States. To this we now turn, and to the complex question of its impacts.

MASS IMMIGRATION, AGAIN, AND PUBLIC CRITICISM, AGAIN

By the end of the twentieth century, the pivotal importance of immigration policy reform in the 1960s was becoming apparent. Annual totals of legal immigration, which had averaged 178,000 over the duration of the National Origins System, rose to 400,000 by 1973, to 600,000 by 1978, reaching 1 million by 1989 and hovering in that magnitude through the 1990s. These figures exclude illegal aliens, refugees who have not filed for permanent status, and an estimated half-million "non-immigrant" aliens working in the country at any given time. By the 1990s, immigration was adding between 1 and 1.5 million persons (3–500,000 of that illegal) to the American population every year, and accounting for 60 percent of America's population growth, a proportion steadily rising.

The source nations of the new Americans were no longer England, Germany, Ireland, Italy, and Poland, but (as of 1990) Mexico, the Philippines, Vietnam, China/Taiwan, the Dominican Republic, Korea, India, the USSR, Jamaica, and Iran. Throughout the 1980s and 1990s, 82 percent came from Latin America and Asia, 13 percent from Europe.

By the 1980s these changes began to gain media and political attention. Historian John Higham reminds us of the starting point in understanding immigration, when he writes that "immigrants are an unsettling force wherever they appear," especially in large numbers from culturally diverse backgrounds and over an extended time. The numbers were startlingly large and rising, and it was the numbers of immigrants, not where they came from, that first generated concern and, in the late 1970s, the beginnings of a restrictionist reform effort.

A pioneering first (and thus far, only) National Commission on Population Growth and the American Future, chaired by John D. Rockefeller III, reported to President Nixon in 1972 that "in the long run, no substantial benefits will result from further growth of the Nation's population, rather that the gradual stabilization of our population would contribute significantly to the Nation's ability to solve its problems." Thus, we should "welcome and plan for a stabilized population," which clearly implied bringing immigration policy into alignment with that goal. The Commission recommended controlling illegal immigration and capping legal immigration at the current level of 400,000 annually, which it noted as the source of one-quarter of current U.S. population growth. When the commission also recommended liberalized abortion policies, President Nixon sensed a political liability and rejected the entire report. Some environmentalists persisted. National Parks and Conservation Association (NPCA) President Anthony Wayne Smith said in a 1978 editorial in *National Parks and Conservation Magazine* that "the pressures of a steadily rising population preclude adequate long-term solutions to conservation issues" and that with the domestic birthrate below replacement level at 1,8 total fertility rate (average number of live births per woman), the 400,000 legal plus 800,000 illegal immigrants entering the United States annually matched, and doubled, natural increase. The NPCA in 1978 formed a coalition of labor and environmental groups to press for measures to control illegal immigration.

In this, the organization moved against the shifting tide. Although the population growth impacts of the post-1965 immigration system were rising, willingness to discuss them was fading. The environmental and labor groups briefly convened in NPCA's coalition were concluding that calls for immigration reform would get them attacked by Catholic, Protestant, and Jewish religious leaders and civil rights activists as somehow anti-immigrant, which might mean anti-Mexican, which might mean "racist," a risk these organizations, overwhelmingly run by liberal Washington-based staff, were afraid to run. The immigration-population growth connection was factually unassailable and growing stronger, but the topic was thought to be taboo. Some of the staff and board of the nation's foremost organization working for population stabilization, Zero Population Growth (ZPG), resisted the pressures from its president (1975–77), Dr. John Tanton, and others to make immigration a permanent part of ZPG's lobbying program. Frustrated at the organization's reluctance to address the part of population growth directly assigned to government control, Tanton, a Michigan ophthalmologist, in 1978 joined with other environmentalists and populationists (with ZPG's blessing) to launch a small organization (of which I was a founding board member) in Washington, the Federation for American Immigration Reform (FAIR), the organizational beginnings of what was called the "new restrictionism."

Critics of the status quo first raised questions not about the immigration flows permitted by the policy in place, but illegal entries around it. NPCA President Smith's editorial had mentioned the figure of 800,000 illegal aliens annually, and here he touched on an issue of rising public concern, even if his numbers were only an educated guess. Large scale illegal entry into the United States, a wealthy country with a generous welfare state whose lowest wages were ten times those in the Third World, should have been anticipated at the southern border by those who knew anything about U.S. twentieth-century history there. The Bracero Program had built enormous immigration momentum through seasonal agricultural jobs and family networks, and ending the program in 1964 did nothing to alter the allure of a migratory relationship that looked like low wage workers to American growers and jobs at high wages to Mexicans. The Immigration and Naturalization Service (INS) reported the annual apprehension and removal of 500,000 illegal aliens in the late 1960s, most from Mexico but many from Central America and the Caribbean, and INS Commissioner Leonard Chapman, a retired Marine Corps general, spoke of an "invasion." By the mid-1970s illegal immigration had become "a hot second tier issue," in journalist Roberto Suro's words. Visual and print media conveyed pictures of illegal aliens, overwhelmingly young males, climbing fences or sprinting through highway checkpoints at the U.S.-Mexican border in California and Texas. Estimates of illegal individuals entering the U.S. ran from 200,000 to a million a year.

Corrective reform efforts seemed inevitable, as public opinion ran strongly against a large-scale human invasion that was illegal, displaced some American workers at the bottom of the wage scale, exerted downward pressure on wages in affected industries, was a government subsidy to large growers in the southwest, encouraged the development of criminal rings for smuggling, and created a growing class of underground noncitizens in the country who had little recourse to the law. In the words of economist and Secretary of Labor (1977–81) Ray Marshall, the deal offered to the United States by access to illegal Mexican farm workers is that "there is more product, it costs less to produce, and the only losers are low income American citizens with Hispanic names." California labor leader Cesar Chavez and his United Farm Workers agreed that a porous border undercut the economic and social gains of Americans of Hispanic descent. "This immigrant labor subsidy encourages the expansion of an industry in which the majority of workers earn below-poverty-level incomes," UC Davis economist Phil Martin observed, and "holding down food prices by holding down farm worker wages . . . is morally wrong." It was also saving consumers very little—tomato prices would rise 3 percent if illegal workers were removed from the fields, according to a Center for Immigration Studies report. Illegal Mexican workers brought larger problems than lowered wages, Hispanic writer Roberto Suro argued. Their presence in Latino communities created permanent tensions with the larger society: "Latinos will always be handicapped so long as a large proportion of the Latino population is made up of people who have no legal standing in the United States."

Astonishingly, illegal entry and work force participation had defenders, although with flimsy arguments. The term should not be "illegal aliens," it was argued, but "undocumented workers," recognizing their service to America. Entering illegally was not really illegal, if we recognize a higher human right to "feed families" and "have a better way of life"; they did work "no Americans will do"; and most returned to Mexico at the end of the growing season, fulfilling the old dream of cheap, docile workers who did not really live here.

Thus, the arguments against the large and sustained flow of illegal labor were overwhelming, and no government could ignore them. Sensing what might lie ahead and, as a Jew "particularly troubled by [the anticipation of] identity cards and roundups," in Suro's telling of it, President Ford's Attorney General Edward Levi appointed a committee and passed the problem to Jimmy Carter, who agreed to pass it to a congressional Select Commission on Immigration and Refugee Policy headed by Notre Dame University President Father Theodore Hesburgh. The commission's 1981 report noted opinion surveys showing public opposition to current high levels of immigration both legal and illegal, but affirmed the positive value of legal immigration and proposed that "closing the back door" of illegal immigration was required in order to preclude a public backlash against all immigration. Because illegal individuals came for jobs, the "jobs magnet" must be cut off. This magnet was the American workplace, where employers were free to hire illegal individuals under a little-noticed "Texas Proviso" of 1952. Enact penalties on employers of illegal aliens, the commission recommended (an idea put forward by liberal Senator Paul Douglas in the 1950s), and the flow northward will abate.

Senator Alan K. Simpson (R.-Wyo.) and Representative Romano Mazzoli (D-Ky.) commenced in 1982 what proved to be a contentious four-year battle over immigration legislation. Nobody defended illegal immigration, but a strange coalition benefiting from the northward flow (seasonal crop growers and Latino activists) joined with church groups and the civil liberties lobby in objecting to worker identification proposals and arguing that an "amnesty" was far preferable to the mass deportation of an illegal population now estimated between 3 and 5 million. Public opinion may have been strongly supportive of any necessary measures to end illegal entry, but the public does not testify before Congress, and the only organized support for effective controls was FAIR, a small and fledgling lobby. In 1986 Congress passed and President Reagan signed the Immigration Reform and Control Act (IRCA), in retrospect a public policy failure of major proportions. Sanctions on employers of illegal aliens entered American law where they should have been all along, but a proposed system of worker verification based upon a computer registry of Social Security numbers was defeated by objections to "a national ID card" (which was never proposed) and the claim that Hispanics would be "singled out" for special scrutiny. The final measure allowed employers to accept as proof of legal residence any two of a wide range of documents, most easily counterfeited. "The change in the farm labor market made by IRCA," wrote economist Phil Martin, "is the switch from undocumented workers to falsely documented workers." For this toothless provision, Congress traded an unprecedented "amnesty" for lawbreakers who had been in continuous residence since 1982 (to capture "long-term" residents only) plus a special program to legalize already present illegal workers. The double amnesty was justified on the theory that blanket "legalization" was preferable to mass deportation, that the bad precedent would not matter, and that the problem would not build up again because the magnet would be cut off. Almost nothing promised by the legislation turned out as expected. The amnesty covered only 60 percent of the illegal population, still 2.7 million people, most of them male, who could then apply for visas for their relatives. Demographer David Simcox estimated that federal assistance, welfare benefits, and costs of schooling the children of amnestied workers added up to $78.7 billion, or a subsidy of nearly $30,000 for each legalized alien.

For illegal aliens who were ineligible for amnesty, enforcement by INS of the ban on hiring them was spotty, and document fraud quickly became almost universal. The Border Patrol reported that illegal entries dropped off in 1987, as the networks channeling cheap Third World labor into the United States (Mexico was the staging ground and chief source country, but on a given week the Border Patrol at San Diego arrested nationals from over 100 countries) waited to see whether the United States was serious about illegal immigration. It was not. Driven by Mexican economic crisis and civil wars in Central America and lured by a magnet of jobs in low-wage industries from agriculture to food service, lawn-home maintenance, and child care (and, some said, also welfare benefits, free public schooling, and free hospital emergency room care), illegal immigration rose again to former levels and continued as a heated topic of immigration debate.

Historian Reed Ueda rightly calls IRCA "the most generous immigration law passed in U.S. history," with "novel and generous provisions for the legalization of illegal aliens and [enlarging] a host of quota allotments based on special needs and status." It conferred legal status on millions who had, in the critics' terms, "butted in line" ahead of other millions abroad who were on waiting lists for visas and allowed the flow of illegal individuals to continue at levels estimated by the INS at 500,000 annually by the mid-1990s—approximately half of legal immigration itself, which had reached levels matching the flows prior to World War I.

IRCA proved to be no aberration. As policy decisions in the following years would prove, American immigration policy making had entered a long era of permissiveness toward massive legal and illegal entry, policy makers in the 1980s and 1990s repeatedly expanding the opportunities and inducements to migration. This occurred in the teeth of public opinion polls showing the American public in all parts of the country and across all racial and ethnic groups opposed to such high numbers and especially angry with illegal entry. The Border Patrol was underfunded no matter which party was in power, and the one in three (estimated) illegal border crossers who were apprehended were penalized only by a bus trip back across the border, there to try again. And then there was the opening door to a potentially limitless supply of volunteers to join America: "refugees."

THE EVER-WIDENING GATE

During the Cold War, international events had more to say about immigration trends than the intentions of policy makers. The 1965 act was ignored and then bypassed before it was a year old. Cuban dictator Fidel Castro, facing political turmoil in the fall of 1965, announced that any Cuban wishing to leave was free to do so. To embarrass Castro, Congress quickly passed the Cuban Adjustment Act of 1966, placing all arriving Cubans in their own special category as if they were refugees and welcome to the United States in any numbers. This "discrimination" by nationality was unopposed. By the time Castro reversed policy in 1973, 270,000 Cubans had entered the United States, 677,000 since 1959, when Castro took power. In 1980 thousands of Cubans stormed the Peruvian embassy in Havana seeking asylum, Castro opened the port of Mariel for departing boats, and 125,000 Cuban "Marielitos" (many of them the discharge of Cuba's prisons) sailed to Florida with President Carter's hearty welcome.

Other large migratory flows from this hemisphere had nothing to do with making points against communism and exposed the confusion in refugee and asylum policy. Impoverished, overpopulated Haiti entered a period of political instability in 1971, and Florida's beaches received 60,000 Haitians in the 1970s (perhaps that many died at sea), with irregular large flows in the 1980s and 1990s. These were not refugees fleeing a Hitler or Stalin, it was pointed out, but "economic refugees," or in other words not refugees in the legal definition. A Marxist takeover of Nicaragua in 1979 and civil war in El Salvador and Guatemala produced streams of migrants into the United States during the 1980s, few of whom could demonstrate direct political persecution. Were all people fleeing from something unpleasant in their home country toward life in the United States to be considered refugees? President Reagan justified his interventionist Central

American policy in part by producing the figure of 2.3 million "refugees" ("foot people") that would be created if communism took over in the region, and a prominent historian estimated that by the 1990s there were 2 million Central American "refugees" or l of 8 people in the region, although most of these millions had not yet left.

With American refugee policy nonexistent or incoherent, immigration policy was out of control, jerked about as international political events dislodged the world's poor. U.S. military intervention in Indochina ended in defeat and withdrawal in 1975, and at least 130,000 Vietnamese, Cambodians, and Laotians immediately fled the victorious communists, some Vietnamese clinging to the wheels of U.S. helicopters evacuating the embassy in Saigon, most fleeing the country in boats. These had been our allies, and their lives were certainly in danger as communist rule began. Nevertheless, the question remained: If many or all were genuine refugees from almost certain political persecution (though, having fled before the communists arrived, they could not prove it on an individual basis), how many of them should the United States take? Monthly flows reached 14,000 in 1980–81, 550,000 in all within seven years, 1 million Indochinese by 1991. Whether or not the increasingly familiar sight of people fleeing communist dictatorships to live in the United States embarrassed Red regimes, it was expensive to this country in dollar terms. Resettlement costs were disguised and not well publicized, but have been estimated at $1.4 billion for Cubans even before the Mariel exodus, and Vietnamese relocation costs were conservatively reckoned at $1 billion.

Painfully aware of the incoherence of U.S. refugee policy, and irritated that it was set by the White House and State Department, Congress passed the Refugee Act of 1980, which adopted the UN definition of a refugee as "any person who is outside any country of his nationality . . . and who is unable or unwilling to return . . . because of persecution, or a well-founded fear of persecution, on account of race, religion, nationality, membership of a particular social group, or political opinion." The definition was little help in setting U.S. policy. The worldwide number of refugees by such a definition was variously estimated from 10 to 24 million people in the early 1980s, a number easily multiplied many times if, as some refugee relocation activists urged, one included as "persecution" a country's cultural hostility to homosexuals, China's one-child policy that forced some parents into sterilization or abortion, or cultural sanction in Africa and parts of the Islamic world for female genital mutilation. The category "refugee" was thus elastic and infinitely expandable. To establish the American annual share, Congress resorted again to what it is congenitally incapable of doing, setting a "ceiling." The 1980 Refugee Act replaced the 17,400 refugee annual quota set in the 1965 act with the figure 50,000. However, the president was authorized to exceed that number after consultation (which meant that it was no ceiling at all). The number 50,000 has been exceeded every year since 1980, the numbers ranging from 67,000 to 217,000 over the next ten years, not counting the Cubans, who enjoyed what the 1965 act was supposed to have abolished, a place in U.S. law where they were discriminated in favor of because of their nationality (from 1966 to 1994, when President Clinton limited the range of the Cuban Adjustment Act by directing that Cubans arrested at sea would be returned to Cuba). Unpredictable large pulses of Cold War refugees continued—among them a quarter of a million Iranian students unwilling to return home when the Shah was overthrown in 1979 and thousands of Russian Jews arriving in the 1990s from the former Soviet Union. Acceptance of a substantial percentage of the world's "refugees" was an important part of U.S. policy, but setting limits was beyond the policy system's abilities.

THE CASE FOR REFORM

ECONOMICS

Sustained illegal immigration, spasmodic refugee crises, legal immigration hovering by the 1990s around 1 million a year and in 1990 and 1991 reaching the largest totals in national history—these were the large openings in the American immigration system through which has been surging the Second Great Wave out of the world's impoverished and overpopulated regions. The United States received more immigrants than any country in the world by a large margin, but the Second Great Wave washed across multiple national boundaries, especially drawn to Europe, Canada, and Australia. In all countries feeling the sustained impact of the Second Great Wave, there were major impacts and rising levels of criticism and debate. Ironically, absorbing the Second Great Wave did almost nothing to remedy the problems of the billions who lived in poverty and political oppression, because Western countries were receiving only about 1–2 percent of the annual increase in human populations. Immigration to the West was no solution to any developing society's problems (some argue that Mexico may be a special case) and may have been on balance an injury, as the "brain drain" of doctors, scientists, and other trained professionals depleted precious human capital desperately needed at home.

In the United States, critics of the immigration situation first focussed, understandably, on illegal immigration and met a puny intellectual resistance that soon collapsed. By the 1990s virtually everyone agreed (some reluctantly) that illegal immigration must be stopped. The U.S. Commission on Immigration Reform, chaired (until her death in 1996) by former Texas congresswoman Barbara Jordan, published a 1996 report lined up generally with the reformers, endorsing a fraud-proof system of verification and large increases in border and workplace enforcement. Although there was no real debate, there were disagreements over whether this harmful and illegal phenomenon was preferable to the steps necessary to control the borders and insure that everyone who worked in America was a legal resident.

Legal immigration was a more complicated issue, generating argument along a broad front. Policy debate centered initially on economics and on an effort to establish what might be called a cost-benefit analysis. At the metropolitan level, immigrant revitalization of entire neighborhoods was often cited—rebuilt and thriving sections of the formerly devastated Bronx or Brooklyn in New York, vibrant Koreatown in Los Angeles. But over against such examples there was the crowding and squalor in many immigrant communities, especially along the Mexican border. The media carried stories of flourishing Korean groceries and claims that American entrepreneurship required periodic revitalization from abroad. However, sentimental anecdotes of immigrant success made a flimsy argument. Economists turned to labor market impacts, and an old argument, based on the theory of supply and demand and the experience of American labor, was heard again: mass immigration of low-skill, low-wage labor harms American workers and adds to poverty. "Post-1965 immigrants," Cornell University economist Vernon Briggs wrote, most of them "coming from the poorer nations of the world, where average education, wages, and skill levels are far below those in the U.S., are suppressing the wages of all workers in the lowest skill sector of the labor market." Early metropolitan studies on wage suppression were inconclusive.

By the 1990s, the picture had clarified. Economists such as George Borjas had been documenting a steady decline in what economists called the "social capital" (or sometimes "human quality") of immigrants after the early 1970s, with declining average educational levels and low social mobility (the key word is "average"; the shape of immigrant skills was an hour-glass, economist Phil Martin pointed out, with a large low-skilled bottom, a thin middle, and a small bulge at the top of computer programmers, doctors, and other professionals). In 1997 the National Research Council (NRC) published an analysis of the accumulated evidence on immigrants' economic impacts, *The New Americans* (1997). It concluded that immigration may have produced a tiny net gain in economic output, perhaps as small as $1 billion or as much as $10 billion (in an $8 trillion economy, this sum is insignificant). This was offset by a $15–20 billion fiscal drain from heavy immigrant use of welfare and social services. Two Harvard economists working on that study, George Borjas and Richard Freeman, found the chief impact of immigrants was on low-skilled high-school dropouts who were forced to compete with them directly. The result: twenty million American low-skilled workers saw their average hourly wage drop 30 percent between 1979 and 1995. Half of this drop was due to immigration. "Immigration creates winners and losers," Borjas and Freeman continued: "Low income workers and taxpayers in immigrant states lose; those who employ immigrants or use immigrant services win." The impact was substantial, because the scale of immigration pushed the foreign-born population to nearly 10 percent of the population, almost one in every eight American workers, as measured by the 1990 census. The NRC study concluded that "the magnitude of the current flows—and the flow's disproportionate share of poorly educated immigrants . . . has increased the costs of immigration, and harmed many native-born workers." In his 1999 book, *Heaven's Door,* Borjas found that previous social science researchers had "greatly exaggerated" contemporary mass immigration's economic benefits and looked away from its costs. Himself an immigrant from Cuba, Borjas charged that those defending the immigration status quo were in effect "supporting an astonishing transfer of wealth from the poorest people in the country, who are disproportionately minorities, to the rich." "Immigration is an income redistribution program" inside America, he bluntly concluded, "a debate over how the pie is split." The wage drag of low-skilled immigrant labor shifted about $160 billion from workers to users of immigrants' services—employers in low-wage industries, consumers of cheap strawberries and tomatoes, hirers of nannies and gardeners.

That the losers from the immigration status quo were "low income workers and taxpayers," in Borjas and Freeman's words, suggested that the policy would be hard to reform, as these losers were politically weak. It was often said that if half of the million-plus immigrants arriving each year were lawyers, immigration restriction would be enacted overnight. A small version of that scenario of professional-class competition with immigrants emerged in the 1990s as high-tech companies in California's Silicon Valley and elsewhere were charged with laying off high-wage American computer programmers and replacing them with cheaper and more pliable "temporary" foreign workers—"indentured servants," FAIR's Dan Stein called them—brought in under the controversial H1-B visa program. However, a more potent constituency for immigration reform was taxpayers, who might be mobilized by mounting evidence about the fiscal burden of immigration. A war of studies raged through the 1970s and 1980s over whether immigrant families were heavy users of the public schools and welfare and thus cost state and local governments more than they paid in taxes. The NRC study confirmed the fears. In California, where 43 percent of the school-age population (5–17) were children of immigrants (the national figure was 16 percent), education and other social services were subsidized by native taxpayers—in that state costing natives an immigrant subsidy of $3,463 (per household) annually. This was likely to get worse. A 1999 study by Steven Camarota of the Center for Immigration Studies confirmed Borjas's findings that immigrants' share of the total poverty population had grown 123 percent since 1979, the rate among immigrants now roughly double that of natives.

"The fact that immigration hurts the poor and benefits the rich doesn't necessarily make it a bad thing," observed John Cassidy in reviewing the NRC report and other scholarly studies in the *New Yorker,* but "these are worrisome findings" and "the new economic research suggests that the intellectual case for immigration needs bolstering." This was especially so when it was realized that among the working-class Americans harmed by economic competition with immigrants were African Americans whose well-being was supposed to be a special national concern. Black complaints about immigrant job competition were more than a century old, but they were heard again as mass immigration surged through the 1980s and 1990s. "They brought in all these Guatemalan and Mexican workers," said a black worker at Case Farms poultry plant in Morgantown, North Carolina, "because they figured they'd work for nothing," and before long the plant work force was virtually all Latino. Los Angeles writer Jack Miles, struck by the anger and violence directed against recent Latino and Asian immigrants by blacks during the 1992 "Rodney King" riots in LA, concluded that "America's older black poor and newer brown poor are on a collision course." Blacks were being displaced in the lower rungs of the economy by browns, because "nonblack employers . . . trust Latinos. They fear or disdain blacks. . . . By an irony I find particularly cruel, unskilled Latino immigration may be doing to American blacks at the end of the twentieth century what the European immigration that brought my own ancestors here did to them at the end of the 19th century." Latinos in southern California told journalist Roberto Suro that the blacks had only themselves to blame, for they are "lazy, defeated, and corrupt, . . . jerks who stand on the street corners all day," while "we have a work ethic." Suro agreed that Latinos "colonize whole factories" and occupations, with the silent collaboration of white employers.

The irony was even deeper. Latinos themselves, once with a foothold in the United States, shared an objection to recent immigrants from Mexico and Central America, primarily on the ground—does this sound familiar?—of labor market competition. Polls reported consistent black and Latino support for lower levels of immigration, a Latino National Poll of 1992 finding that 65 percent of Hispanics feel that too many immigrants are entering America. The color of their skin protected them from being accused of motivation by anti-foreign prejudice, which left only concrete economic and social conflict as a basis for these attitudes.

CONCERNS OVER NATIONAL COHESION AND IDENTITY

The restrictionist reform movement of the first part of the twentieth century was one aspect of a vigorous American nationalism that, among other things, assumed and asserted the superiority of the dominant culture. Yet at that very time American intellectuals, always attracted to the subject of American identity, began to argue that it ought to be reconceived. A body of ideas that would be called cultural pluralism was given a foundational statement in a 1915 essay by Horace Kallen, augmented by the wartime and postwar writings of Randolph Bourne and others. They argued that America ought to abandon all efforts and hopes of being a melting pot producing Anglo-Americans or even Anglo-plus a few other European things. It should instead see itself as a place where every culture that immigration brought to these shores (plus the Native American culture almost extinguished) should be allowed to sustain itself within the larger society, because all were equal and valuable. As some envisioned it, America would not be a pot to blend all cultural inputs but instead a salad bowl (a term invented a bit later) to preserve all of them. Kallen imagined a very different America, "a federation of distinct nationalities . . . an orchestration of mankind."

Melting pot imagery and the desirability of rapid Americanization persisted for decades in mainstream society, but cultural pluralism or cultural relativism was increasingly popular among intellectuals. As in so much else, the 1960s were a watershed in the evolution of thinking about American identity. The revolution in thinking about race relations fatally undermined older conceptions. If African Americans were human equals to be treated as social equals, who could still maintain that some cultures were preferable to others? Cultural relativism was triumphant everywhere, and the ideal of "Anglo-conformity" was increasingly denounced by intellectuals, including those who wrote the histories and social science texts for the schools and the larger society. An "ethnic revival" surged through the nation's emotional life or was at least summoned and touted by books like Michael Novak's *The Rise of the Unmeltable Ethnics* (1972). "The spirit of ethnicity . . . begs for reawakening," said Congressman Roman Pucinski of Chicago in 1972 as he sponsored federal support for ethnic heritage studies in the schools, because "there is a growing sense of sameness permeating our existence." Writers, members of Congress, and other shapers of the social discourse urged all non-WASP ethno-racial groups to hold firm to and accentuate their differentness, and federal money flowed into this project.

What followed from such ideas was the growing conviction that what America needed was more ethno-racial and cultural diversification away from the WASP norm, which itself was increasingly seen as tainted by association with a racist and indigenous people-exterminating history. In the 1950s and 1960s this impulse toward nation-broadening took the inclusive form of integrating the African American minority into white society. In time the goal expanded and took on the name multiculturalism, a term that one scholar found in forty newspaper articles in 1981 and in 2,000 eleven years later, a fiftyfold increase. The term means more than one thing, but it may be called the belief, among other things, that the more distinct and different cultures that are encouraged to vibrate through and be welcomed and nonjudgmentally tolerated within American life, the better. This romantic sentiment and body of ideas, ultimately centrifugal in its thrust, is more a critique of American life and history than an affirmation of anything in particular beyond unfailing cultural tolerance. It had no goal but more diversity, unless one can make sense of such passages as this from Michael Novak: "Struggling to be born is a creature of multi-cultural beauty, dazzling, free, a higher and richer form of life." Still, cultural pluralism in the form of multiculturalism remains perhaps the strongest current running in the great river of American thought and emotion in the last third of the twentieth century.

These currents of thought and feeling did not produce the 1965 act, whose architects had explicitly denied any intention to revise America's cultural makeup. However, multiculturalists welcomed the results of the new immigration policy, which became the great demographic engine of their project. It was fateful for discussion of immigration policy that multiculturalism set the tone for American intellectual life as the Second Great Wave of migration arrived. It meant that, whereas the economic and fiscal impacts of immigration might be legitimate subjects for policy debate, questions about cultural impacts were taboo. Even concerns about social cohesion were immediately said to be the old superiority-inferiority poisons, stigmatization of The Other, (bad) nationalism. "We seem incapable yet (still) of addressing the important issue of what holds this society together (and therefore what needs attention and nurturing) . . . ," wrote sociologist Charles Keely. "When raised, the question usually seems to have a bigoted tone. . . ." Surely he meant that those who raised "the important issue of what holds this society together" were *said* "to have a bigoted tone" by those who would prevent discussion of the "diversity" agenda.

Although this was true for the 1970s and 1980s, the taboo on discussion of whether endless cultural diversification might possibly have unfortunate consequences or necessary limits lifted somewhat in the 1990s as the immigration debate entered its third decade, and for several reasons. Multiculturalism was increasingly identified with the arrogant thought policing of "political correctness," and this association of extreme multiculturalism as "left-wing McCarthyism" encouraged dissenters who had earlier been intimidated. Disturbed by certain social trends, many within the United States began to complain of the fragmentation of society—along sharper class lines as the gulf between rich and poor seemed to widen and along tribal lines as groups asserted their distinctiveness, separateness, and grievances. Historian Arthur M. Schlesinger Jr. in a best-selling book, *The Disuniting of America* (1991), called attention to signs of social division and found as their chief source "a new conception . . . of a nation of groups, differentiated in their ancestries, inviolable in their diverse identities." This was multiculturalism, initially a welcoming spirit towards ethnic and racial diversity, but growing into an almost anti-American critique of assimilation and the denial of a single national history and identity. "Something good—movement towards a more inclusive society and broader concepts of what an educated person should know," wrote Robert Pickus of the World Without War Council, "is producing something bad—the disuniting of America." What Pickus called "the profound erosion of common ground in America" concerned many people in the 1990s, and of course radical multiculturalism was by no means the only contributor. He offered a list including "Duke's English Department, corporate America . . . religious decay or religious assertiveness, Hollywood, and the media," just some of the "separatist realities in American life." Schlesinger added to the list many contemporary historians who were no longer presenting nor their schools teaching a common history, but in its place celebratory stories of America's separate races and ethnic groups. "The balance," he said, "is shifting from unum to pluribus" across the entire range of American thought. Historian John Higham noted in 1997 that "ethno-racial tensions are acute and in some ways growing. Are we witnessing an approaching end of nation-building itself? . . . An erosion of the nation-state, as its capacity to maintain national borders and an effective national center weakens?"

Outside America, as we have seen, recent world history seemed a tale of nations breaking apart into their separate religious or ethno-cultural elements, or engaged in bloody wars inside old borders. The world, including (and in an especially violent way) the Balkans themselves, seemed to be Balkanizing on a rising curve of ethnic group-nationality animosity. Could even America be vulnerable? Journalist Kevin Phillips had written an article in 1978 entitled "The Balkanization of America," and he and a crowd of others like Schlesinger who were taking up this theme saw Balkanization in the strengthening of trends toward a widening of class gaps as well as the centrifugal internal forces of multiculturalism, bilingual education-supported language maintenance, and the writing and teaching of a new American history in which a national narrative had been dissolved into subgroup celebrations. Senator Daniel P. Moynihan, noting in his 1993 book *Pandemonium* that the splintering of nations would perhaps form 50–150 new countries in the next fifty years, wrote: "Some of them in North America? Possibly." Among the sources of a national fragmentation that was now taken seriously by American intellectuals, mass immigration over four decades, most of it from Latin America and Asia, could not be forever ignored as possibly another, perhaps the preeminent, source of challenge to national cohesion and traditional identity.

The immigration debate expanded to address these questions. Was *E Pluribus Unum* (out of many, one) still working in the late-twentieth century mass immigration era? Or was immigration contributing to a cultural and class fragmentation of America?

These questions, put forward by many writers and speakers in different ways, were in reality a rebirth of "the national question," absent from America since the beginning of the twentieth century. "If the American people truly want to change their historic European rooted civilization into a Latin Caribbean-Asian 'multi-culture,' then let them debate and approve that proposition through an informed political process," wrote Lawrence Auster. "And if Americans do not want their society to change in such a revolutionary manner, then let them revise their immigration laws accordingly." That reasonable point was clouded, some thought, by the excess in the title chosen for Auster's book, *The Path to National Suicide* (1990). New York economic writer (and recent immigrant) Peter Brimelow, in *Alien Nation: Common Sense about America's Immigration Disaster* (1995), was another author who reaffirmed the conviction of many restrictionists of a century earlier that American nationality was not independent of but bound up with not only a specific historic culture (Anglo-European) but also "blood," ethno-racial nationality, or, a "white majority" seeing itself as a nation. Auster and Brimelow made no claims about group racial superiority or inferiority. However, to them it was Anglo-European cultural hegemony that had made America a place of freedom, democracy, and social trust and cooperation. Brimelow agreed that small numbers of Chinese, Mexicans, and other non-Europeans had assimilated nicely and "disappeared" into America, but with mass migration from non-European sources after 1965, the United States was being transformed into something else—and, he seemed to think, something unworkable. "It is commonly said that America is more than a nation; it is an idea," he quoted *National Review* editor John O'Sullivan: "My thesis . . . is the precise opposite: America is more than an idea; it is a nation." Immigration waves were changing that. "There is no precedent," Brimelow wrote, "for a sovereign country undergoing such a rapid and radical transformation of its ethnic character in the entire history of the world," and he argued that history delivers a mostly negative verdict on whether multiracial societies (America had been biracial) work. What should be done? "Americans ought to be asked" about this risky and unprecedented experiment. Brimelow was confident that there was little public support for a government-engineered project of demographic transformation.

Racist stuff, some reviewers wrote, perhaps hoping to squelch any debate on the national question. Race-conscious about the cohesive ties of nationality is a better description, a legitimate topic to detached scholars but not to those whose memories of Europe in the 1930s and 1940s convinced them that the topic was dangerous and should be delegitimized. On the fundamental question of what makes and perpetuates a nation, *Alien Nation* gave an out of fashion (to say the least) ethno-racial-historical answer, one that pointed immigration policy back to the "like-mindedness through national origins preferences" logic of 1924.

To others who agreed that immigration levels were far too high, this form of concern over immigration's sociocultural impacts was misplaced. It implied the necessity of a permanent white European majority for a working national cohesion. Yet America had always been a society in ethnic and racial transformation away from an English core, wrote Center for Immigration Studies' Director Mark Krikorian, one of those on the reform side who believed that an American could be made out of anyone of any color or culture. Krikorian's center declared itself "pro-immigrant" but also "pro-lowering of the numbers," because, in Krikorian's words, we *do* have a problem, "the difficulty of assimilating large numbers of foreigners into a society that promotes ethnic division and snickers at the idea of Americanization." Restrict the inflow and work harder at Americanization, he urged. Leon Bouvier and Lindsey Grant agreed that current immigration posed cultural problems, but these had nothing to do with color and everything to do with rates of cultural assimilation to American norms and allegiance, and rising ethnic conflict in areas of highest immigration. Worrying that the "glue of a sense of community" was giving way to "belonging to subgroups," they vaguely urged "a move toward a more communitarian mode of social interaction" and reducing immigration to 200,000 a year.

Even President Clinton admitted some uneasiness about the scale of immigration over which he presided for two terms. Speaking at Portland State University in 1998, he said that "a new wave of immigration larger than any in a century, far more diverse than any in our history," means that there will be "no majority race" in California in five years and in the United States in fifty. "No other nation in history has gone through demographic change of this magnitude in so short a time" and "unless we handle this well, immigration of this sweep and scope could threaten the bonds of our union." Clinton had nothing to say about how to "handle this well," but the U.S. Commission on Immigration Reform recommended in 1997 reducing immigration levels to about 550,000 per year, along with measures to shut down illegal immigration. With lower numbers, the commission endorsed what they called an "immigrant policy"—stronger Americanization efforts by governments and private groups. "Americanization," Barbara Jordan wrote in a *New York Times* Op-Ed, "that word earned a bad reputation when it was stolen by racists and xenophobes in the 1920s. But it is our word, and we are taking it back," to help "those who choose to come here . . . embrace the common core of American civic culture." Reform convictions had taken hold at the highest levels of deliberative policy making.

Having a President and a national commission express concern over the cultural assimilation of immigrants represented a setback for the defenders of continued mass immigration. They had attempted to ridicule the entire discussion with an appeal to history. "The U.S. has experienced these effects over and over again from previous waves of immigration," insisted Sidney Weintraub: "In each case, the wave was accompanied by dire predictions of the economic, political and social consequences on the U.S., only to be contradicted in practice." Our successful, even triumphant national story makes such worries seem silly, even reprehensible. In this view, the nation's assimilative forces—a compelling popular culture, the world's most successful and attractive economy, a compelling core ideal called by Swedish sociologist Gunnar Myrdal (and others) "the American creed," plus intermarriage—had arranged more than sufficient national unity to allow America to lead the West to victories over fascism and communism. Our national culture had not been splintered and weakened, but was immensely enriched while remaining cohesive. Why should the present and future be any different? Furthermore, the foreign-born percentage of the population was still below the levels of 1900 or 1910.

History lessons of this kind settle arguments only when none of the facts have changed, which is next to never, and not in this case. Critics of the immigration status quo pointed out that assimilation of the first Great Wave was greatly facilitated by its sharp curtailment by war and restriction, providing a "breathing space" of forty years of very low levels of immigration during which the forces of assimilation regained the upper hand. There was no prospect of this sort of reform-generated breathing space in the 1990s, as mass immigration entered a fourth decade, and the foreign-born percentage of the population had reached 25 percent in California, 19.6 percent in New York, and 16.4 percent in Florida. The post-1965 immigrants came into a very different America, one that lacked the strong integrationist institutions and occasions of a century before—a powerful, confident host culture based upon English beginnings with European borrowings and insisting upon assimilation; a strong public school system, conducted in English; the unifying experience of total war in the 1940s, followed by a period of universal military service.

The Second Great Wave had another new characteristic: one ethnic group, Hispanics, made up more than half the immigration and had the highest fertility rates. The Puerto Rican, Cuban, and Caribbean components were separated from their cultural base only by coastal waters. The Mexican border, a staging ground for Mexican, Central American, and Latin American migration, provided a 2,000 mile land boundary allowing the quick and constant replenishment of cultural influences.

This southwest border was the new Atlantic crossing, and this was quite unprecedented, noted historian David Kennedy in a 1996 *Atlantic Monthly* article. More than a third of the immigrants to the U.S. came "flowing into a defined region from a single cultural, linguistic and national source: Mexico." Hispanic immigrants had always dispersed to other regions, the Midwest and Pacific Northwest, and in the 1980s and 1990s they were moving in large numbers into the South. In the Southwest the sheer demographic power of concentrated Hispanic, mostly Mexican, immigration (California contained half the Hispanic immigrants to the United States), created a new situation in a part of America that had once belonged to Mexico.

Did the new situation mean that the southwestern region of the United States was experiencing Mexican Reconquista? The picture was extraordinarily complex. Historically, the Mexican American—that is, resident, not migratory—population in California, Arizona, New Mexico, and Texas, although naturalizing at a lower rate than other immigrant groups, had aspired to be U.S. citizens and made an impressive record in that direction against considerable resistance. Mexican American leadership had come together in 1929 in Texas to form the largest Latino civil rights group, the League for United Latin American Citizens (LULAC), stressing Americanization, participation in U.S. political life, and opposition to Mexican immigration. By the 1960s this strategy, combined with strong socioeconomic currents, had produced an encouraging record of the social integration of resident Mexican Americans, evident in English language facility among the young, and in most places a daily community life in which cultural distinctiveness was diluted by economic and social mixing, upward mobility, and intermarriage.

By the 1990s many things had changed. A large and growing population of Mexicans who were not in self-identification or often even in law Americans had built up in the southwestern United States where Mexican American advocacy groups no longer spoke LULAC's earlier integrationist language. A new generation of activists emerged after the 1960s, attempting to speak for and to the Mexican diaspora as a permanent ethnic power base. Often (especially in California) calling themselves "Chicanos" rather than Mexican Americans, these activists embraced an open-border immigration position that Cesar Chavez had rejected in the 1960s as harmful to Mexicans already part of the American working class. "Reconquista" by northward migration was in the air of politics and the media. Ambitious Hispanic politicians could not resist mobilizing their ethnic constituency, and a language of separatist nationalism came from the new generation of university-based and urban Latino activists in the 1980s and 1990s. Encouragement for Mexican cultural maintenance and political identification with the homeland came from Mexican governmental officials through a new Program for Mexican Communities Abroad launched in 1990. Occasional Chicano activists or politicians talked aggressively of irredentism, of reversing through massive migration the results of the 1848 war. "These population dynamics," said Henry Cisneros, former mayor of San Antonio and secretary of Housing and Urban Development in the Clinton administration, "will result in the browning of America, the Hispanicization of America. It's already happening and it's inescapable." "California is going to be a Hispanic state. Anyone who doesn't like it should leave," said Mario Obledo of the Mexican American Legal Defense and Education Fund. A 1994 parade of 70,000 Latinos in Los Angeles protesting Proposition 187 was festooned with the red, white, and green flag of Mexico, with hardly an American flag to be seen. "Somos Mexicanos!" shouted Antonio Villaraigosa, the speaker of the California State Assembly, at a 1997 rally. "The question is not whether *reconquista* will take place, but how and with what consequences," wrote one journalist. "The possibility looms that in the next generation or so we will see a kind of Chicano Quebec take shape in the American southwest," David Kennedy wrote in an article for *Atlantic Monthly.* "This constant influx from a single country is unprecedented in American history," writer Linda Chavez commented, and "is unquestionably a factor inhibiting the successful assimilation of Mexicans already here." In 1999, a Texas town passed an ordinance declaring that all city meetings and functions would be held in Spanish.

All of this was a mix of posturing and deep cultural divisions in a border region experiencing its part of the Second Great Wave from south to north. Close observers in California, the most immigration-impacted state, foresaw the "transnationalization" of the regional population (the term was coined by University of California at San Diego historian David Gutierrez) rather than the ascendancy of either the United States or the Mexican identity, a population less nationalistic than oppositional and alienated. It seemed clear that history lessons about how easily America had resolved centrifugal forces a century ago had little relevance to end-of-century realities.

IMMIGRATION'S POPULATION-ENVIRONMENT CONNECTION

In one area of mass immigration's influence upon the U.S., its contribution to population growth and the problems this creates, a genuine argument had never developed. The Rockefeller Commission's 1972 report, having set out the multiple advantages of population stabilization, noted that immigration contributed 1/4 of America's population growth and recommended tying annual immigration totals to a national population policy. The number of immigrants they recommended for annual entry—400,000—would today represent a cutback to one-third of the end-of-century volume. This recommendation, and the fundamental necessity of seeing immigration as a key part of the nation's more important population policy, was never intellectually challenged with different numbers. The very idea of "adopting" a "national population policy" was denounced, blindly ignoring the fact that immigration was our legislated population policy, aimed at growth and ethno-racial and cultural transformation.

The media missed this crucial point and gave space to what was depicted as a serious intellectual disagreement over the existence of "the population problem" itself. Indeed, there was (and probably always will be) much controversy and little agreement on what the "sustainable" level of population should be. Paul and Anne Ehrlich, pointing out that optimum population size depends upon the technology and consumption patterns of society, thought 75 million in the United States about right, and Cornell ecologists David and Marcia Pimentel defined the range as between 40 and 100 million. Others either arrived at different numbers or scoffed at the exercise as beyond rational calculation. However, there was no real controversy at all among serious students of America's environment-resource position regarding the desirability of the earliest possible stabilization of population, prior to determining a sustainable level.

Making it appear otherwise for a decade or more was one of the remarkable stories of successful entrepreneurship in modern public affairs. A professor of marketing and economics, Julian Simon, who confessed that he was able to recover from deep personal depression only when he wrote positive things about bringing new babies into the world, in the early 1980s launched an audacious career of writing and lecturing around the message that there were no population, growth, or natural resource problems. Both population and economic growth should continue endlessly: "There is no meaningful physical limit . . . to our capacity to keep growing forever." Simon was tireless and articulate, and his was a message meshed with the free-market ideology of the Reagan years. His outlandishly unqualified (but, for him, therapeutic) optimism that things would work out fine with more people and endless growth brought him conservative foundation support, much media coverage, and some influence within an optimism-keyed Reagan administration. His much-publicized views made it appear that there was an actual scientific controversy over the costs of population growth.

To the contrary, there was a large consensus that world population growth—having reached 6 billion in 1999 and according to the UN Population Division (in 1998) headed toward a range between 7.5 and 16 billion by the end of the twenty-first century—was broadly harmful and should be ended and then reversed toward sustainable levels. "Human beings and the natural world are on a collision course" and the driver behind it is unprecedented human population growth, said a group of 1,500 scientists, including ninety-nine Nobel Laureates, in a "Warning to Humanity" issued in 1992. Simon's views were universally seen by informed people as an absurd exaggeration of one important truth, that the "Doomster" fringe of the population and environment worriers had exaggerated the scale and pace of the population problem because they forgot that human ingenuity could considerably lengthen the period before limits and costs became a real crisis. However, the rest of the Simonite message collapsed under criticism and the weight of data. Simon's death in 1998 came at a time when the scientific consensus on the desirability of population stabilization and possibly reduction had finally isolated him on the far edge with imitators such as journalist Ben Wattenberg and talk-show host Rush Limbaugh.

What did the consensus on stabilizing population have to do with immigration, which was a matter of existing people switching countries? The Rockefeller Commission had concluded that immigration should not be allowed to prevent U.S. population stabilization. In the year of that report the U.S. total fertility rate for the first time dropped below replacement level (2.1), reaching 1.7 by the end of the decade and remaining below replacement level through the 1980s. The Baby Boom was over. The American people were choosing smaller families and, inevitably, an end to population growth (which would occur after fifty to sixty years of "population momentum"). Projecting these fertility rates forward, demographer Leon Bouvier estimated that U.S. population would peak at about 250 million by 2030 and then begin a gradual decline (the happy goal of the Rockefeller Commission) if immigration remained at "net replacement levels" or about 250,000, the number thought to leave the country annually.

That path to population stabilization by 2030, voluntarily chosen by Americans in the 1970s and after, was radically altered by politicians in Washington. They did this by expanding immigration, so that its contribution to population growth (immigrants plus births to foreign-born women), which had been 13 percent in 1970, rose to 38 percent by 1980, and to 60–70 percent, and rising, by the end of the 1990s. From 1970 to 1996, immigration added 62 million people to the U.S. population, and the Census Bureau in 2000 projected a doubling of population to 571 million by 2100, and then only if immigration (and fertility) were essentially unchanged. With zero net immigration, the population would have stabilized at 307 million in 2050. "Do we really want an America of 500 million people?" asked Colorado Governor Richard Lamm, a leading environmentalist: "Immigration will decide whether we stabilize or whether we continue to grow." By 2040, concluded a California Department of Finance study, "California," the chief immigrant-receiving state, "will be twice as crowded as it is today [and] Latinos will be the dominant ethnic group."

This is the arithmetic not only of demographic transformation, but of a daunting tangle of ecological deterioration, resource shortages, and crowding foreseen by the Rockefeller Commission in 1972, by the Global 2000 report in 1980, and by a long list of scientific panels and individual authors as immigration-driven population growth gained momentum. As these numbers, projections, and their implications filtered out to the public, there was no counterargument. Immigration policy had become America's unacknowledged U.S. population policy, and it had been full-throttle expansionist since the 1960s.

Stunned by the ominous environmental implications of such growth, and worried that it made their mission to protect and restore the American landscape more difficult if not impossible, a group of Sierra Club members in 1998 urged the club's national board to make immigration restriction a goal of the organization. Rebuffed, they demanded a 1999 referendum, and lost 60–40 percent against unanimous board and staff opposition. An argument had actually been forced to the surface on the immigration-population-environment connection and was reflected in Sierra Club materials, and magazine and news stories. On record for population stabilization, the club's officialdom did not dispute that current levels of immigration—"overimmigration," in environmentalist David Brower's phrase, who subsequently resigned from the club—prevented that goal and made more difficult the environmental protection that was the group's core mission. They argued instead that any restrictionist position on immigration would alienate "people of color" and make the club's political position weaker (although polls consistently showed that the majority of Hispanics support immigration restriction). Less than 15 percent of club members voted; immigration reform sentiment simmered among an unknown proportion of the rest.

THE POLITICS OF IMMIGRATION REFORM IN THE 1990s

Historian David Reimers, in a chapter on the 1990s entitled "A Broken Immigration System" in his book *Unwelcome Strangers* (1998), points out that although the 1965 law was responsible for a large increase in the numbers of immigrants, Congress, presidents, and courts continued for decades to turn up the volume and ignore porous borders. The immigration flood of the 1990s—with million-plus flows, southern and northern borders and ports of entry still open to illegal aliens, periodic refugee and asylum episodes—was the work of years of policy "liberalization." Exemptions were made to admit large numbers of Cubans, followed by Vietnamese, Salvadorans, and Nicaraguans, then the 1986 law aimed at controlling illegal immigration amnestied nearly 3 million illegal aliens and failed to restrict the future flow. Some political dynamic was at work undermining limits through a period when the public, when asked by pollsters, repeatedly supported smaller numbers. Responding to pressure from ethnic lobbying groups, Congress in a 1990 law widened the gates again, expanding per country limits, granting Salvadoran "temporary" illegal entrants a longer stay, and making other changes resulting in a large expansion of legal immigration.

Public frustration boiled over. Grassroots citizens organizations calling for immigration reform had been springing up in the most immigration-impacted states and cities, such as Florida, Texas, Chicago, and New York, a few with the support of FAIR, most independently. In California, however, the new restrictionism found its most potent political voice. A group in Orange County, frustrated that writing letters protesting illegal immigration to their congressman in Washington produced no results, wrote Proposition 187 or the "Save Our State" initiative, which would deny public services to illegal aliens. With little money but the help of a network of over forty such groups statewide gathering the necessary signatures, Proposition 187 went on the ballot in 1994. Condemned by ethnic lobbies and religious and educational leaders as "racist" and "divisive," Proposition 187 was supported by Republican Governor Pete Wilson, a frequent critic of illegal immigration who was skilled at directing his and the public's indignation against inept policy makers in Washington rather than the illegal immigrants themselves. Proposition 187 passed by a resounding vote of 59 percent "for" to 41 percent "against." Most Hispanic voters favored the measure in early polling, and whereas only 31 percent voted for it after a long campaign in which Hispanic political leaders branded it as "anti-Hispanic," geographer William Clark found that suburban Latinos joined all the state's ethnic and racial groups in favoring 187. Wilson was overwhelmingly re-elected, and Proposition 187, having "sent a message" to politicians everywhere concerning the public sentiment on at least illegal immigration, was at once tied up in court.

The 1994 election also gave Republicans control of both houses of Congress, and the events in California suggested that the moment might have arrived for restrictionist reform. In March 1995, the U.S. Commission on Immigration Reform chaired by former Congresswoman Barbara Jordan proposed to increase border security, establish a national employment verification system, cut overall legal immigration by 40 percent, shift selection toward skills, and end family chain migration by eliminating preferences for brothers and sisters and adult children of new immigrant citizens. Welcoming this call for reform, a restrictionist convocation in Washington circulated the statement: "We are not against immigration or immigrants. The issue is how many and who, which has always been the issue." FAIR's agenda for reform went farther than the Jordan Commission. Total numbers, refugees and all, should be consistent with the overriding national goal of early population stabilization (which meant about 300,000 immigrants a year, matching out-migration); shift selection from family ties toward skills needed by the U.S. economy, possibly through a Canadian-style system of points for education, language ability, and skills; and control illegal immigration through a national system for worker verification. Of the handful of immigration reform groups, none proposed ending immigration, although some urged a temporary moratorium (except for immediate family members). Restrictionists struggled to convey their positive goals: "We want an America environmentally sustainable, uncrowded," said FAIR's Dan Stein.

Congress seemed to move in the reform direction in 1995 with a Republican task force report declaring that "IRCA had failed" to deter illegal aliens and demanding, among other things, an end to the grant of "birthright citizenship" to "anchor babies" born on American soil to illegal aliens. Chairman of the Senate Immigration Committee Senator Allen Simpson, declaring that "the American people are so very fed up . . . with efforts to make them feel that Americans do not have that most fundamental right of any people: to decide who will join them here and help form the future country," concluded that "it is time to slow down, to reassess." A bill moved through the House that would limit welfare benefits to recently arrived immigrants' elderly parents who had never worked in the United States and make sponsors of new immigrants more responsible for their care.

However, most of the welfare cuts were soon restored, and the likelihood of legal immigration reform faded, as the Republican Party's leadership as well as President Clinton began to respond to aggressive lobbying by business and ethnic forces mobilized by the National Immigration Forum (NIF). Thus, the Illegal Immigration Reform and Immigrant Responsibility Act of 1996 was stripped of all but minor changes: "The pro-immigration coalition desired to preserve the current rate of legal immigration and did so," and thus "won the 1996 battle" while "restrictionists were thoroughly defeated," concluded historian David Reimers. "We kept them [the restrictionists] from getting almost anything," gloated Frank Sharry of the NIF. "The deck was stacked in their favor, but we outfoxed them . . . an astonishing victory," and he was right. The immigration reform impulse was easily contained. In 1996, our laws admitted 916,000 legal immigrants joined by perhaps 400,000 illegal individuals, the largest and most ethnically diverse cohort since 1914, stretching toward the horizon.

HOW CAN THIS BE?
AN UNREFORMABLE UNPOPULAR SYSTEM?

"How can this be," asked Yale law professor Peter Schuck, "when recent immigration trends have presented restrictionists with explosive political ammunition," when most immigrants are non-white and non-English speaking, when they fuel and complicate the debate over bilingual education and affirmative action and contribute to an increase in poverty and a widening of the wage gap between high- and low-skill workers? How indeed, when polls going back to the early 1980s had consistently been critical of immigration levels, a 1996 Roper poll showing one of the highest levels (83 percent) of support for reducing immigration. Hispanic Americans shared this broad and steady public consensus. A Latino National Political Survey in 1992 found that 75 percent of Mexican Americans agreed that there are too many immigrants coming into the country. Our political system often ignores public opinion—but for over three decades, on an issue central to the nation's size, demographic composition, identity, and culture?

Immigration was a prime example of what political scientist James Q. Wilson called "client politics," when a relatively small number of people who stand to benefit organize with energy around an issue, whereas those who pay the costs are a diffuse, large majority who may be disgruntled but whose main concerns are elsewhere. The coalition that came together in the 1980s and 1990s to defend the expansionist policy against restrictionist reformers, as University of Texas political scientist Gary Freeman wrote, "was composed of organizations representing those having a direct interest in outcomes—employers [of low-wage foreign labor], immigrant-rights organizations, the churches, and immigration lawyers," a formidable lineup augmented in the 1990s by a critically important National Association of Manufacturers-led alliance of high-technology corporations eager to import foreign computer professionals.

On the other side, Freeman wrote, the restrictionists "simply lack a serious, organized constituency." The groups most injured by massive low-skilled immigration—blacks, recent immigrants at the bottom of the economic ladder, and low-skilled whites—were politically weak and found no one to articulate their concerns. The leadership of organized labor and Mexican Americans (although not, in either case, the rank and file) had moved away from their historic restrictionist positions. Ethnic lobbies claiming to speak for minority populations were universally aligned with expansionist immigration policy in order to enlarge their groups' political influence. Black political leadership was persuaded to shun the issue in order to hold "the civil rights coalition" together. The "patriotic societies" so vigorous at the turn of the century were dedicated to the national interest as they conceived it, but their history of arid anticommunism during the decades after World War II had greatly reduced their social and political influence. Environmentalists like members of the Sierra Club, losing in their struggle to preserve habitat and wildlife because of a growing population, could or would not rally their organizations to the prerequisite for population stabilization, which was immigration restriction. The tax-paying general public's interest in and knowledge of the issue was diffuse. Polls found Americans in general opposed to the high volumes, but, when asked for details, they were uninformed on immigration, unable to comprehend demographic facts or trends, restrictionists without deep convictions or knowledge—and on this as on many issues affecting public and national interests, an unorganized majority in a system responding to organized groups with deep pockets.

This left immigration policy making to distant, obscure legislative maneuvering in Washington, where special interest lobbying invariably produced expansionist outcomes. However, the dynamics of "client politics," whereby small, intense, and well-financed interest groups repeatedly outmaneuver a "diffuse majority," explains only a part of the four-decade dominance of expansionists over restrictionists. Until the early 1990s the issue was somehow kept out of electoral politics where the public could register opinions. Politicians evidently feared ethnic voting blocs whom they (on little evidence) assumed to be "offended" by talk of an immigration problem and knew there had not yet developed a restrictionist voting bloc.

Then California's Republican Governor Pete Wilson made curbing illegal immigration a winning issue in his 1994 reelection campaign, attacking Congress for allowing a porous border rather than illegal immigrants themselves. Had Wilson shown the way for immigration reform to become a political winner? The expansionists counterattacked to contain the issue. Republican politicians in the state (and elsewhere), who in 1996 subsequently criticized (only) illegal immigration, lacking Wilson's verbal skills, were demonized by Democrats and the media as "harsh" and "divisive" and the issue as somehow rooted in that overworked word, "racism." Journalists and politicians, ignorant of history, increasingly referred to restrictionists as "nativists," implying that all that was involved was xenophobia, hatred of foreigners. When respected Senator Alan Simpson proposed legislation in 1996 to authorize pilot projects testing ways to verify employment eligibility, the expansionist coalition distributed peel-off bar-code tattoos on Capitol Hill to associate Simpson's proposal with Hitler's treatment of the Jews, indeed with the Holocaust itself. Such tactics bring to mind Hannah Arendt's warning that the dictators of the 1930s and 1940s controlled their critics by "turning every statement of fact into a question of motive."

Such efforts to shut down discussion with invidious labeling aroused the Jordan Commission on Immigration Reform to declare in 1994 that "we disagree with those who would label efforts to control immigration as being inherently anti-immigrant. Rather, it is both a right and a responsibility of a democratic society to manage immigration so that it serves the national interest." The "restriction is nativism" taboo also came under attack from scholars. Immigration reformers may not be numerous enough to constitute "a movement," wrote historian David Bennett, but "they certainly do not represent a return to the nativist traditions of the past," a tradition "all but finished" by the end of World War II. "The immigration debate was being conducted at a higher level than ever before," wrote Yale's Peter Schuck. He found "few traces of racism or nativism," but rather "principled restrictionism" which "contributes significantly to the overt debate." "What do you make of the nativists?" a journalist asked historian John Higham as the grassroots immigration reformers in California and elsewhere gained press coverage in the 1990s. "I don't know any nativists," Higham replied, in a subtle rebuke for such tortured and misleading, as well as argument-closing labels. In only one respect did the immigration reformers at the end of the century resemble those 100 years earlier—they could be found across the political spectrum. Some were conservative Republicans, like Senator Simpson, writers Peter Brimelow and John O'Sullivan at the *National Review,* or the Orange County grassroots organizers of California's Proposition 187. Others were "liberal nationalists" like the *New Republic* writers John Judis and Michael Lind, the latter reminding other liberals that "mass immigration . . . keeps wages low and unions weak—to the benefit of the white overclass."

A key to the stifling of immigration reform is "elite disconnect," a phrase entering American discourse (see Thomas and Mary Edsall, *Chain Reaction,* 1991, and E. J. Dionne, *Why Americans Hate Politics,* 1991) to draw attention to the remarkable gap that has opened between America's liberal-cosmopolitan elites in government, media, and the universities' and the Democratic Party's working and middle-class base. One of those elite liberal Democrats, prolific author, Harvard professor, and Bill Clinton's secretary of labor (1993–97), Robert Reich, correctly pointed out that the Republicans who ran America's corporations were also in the disconnected elite, which he designated not by political party or ideology but by education and social class. One-fifth of the American people were the lucky, well-educated "symbolic analysts" whom globalization was making rich and entirely cosmopolitan, transnational in their outlook. He feared they were withdrawing into gated communities and private clubs and schools, "seceding" from the four-fifths of "routine producers" whose incomes were under mounting pressure from a global work force. Immigration, Reich pointed out in *The Work of Nations* (1991), brought that labor competition home and was good for the top fifth, who needed nannies, gardeners, and cheap employees (and probably agreed with the *Wall Street Journal* when it editorially asked on 3 July 1989 for a new constitutional amendment, in "There Shall Be Open Borders"). However, it was costly to the rest of America, and Reich predicted that immigration "will be a point of growing contention" between the disconnecting elite who make the policies and those at the middle and bottom. Identifying with the latter, novelist and ardent environmentalist Edward Abbey complained that, with mass immigration, "the conservatives get their cheap labor and the liberals get their cheap cause."

FOR A CROWDED NEW FUTURE, A GRIDLOCK OF OBSOLETE IDEAS

In the astonishing prosperity, Wall Street boom, and expanding job markets that ran through the 1990s after an early and brief recession, it seemed that the nation's political system was incapable of grappling with any long-term problems, including mass immigration. It was understandable when one observer, sociologist Douglas Massey, declared in 1999 that the United States was now "a country of perpetual immigration," because "a significant reduction in the immigration rates no longer can be legislated." There will be no pause; the stream will only grow. Any "migration flow," noted Myron Weiner, "once begun, induces its own flow" through networks of information and contacts as well as organized smuggling rings. The momentum built up by three decades of mass immigration was augmented by the "chain migration" feature inserted carelessly into U.S. law in 1965 allowing even brothers and sisters abroad to "reunify" with naturalized immigrants. The unique porosity of America's borders made it the leading, although not the only, Western society struggling in the 1980s and 1990s with mass immigration. Having themselves launched the First Great Wave, Germany, the Scandinavian countries, the United Kingdom, France, Italy, and the rest of Europe were—with the Neo-Europes (the United States, Canada, and Australia)—the favored destinations of the Second Wave, estimated by Harvard's Samuel P. Huntington as 100-130 million people in the year 1990 alone.

Huntington asked: "Can either Europe or the U.S. stem the migrant tide?" Could liberal democracies in the West summon the resolve to limit and manage immigration, taking from it only the small amounts desired to augment declining populations? In Europe at the century's close, the inability of established governments to limit immigration produced fast-growing restrictionist parties in France, Germany, Italy, the Low Countries, Switzerland, and Austria. In the late 1990s, several European countries tightened their asylum procedures. However, in Europe as in the United States, immigration momentum had been allowed to build up over decades, and mainstream politicians seemed paralyzed. We are "destined to be overwhelmed by people from the failed societies of the South," commented France's Pierre Lellouche. You are indeed, said Malaysian prime minister Mahathir Bin Mohamad in 1997: "We do have the ultimate weapon. People are more mobile now. They can go anywhere . . . If we are not allowed a good life in our countries . . . we should migrate north in our millions, legally or illegally. Masses of Asians and Africans should inundate Europe and America." As the century ended the press carried and travelers returned with stories from China, with its 1.2 billion population—reports of unrest, discontent, massive rural displacement generating a restless flow of perhaps one hundred million or one-tenth of the population toward the cities, as China slipped from a controlled communist society toward the chaos of transition. Harbingers of a potentially immense overseas migration of Chinese began arriving in the 1990s in rusty steamers carrying smuggled immigrants again to the Golden Mountain—to Vancouver, New York, even Savannah, Georgia. Another potential source of even larger immigration pressures was nearby Mexico. That nation's population ended the century at 100 million and a doubling time of thirty-two years, massive unemployment, political unrest, and millions of channels to family and kinship anchors north of the border in what was often called Greater Mexico. "We are really just at the start," observed writer David Simcox, "of a worldwide phenomenon that is going to intensify and irrevocably change many countries."

This was the new world beyond our borders, generating, through population growth and societies disabled by civil strife and ecological breakdown, a Second Great Wave far surpassing the first. When the first arrived, we were awakening to our own assault upon the continental environment through relentless forest clear-cutting, air and stream pollution, the beginnings of species extinction as the bison shrank to a few hundred and the last Carolina Parakeet and passenger pigeon died, oddly enough, in the Cincinnati Zoo in 1914. The Second Great Wave spurs American population growth upward as we attempt to rein in our ongoing assault upon our ecological foundations—more than half our original wetlands drained, coastal fisheries depleted, hazardous waste cleanup outpaced by its generation, national parks crowded and ecologically strained, and now the greenhouse gases we generate by fossil fuel burning and industrial emissions bringing a long era of unpredictable global warming and its own ecological stresses. A few signs are encouraging: cleaner metropolitan air in places, fish returning to some lakes and rivers. There is a broad, international consensus among scientists and specialists in global trends that making our economic processes "sustainable" is an urgent goal within reach, if nations not only alter lifestyles but cap their population growth, then move toward stable populations a safe margin below sustainable carrying capacity. As we have seen, estimates of optimal U.S. population depend on many assumptions about resource use and lifestyle and production changes, and range from 50 to 135 million. The public has not yet absorbed the implications, but a task force of President Clinton's Council on Sustainable Development concluded in 1996 that "reducing immigration levels is a necessary part of population stabilization and the drive toward sustainability."

Necessary, but at the end of the twentieth century, still politically out of reach.

This had been the situation once before, at the beginning of the twentieth century. Then Americans—always ambivalent about immigration, knowing that it brought benefits and imposed costs—changed their minds about the open door to overimmigration, and, after four decades of effort, curbed it to annual numbers still above pre-Civil War averages. Changed realities again bring calls for immigration reform toward lower numbers. Yet there is no sign of the political capacity or leadership to enact it, in the shallow, short-horizon politics of the end of the century. Change might

come through some global economic paralysis or border-crossing epi-
demic. At a deeper level, however, reform in the United States awaits a rethinking of the role of immigration itself.

A growing immigration reform literature has made a beginning, arguing that, whatever the benefit-cost ratio of essentially unmanaged mass immigration during our earlier national experience in a population-thinner
time, it must now be seen as solving no international or national problems
yet at the same time intensifying or creating many difficulties. Small-scale,
managed immigration can enrich a nation's life without draining reservoirs
of trained and talented people from struggling societies and straining the
social fabric of receiving countries whose best service to themselves and the
earth is early population stabilization.

William Leach argues, in an important recent book, *The Destruction
of Place in American Life* (1999), that Americans have always been both
restlessly migratory and place-centered, their society at times in a centrifugal and at others a centripetal pattern. In the late twentieth century "the
centripetal pull that always seemed to check the centrifugal side of the
American experience . . . no longer has the strength it once had," and we
live amid "the weakening of place as a centering presence in the lives of or-
dinary people." Americans increasingly are drifters and movers, changing
jobs and homes, affiliations, relationships. Larger migration flows, both internally and from abroad, are at the center of this pattern, although beneath
it are the real culprits, globalization of economies and mass communication. Leach regrets the costs of this cycle of rootlessness, as does economist
Albert O. Hirschman, who acknowledges in *Exit, Voice and Loyalty* (1970)
that "exit"—cutting and running, bailing out, leaving the problems behind
and moving west—"has been accorded an extraordinarily privileged position in the American tradition." He argued for an appreciation of and re-
balancing with more of the other, non-migratory options, "voice"—stay-
ing where you are and joining the effort to resolve problems—and
"loyalty," which perhaps needs no elaboration. This is what western writer
Wallace Stegner meant when he deplored that there were so many "wan-
derers" in America and so few "stickers." Faced with difficulties, we Americans migrate away from them, choosing a solution (of sorts) for individuals or families while we leave social problems rooted in the place abandoned
by the young and the dreamers of greener grass. However, our heritage also
contains the stickers, for whom the act of migration is a sort of defeat. Both

impulses are woven into the American grain, but Stegner found them badly out of balance.

We are deep into an era in which immigration itself requires rethinking, globally and especially in the United States, where it decimated an indigenous civilization, played a part in building an unprecedentedly free and successful society, and now in a second mass wave augments the centrifugal forces and environmental harms that are emerging as America's chief challenges.

Documents

1

EXCERPT FROM *THE BOOKER T. WASHINGTON PAPERS*

A ship lost at sea for many days suddenly sighted a friendly vessel. From the mast of the unfortunate vessel was seen a signal, "Water, water; we die of thirst!" The answer from the friendly vessel at once came back, "Cast down your bucket where you are." A second time the signal, "Water, water; send us water!" ran up from the distressed vessel, and was answered, "Cast down your bucket where you are." And a third and fourth signal for water was answered, "Cast down your bucket where you are." The captain of the distressed vessel, at last heeding the injunction, cast down his bucket, and it came up full of fresh, sparkling water from the mouth of the Amazon River. To those of my race who depend on bettering their condition in a foreign land or who underestimate the importance of cultivating friendly relations with Southern white man, who is their next-door neighbour, I would say: "Cast down your bucket where you are"—cast it down in making friends in every manly way of the people of all races by whom we are surrounded.

Cast it down in agriculture, mechanics, in commerce, in domestic service, and in the professions. And in this connection it is well to bear in mind that whatever other sins the South may be called to bear, when it comes to business, pure and simple, it is in the South that the Negro is given a man's chance in the commercial world, and in nothing is this Exposition more eloquent than in emphasizing this chance. Our greatest danger is that in the great leap from slavery to freedom we may overlook the fact that the masses of us are to live by the productions of our hands, and fail to keep in mind that we shall prosper in proportion as we learn to

---

Source: Excerpted from *The Booker T. Washington Papers,* Vol. 3 1889–95. ed. Louis R. Harlan, Stuart B. Kaufman and Raymond W. Smock. Urbana, Ill.: University of Illinois Press, 1972, 584–85.

dignify and glorify common labour, and put brains and skill into the common occupations of life; shall prosper in proportion as we learn to draw the line between the superficial and the substantial, the ornamental gewgaws of life and the useful. No race can prosper till it learns that there is as much dignity in tilling a field as in writing a poem. It is at the bottom of life we must begin, and not at the top. Nor should we permit our grievances to overshadow our opportunities.

To those of the white race who look to the incoming of those of foreign birth and strange tongue and habits for the prosperity of the South, were I permitted I would repeat what I say to my own race, "Cast down your bucket where you are." Cast it down among the eight millions of Negroes whose habits you know, whose fidelity and love you have tested in days when to have proved treacherous meant the ruin of your firesides. Cast down your bucket among these people who have, without strikes and labour wars, tilled your fields, cleared your forests, builded your railroads and cities, and brought forth treasures from the bowels of the earth, and helped make possible this magnificent representation of the progress of the South. Casting down your bucket among my people, helping and encouraging them as you are doing on these grounds, and to education of head, hand, and heart, you will find that they will buy your surplus land, make blossom the waste places in your fields, and run your factories. While doing this, you can be sure in the future, as in the past, that you and your families will be surrounded by the most patient, faithful, law-abiding, and unresentful people that the world has seen.

2

EXCERPT FROM *THEODORE ROOSEVELT: AN AUTOBIOGRAPHY*

In the present state of the world's progress it is highly inadvisable that peoples in wholly different stages of civilization, or of wholly different types of civilization even although both equally high, shall be thrown into intimate contact. This is especially undesirable when there is a difference of both race and standard of living. In California the question became acute in connection with the admission of the Japanese. I then had and now have a hearty admiration for the Japanese people. I believe in them; I respect their great qualities; I wish that our American people had many of these qualities. Japanese and American students, travelers, scientific and literary men, merchants engaged in international trade, and the like can meet on terms of entire equality and should be given the freest access each to the country of the other. But the Japanese themselves would not tolerate the intrusion into their country of a mass of Americans who would displace Japanese in the business of the land. I think they are entirely right in this position. I would be the first to admit that Japan has the absolute right to declare on what terms foreigners shall be admitted to work in her country, or to own land in her country, or to become citizens of her country. America has and must insist upon the same right. The people of California were right in insisting that the Japanese should not come thither in mass, that there should be no influx of laborers, of agricultural workers, or small tradesmen—in short, no mass settlement or immigration.

Unfortunately, during the latter part of my term as President certain unwise and demagogic agitators in California, to show their disapproval of

Source: Excerpted from *Theodore Roosevelt: An Autobiography*. New York: Charles Scribner's Sons, 1926.

the Japanese coming into the State, adopted the very foolish procedure of trying to provide by law that the Japanese children should not be allowed to attend the schools with the white children, and offensive and injurious language was used in connection with the proposal. The Federal Administration promptly took up the matter with the California authorities, and I got into personal touch with them. At my request the Mayor of San Francisco and other leaders in the movement came on to see me. I explained that the duty of the National Government was twofold: in the first place, to meet every reasonable wish and every real need of the people of California or any other State in dealing with the people of a foreign power; and, in the next place, itself exclusively and fully to exercise the right of dealing with this foreign power.

Inasmuch as in the last resort, including that last of all resorts, war, the dealing of necessity had to be between the foreign power and the National Government, it was impossible to admit that the doctrine of State sovereignty could be invoked in such a matter. As soon as legislative or other action in any State affects a foreign nation, then the affair becomes one for the Nation, and the State should deal with the foreign power purely through the Nation.

I explained that I was in entire sympathy with the people of California as to the subject of immigration of the Japanese in mass; but that of course I wished to accomplish the object they had in view in the way that would be most courteous and most agreeable to the feelings of the Japanese; that all relations between the two peoples must be those of reciprocal justice, and that it was an intolerable outrage on the part of newspapers and public men to use offensive and insulting language about a high-spirited, sensitive, and friendly people; and that such action as was proposed about the schools could only have bad effects, and would in no shape or way achieve the purpose that the Californians had in mind.

. . . After a good deal of discussion, we came to an entirely satisfactory conclusion. The obnoxious school legislation was abandoned, and I secured an arrangement with Japan under which the Japanese themselves prevented any emigration to our country of their laboring people, it being distinctly understood that if there was such emigration the United States would at once pass an exclusion law. It was of course infinitely better that the Japanese should stop their own people from coming rather than that we should have to stop them; but it was necessary for us to hold this power in reserve.

. . . But this is not because either nation is inferior to the other; it is because they are different. The two peoples represent two civilizations which, although in many respects equally high, are so totally distinct in their past history that it is idle to expect in one or two generations to overcome this difference. One civilization is as old as the other; and in neither case is the line of cultural descent coincident with that of ethnic descent. Unquestionably the ancestors of the great majority both of the modern Americans and the modern Japanese were barbarians in that remote past which saw the origins of the cultured peoples to which the Americans and the Japanese of today severally trace their civilizations. But the lines of development of these two civilizations, of the Orient and the Occident, have been separate and divergent since thousands of years before the Christian era; certainly since that hoary eld in which the Akkadian predecessors of the Chaldean Semites held sway in Mesopotamia. An effort to mix together, out of hand, the peoples representing the culminating points of two such lines of divergent cultural development would be fraught with peril; and this, I repeat, because the two are different, not because either is inferior to the other. Wise statesmen, looking to the future, will for the present endeavor to keep the two nations from mass contact and intermingling, precisely because they wish to keep each in relations of permanent good will and friendship with the other.

3

EXCERPT FROM *AMERICA: NATION OR CONFUSION?*

It has long been the assumption of the American people that immigration was a necessity for our industries, that our country would have stifled and decayed if it had not received a steady stream of immigration, and that now we will destroy our prosperity if the flow is cut off.

It is assumed also that the question is one of race inferiority and superiority. A few ardent advocates may have . . . given some basis for this assumption. But the demand for immigration restriction is based on no such claim. It is based on racial difference. It cannot be repeated too often that I make no claim of racial superiority of North European over South European. I do not claim that the North European is braver in war, stronger physically, keener mentally, more moral or more lovable than the South European. I make this claim no more than I claim that the white man is superior to the yellow man or the black. I make only one claim of superiority in the old colonial stock over the later comers. I do believe that the colonial stock has a superior political aptitude, or at least an ingrained political tradition and training superior to any of the immigrants from southeastern Europe or indeed from northwestern Europe, save only those coming from Great Britain. I will consider this point more fully later on. Aside from political tradition or habit, the argument in this book makes no claim of superiority in the white man over the black or yellow man, or in the Northwestern European over the Southeastern European or in the old-stock American over the new stock. The essential point is not superiority or inferiority, but difference—a profound difference between races—more

Source: Edward R. Lewis, *America: Nation or Confusion?* New York: Harper Brothers, 1928 pp. 16, 122–33, 42–43, 52–53, 139, 143–44, 165.

deep and profound, it is true, of course, in a comparison between the black and yellow man and the white man than between the old-stock American and the Greek, Armenian or the South Italian, but a deep and profound difference all the same.

The differences are so pronounced that it is impossible to say that mixture would result advantageously. That is all that it is necessary to say. It is not necessary to prove that mixture is undesirable. The burden of proof is on the other side. It is for the advocates of mixture to prove that the unprecedented mixture of races which would result in our country from a fusion of all the races that they would bring to us would result in a race superior to that we have now. . . .

. . . The evil doctrine has actually obtained currency in our country that common labor is menial and unworthy. I think it can be traced to immigration. Each new race of immigrants, as it has come in, has turned to the work it could do, and as it was new and untrained, largely from rural surroundings and ignorant of our language, in all cases save the Jews, it has turned to manual labor for its start in this country. The American did common labor before the immigrant came. But when the latter came, he refused to work with the immigrant. He refused to be classed, in the old days, with the Irish and the German, and then the Irish and the German refused to be classed with the "dagos" and "wops" and "Hunkies," and if we go on the "dagos" and "wops" will refuse to be classed with the Japs, Chinese and Hindoos. The natural and understandable antipathy of races to each other has accordingly been interpreted as an antipathy to common labor. Because Americans will not work at manual labor alongside of foreigners, it is said that they will not work at manual labor at all.

If this is so, then we are the first nation in the history of the world that has not been able to produce its own labor. The French, the English, the Scotch, the Germans, while they import some labor, supply basically all their common labor. The United States has been able to glut its labor market because of its immigration supply, but no other nation has been able to do so in any comparable degree. Our power to do so has been due to adventitious and artificial conditions, which is one proof that it is, if not an evil, certainly not a permanently possible policy. . . .

We cannot, therefore, subscribe to all the tenets of the faith of the free immigrationist. He sees a perpetual labor shortage. He would make a surplus in time of expansion, which would become a plague in time of depression. If he loses labor to another industry, or another section of the country, he does not bid for his old labor but seeks a new, cheap supply. There would be no limit to his demands until the country was filled to overflowing as England and Belgium are filled now. He wants hands and not citizens. He would perpetuate the evil tradition that Americans will not work with their hands. . . .

Some declare that a nation is only a people living in a definite territory, subject to the same government. It is not necessary that they be the same race. It is not necessary that they have the same traditions. A nation is a people in a definite territory, subject to the same government, but it is more than that. A common government and a common territory are necessary for a nation but they are more often the result of nationality than the cause of it. . . .

A nation is knit closer by common economic interests. The spirit of nationality in the United States was aided, or perhaps made possible, by the steamboat and the railroad ministering to trade and travel. But, after all, economic unity arises from spiritual unity, or rather spreads it farther. Economic interests do not make the group. They may aid the group to expand. But they often run athwart national boundaries. There is a stronger force, one which aids the economic interests within the nation and which often defeats or ignores the economic interests between various nations. Back of all is like-mindedness, a common psychology, a veritable consciousness among the people of kinship with each other. . . .

. . . [It] is surely clear that no country can be a coherent and harmonious nation where the majority at least does not have a common tradition and a common past. We can allow a portion of the population to be aliens, a portion to be of alien descent who no longer have an alien bias, who no longer take part in alien or hyphenated groups, but who are not yet immersed in the American tradition so that it is an instinctive part of them. But the nation requires and America requires surely at least a majority of people who are wholly native, who think with a native background, to whom the tradition of the country has been passed down for many generations. It depends on like-mindedness, a community of essential standards, a common tradition and a common past. . . .

4

EXCERPT FROM "OUR NATIONAL ORIGINS QUOTA SYSTEM: THE MIRROR FOR AMERICA"

There are four primary factors to be considered in controlling a population, namely: Immigration, emigration, birthrates, and mortality tabulations. Those who would alter our national origins must exert some degree of control over each of these elements of our ethnological composition, in favor of the ethnic or other groups they desire to elevate to a predominant proportion of our people. . . .

The principal target of the advocates of a change in our national origins, however, is immigration. At a time when the nations which have contributed preponderantly to our foreign national origins are not filling their annual immigration quotas, those who are dissatisfied with our national origins find a propitious moment for attacking our immigration laws on behalf of the minority groups they favor. They may, of course, disavow any intention of changing our foreign national origins, but there can be no other result from what they seek to accomplish. They can not repudiate the inescapable effect of their program.

In obvious desperation the disgruntled opponents of our foreign national origins have launched a malicious and calumnious attack on our national origins systems of immigration quotas. They charge that it was conceived in religious bigotry, racial arrogance, xenophobian frenzy, and human intolerance. They allege that it was purposely designed to discriminate against potential immigrants from the small-quota countries. They contend that Congress considered such immigrants to be racially, culturally, religiously, intellectually, physically, or otherwise inferior. Many of

Source: Excerpted from Robert C. Alexander, "Our National Origins Quota System: The Mirror of America," *The American Legion Magazine*, September 1956, 18–19; 52; 55.

these charges—all of which are utterly false—emanate from sources of professional racism, xenomania, and nativist hatred, but are adopted by dupes and disseminated in abysmal ignorance of the true basis of our national origins quota system. Some of the opponents of our national origins—and consequently of our national origins quota system—have been historically and traditionally opposed to all restrictions in our immigration laws.

Our national origins quota system, established under the Immigration Act of 1924, allocates to the mother country of each of our foreign national origins groups an immigration quota of one-sixth of one percent of the number of our people in each group. This is an invariable and exact mathematical formula applicable to the quotas of all groups, subject only to the exception that no country's quota shall be less than 100 immigrants annually.

If some countries have larger or smaller quotas than others this is only because such countries have made different contributions to the foreign national origins of our people. The basic policy and underlying purpose of the national origins quota system is to give each of our foreign national origins groups its fair share—no more and no less— of the annual volume of permissible quota immigrants for its mother country. Those who object to our national origins quota system obviously disapprove the national origins of our people. When they attack our quota system, their cat pops out of the bag.

Our national origins quota system is like a mirror held up before the American people. As the various proportions of our foreign national origins groups are reflected in the mirror the quotas are computed in accordance with that reflection. The opponents of the system manifestly do not look into the mirror with satisfaction, as there they must see themselves as the minority they are among all of our people.

An interesting commentary on the national origins quota system is exemplified in the position of The New York Times, the favorite mouthpiece of those who now seek to discredit that system. On March 1, 1924, when the legislation embodying the national origins quota system was approaching a decision in Congress, that newspaper stated editorially:

> In formulating a permanent policy two considerations are of prime importance. The first is that the country has a right to say who shall and who shall not come in. It is not for any foreign country to determine our immigration policy. The second is that the basic [sic] for restriction must be chosen with a view not to the interest of any group or groups in this country, whether racial or religious, but rather with a view to the

country's best interests as a whole. The great test is assimilability. Will the newcomers fit into the American life readily? Is their culture sufficiently akin to our own to make it possible for them easily to take their place among us? There is no question of "superior" or "inferior" races, or of "Nordics," or of prejudice, or racial egotism. Certain groups not only do not fuse easily, but consistently endeavor to keep alive their racial distinctions when they settle among us. They perpetuate the "hyphen" which is but another way of saying that they seek to create foreign blocs in our midst. . . .

Moreover, it would seem that the opponents of our national origins quota system, who obviously dislike the proportions of our various foreign national origins, are under some moral obligation, when they glibly advocate action which would result in a change in the ethnological composition of our people, to tell us in what respect they consider the immigrants they favor to be superior to those now coming into the United States. Or perhaps they should tell us "*What is wrong with our national origins?*"

5

EXCERPT FROM *CONGRESSIONAL RECORD*—SENATE VOL III.

Mr. BYRD of West Virginia. Mr. President, one of the major issues yet to come before the Senate, before adjournment this year, is the proposed revision of the U.S. immigration laws. . . .

The original objective of the 1924 act was to maintain the ethnic composition of the American people, on the premise that some nations are far closer to the United States in culture, customs, standards of living, respect for law, and experience in self-government. . . .

I have only two objections to the present system. One is that it applies no limitation on immigration from South America and other Western Hemisphere countries and, theoretically, any number of persons could emigrate to the United States from the Western Hemisphere countries immediately. This weakness has not had too great an impact upon our country up to the present moment, largely because South American countries have been absorbing their own population increase very well. Yet, the day is not far off, when the population explosion in Latin American countries will exert great pressures upon those people to emigrate to the United States. It will be my intention, therefore, to support a limitation on the number of immigrants from Western Hemisphere countries. . . . My other objection is that under the present system, certain countries, such as Italy and Greece, for example, whose peoples do assimilate readily and easily into the American society, have been disadvantaged.

Source: Excerpted from *Congressional Record—Senate*, Vol. 111, Senator Robert Byrd, September 14, 1965, 23793–95.

Notwithstanding the two objections I have iterated, I think the basic national origins quota system should be retained. I realize that it has been nullified to a great extent by amendments and special refugee laws and other legislation in the form of private bills. The system has been castigated and vilified by those who declare that it discriminates against other nations, but on the whole, I consider it to be a just and wise system. Relatively larger quotas, of course, are assigned to such countries as England, Scotland, Ireland, Germany, France, and Scandinavia, but this is because the basic population of our country is made up largely of stocks which originated from those countries, and the reasoning back of the present system is that additional population from those countries would be more easily and readily assimilated into the American population. Naturally, those immigrants can best be absorbed into our modern population whose backgrounds and cultures are similar. It is indubitably clear that if the majority of Americans had sprung, not from Western, central, and southern Europe, but from central Africa or southern Asia, we would today have a vastly different country. Unquestionably, there are fine human beings in all parts of the world, but people do differ widely in their social habits, their levels of ambition, their mechanical aptitudes, their inherited ability and intelligence, their moral traditions, and their capacities for maintaining stable governments.

The advocates of this legislation state that the increase in immigration brought about by its passage will be minuscule and will amount to only a few additional thousand persons annually, but I fear that the practical result will be otherwise. In my judgment, it is completely unrealistic for us to be considering legislation that is going to permanently increase our immigration to any degree whatsoever. I grant that the immigrants who have come to this country have made a magnificent contribution to our development. Anyone who attempts to articulate this contribution is doomed to understatement because, certainly, this Nation was put together by immigrants and would not exist if they had not come here.

It is true also that immigrants have continued to play an important role in our Nation's development. But that role has been and is dwindling in importance. Most of us are descendants of immigrants, but this is no longer a nation that needs immigration as it once did. Indeed, the problems we will face in the years ahead will be those of a surplus population rather than needed population. In this respect we are like most other nations of the world. But, unlike other nations, we have not yet learned how to give primary consideration to immigration as it will affect us internally, without developing a guilty conscience. We have yet to make the philosophical transition from an immigrant-seeking nation, which we were until fairly recently, to one whose population has developed to the capabilities of our present resources.

But why, Mr. President, should the United States be the only advanced nation in the world today to develop a guilt complex concerning its immigration policies, when it is already far more liberal than other countries in this respect, and in view of the fact that other advanced nations are selective in dealing with immigrants and without apology?

Every other country that is attractive to immigrants practices selectivity and without apology. . . .

Our first responsibility in matters of immigration, at a time when automation is on the rise and the population explosion is giving cause for concern, is to the people of the United States and not to the entire population of the world. . . .

I think it is rather inconsistent on our part, Mr. President, to permit an increase in immigration—which is sure to be the effect of a more lenient immigration statute—at a time when we are becoming more and more aware of the population problems we are faced with in the world and in this country. These problems are bound to increase in dimension in the years ahead. The continent with the highest birth rate in the world today is South America. Yet, under our present immigration laws, unlimited immigration is allowed to natives of Central and South American countries. It is time we were looking to this aspect of our immigration policy with a view to applying restrictions rather than trying to rectify discriminations against Asian and African countries that exist in our quota systems. As I said earlier, I intend to support the application of a limitation on immigration from Western Hemisphere countries, but any change in our present immigration laws should be largely limited to just this aspect and should not encompass such a wholesale revision as that with which we are about to be faced. . . .

The problems we face due to expanding population may not presently be as serious as those faced by other countries of the world. Our agricultural and other productive capacities have not yet been put to the test. But we are now experiencing a number of troubles which are directly or indirectly attributable to our increasing population. These include pollution of our rivers and streams, and the air we breathe in our great metropolitan areas; the first serious water shortages in the northeastern part of the country; progressive extinction of wildlife; and ever-increasing welfare costs as the nonproductive segments of our population continue to expand. A good deal of the legislation we have enacted in recent years has been directed toward finding solutions to these problems. Liberalizing our immigration policies cannot help but compound such problems. . . .

I fear that the practical results of the new legislation will be a considerably increased immigration, in addition to the many serious concomitant problems, some of which I have discussed.

We take justifiable pride in the heritage of the American melting pot, but, unless the national origins quota system is maintained and unless limitations are placed on immigration from Western Hemispheric countries, the melting pot will no longer melt, and eventually ours will become a conglomerate, characterless society. . . .

Therefore, I intend to cast my vote, when the moment comes, against the proposal to scrap the national origins quota system because the proposed legislation will permit a greater inflow of immigrants from Asian and African countries and because our own problems of chronic and persistent unemployment and underemployment, housing, job retraining needs, growing welfare caseloads, crime, and juvenile delinquency are so great that we should not be considering any liberalization of the immigration laws.

I recognize that this is a very delicate issue and that the position I have taken will not be popular with some people, particularly those who misunderstand my reasons therefor. Nonetheless, I feel it my duty to vote against the proposed legislation, in my judgment, it not being in the best interests of the United States.

6

EXCERPT FROM *PUBLIC PAPERS OF THE PRESIDENT OF THE UNITED STATES: WILLIAM JEFFERSON CLINTON,* VOL I (1998)

Today I want to talk to you about what may be the most important subject of all, how we can strengthen the bonds of our national community as we grow more racially and ethnically diverse. . . .

The driving force behind our increasing diversity is a new, large wave of immigration. It is changing the face of America. And while most of the changes are good, they do present challenges which demand more, both from new immigrants and from our citizens. Citizens share a responsibility to welcome new immigrants, to ensure that they strengthen our Nation, to give them their chance at the brass ring. In turn, new immigrants have a responsibility to learn, to work, to contribute to America. If both citizens and immigrants do their part, we will grow ever stronger in the new global information economy.

More than any other nation on Earth, America has constantly drawn strength and spirit from wave after wave of immigrants. In each generation, they have proved to be the most restless, the most adventurous, the most innovative, the most industrious of people. Bearing different memories, honoring different heritages, they have strengthened our economy, enriched our culture, renewed our promise to freedom and opportunity for all.

Of course, the path has not always run smooth. Some Americans have met each group of newcomers with suspicion and violence and discrimination. So great was the hatred of Irish immigrants 150 years ago that they were greeted with signs that read, "No Dogs or Irish." So profound was the fear of Chinese in the 1880's that they were barred from entering the coun-

Source: Excerpted from *Public Papers of the President of the United States: William Jefferson Clinton,* Volume I (1998), 956–58.

try. So deep was the distrust of immigrants from Southern and Eastern Europe at the beginning of this century that they were forced to take literacy tests specifically designed to keep them out of America. Eventually, the guarantees of our Constitution and the better angels of our nature prevailed over ignorance and insecurity, over prejudice and fear.

But now we are being tested again by a new wave of immigration larger than any in a century, far more diverse than any in our history. Each year, nearly a million people come legally to America. Today, nearly one in 10 people in American was born in another country; one in 5 schoolchildren are from immigrant families. Today, largely because of immigration, there is no majority race in Hawaii or Houston or New York City. Within 5 years, there will be no majority race in our largest State, California. In a little more than 50 years, there will be no majority race in the United States. No other nation in history has gone through demographic change of this magnitude in so short a time.

What do the changes mean? They can either strengthen and unite us, or they can weaken and divide us. We must decide.

Let me state my view unequivocally. I believe new immigrants are good for America. they are revitalizing our cities. They are building our new economy. They are strengthening our ties to the global economy, just as earlier waves of immigrants settled the new frontier and powered the Industrial Revolution. They are energizing our culture and broadening our vision of the world. They are renewing our most basic values and reminding us all of what it truly means to be an American. . . .

Now, some Americans don't see it that way. When they hear new accents or see new faces, they feel unsettled. They worry that new immigrants come not to work hard but to live off our largesse. They're afraid the America they know and love is becoming a foreign land. This reaction may be understandable, but it's wrong. It's especially wrong when anxiety and fear give rise to policies and ballot propositions to exclude immigrants from our civic life. I believe it's wrong to deny law-abiding immigrants benefits available to everyone else; wrong to ignore them as people not worthy of being counted in the census. It's not only wrong, it's un-American.

Let me be clear: I also think it's wrong to condone illegal immigration that flouts our laws, strains our tolerance, taxes our resources. Even a nation of immigrants must have rules and conditions and limits, and when they are disregarded, public support for immigration erodes in ways that are destructive to those who are newly arrived and those who are still waiting patiently to come. . . .

New immigrants also benefit the Nation in ways not so easily measured but very important. We should be honored that America, whether it's called the City on a Hill, or the Old Gold Mountain, or El Norte, is still seen around the world as the land of new beginnings. We should all be proud that people living in isolated villages in far corners of the world actually recognize the Statute of Liberty. We should rejoice that children the world over study our Declaration of Independence and embrace its creed.

My fellow Americans, we descendants of those who passed through the portals of Ellis Island must not lock the door behind us. Americans whose parents were denied the rights of citizenship simply because of the color of their skin must not deny those rights to others because of the country of their birth or the nature of their faith.

We should treat new immigrants as we would have wanted our own grandparents to be treated. We should share our country with them, not shun them or shut them out. But mark my words, unless we handle this well, immigration of this sweep and scope could threaten the bonds of our Union.

Around the world, we see what can happen when people who live on the same land put race and ethnicity before country and humanity. If America is to remain the world's most diverse democracy, if immigration is to strengthen America as it has throughout our history, then we must say to one another: Whether your ancestors came here in slave ships or on the *Mayflower,* whether they landed on Ellis Island or at Los Angeles International Airport, or have been here for thousands of years, if you believe in the Declaration of Independence and the Constitution, if you accept the responsibilities as well as the rights embedded in them, then you are an American. Only that belief can keep us one America in the 21st century.

So I say, as President, to all our immigrants, you are welcome here. But you must honor our laws, embrace our culture, learn our language, know our history, and when the time comes, you should become citizens. And I say to all Americans, we have responsibilities as well to welcome our newest immigrants, to vigorously enforce laws against discrimination. . . .

And together, immigrants and citizens alike, let me say we must recommit ourselves to the general duties of citizenship. Not just immigrants but every American should know what's in our Constitution and understand our shared history. Not just immigrants but every American should participate in our democracy by voting, by volunteering, and by running for office. Not just immigrants but every American, on our campuses and in our communities, should serve; community service breeds good citizenship. And not just immigrants but every American should reject identity politics that seeks to separate us, not bring us together.

7
U.S. POPULATION GROWTH IF
IMMIGRATION AND FERTILITY
DO NOT CHANGE

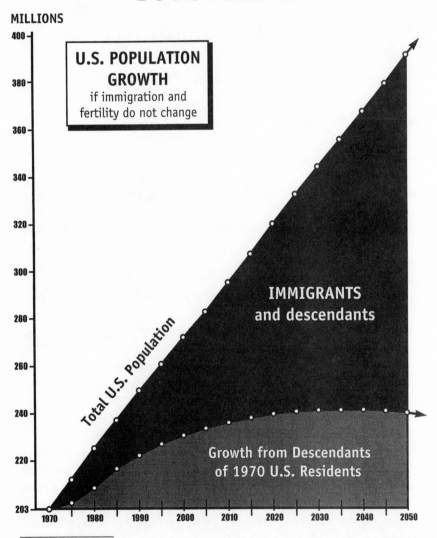

MILLIONS

U.S. POPULATION GROWTH
if immigration and
fertility do not change

Total U.S. Population

IMMIGRANTS
and descendants

Growth from Descendants
of 1970 U.S. Residents

Source: U.S. Bureau of Census and NumbersUSA.com, Roy Berk, "U.S. Population Growth If Immigration and Fertility Do Not Change," *www.numbersusa.com* and U.S. Bureau of Census (February 2000).

207

SELECTED READINGS

Archdeacon, Thomas. *Becoming American: An Ethnic History.* New York: Free Press, 1983.

Baines, Dudley. *Emigration from Europe, 1815–1930.* Basingstoke, UK: Macmillan, 1991.

Barkan, Eliott R. *And Still They Come.* Wheeling, Ill.: Harlan Davidson, 1996.

Baron, Dennis. *The English-Only Question.* New Haven: Yale University Press, 1990.

Bennett, Marion T. *American Immigration Policies: A History.* Washington, D.C., 1963.

Bernard, William S. *American Immigration Policy: A Reappraisal.* New York: Harper, 1950.

Bhagwati, Jagdish. *A Stream of Windows: Unsettling Reflections on Trade, Immigration, and Democracy.* Cambridge, Mass.: MIT University Press, 1998.

Bodnar, John. *The Transplanted.* Bloomington: Indiana University Press, 1985.

Borjas, George. *Heaven's Gate; Immigration Policy and the American Economy.* Cambridge, Mass. (Harvard University Press, 1999).

Bouvier, Leon and Lindsey Grant. *How Many Americans?* (San Francisco: Sierra Club Books, 1994).

Bredbenner, Candice Dawn. *A Nationality of Her Own: Women, Marriage, and the Law of Citizenship.* Berkeley: University of California Press, 1998.

Breitman, Richard & Allan M. Kraut. *American Refugee Policy and European Jewry.* Bloomington: Indiana University Press, 1987.

Briggs, Vernon M. *Mass Immigration and the National Interest.* 2nd ed. Armonk, N.Y.: M. E. Sharpe, 1996.

Brimelow, Peter, *Alien Nation: Common Sense about America's Immigration Disaster,* New York: Random House, 1995.

Brown, Mary Elizabeth. *Shapers of the Great Debate on Immigration; A Biographical Dictionary* (Wesport, Conn.: Greenwood, 1999).

Clark, William A. *The California Cauldron; Immigration and the Fortunes of Local Communities* (New York: Guilford Press, 1998).

Cornelius, Wayne A. *Controlling Immigration: A Global Perspective.* Stanford, Calif.: Stanford University Press, 1995.

Daniels, Roger. *Coming to America: A History of Immigration and Ethnicity in American Life.* (New York: HarperCollins, 1990).

——. *The Politics of Prejudice: The Anti-Japanese Movement in California and the Struggle for Japanese Exclusion.* 3rd ed. Berkeley: University of California Press, 1999.

DeConde, Alexander. *Ethnicity, Race and American Foreign Policy: A History.* Boston: Northeastern University Press, 1992.

Dinnerstein, Leonard. *America and the Survivors of the Holocaust.* New York: Columbia University Press, 1982.

Fitzgerald, Keith. *The Face of the Nation* (Stanford, Calif.: Stanford University Press, 1995).

Garcia, Maria Cristina. *Havana USA: Cuban Exiles and Cuban Americans in South Florida, 1959–1994.* Berkeley: University of California, 1996.

Gardner, Robert W., Bryant Robey, and Peter C. Smith. *Asian Americans: Growth, Change and Diversity.* Washington, DC: Population Reference Bureau, 1985.

Graham, Otis L. *Illegal Immigration and the New Reform Movement.* Washington, DC: FAIR, 1980.

Gutierrez, David. *Walls and Mirrors; Mexican Americans, Mexican Immigrants and the Politics of Ethnicity* (Berkeley: University of California Press, 1995).

Hatton, Timoth J. and Jeffrey G. Williamson. *The Age of Mass Migration; Causes and Economic Impact* (New York: Oxford University Press, 1998).

Higham, John. *Strangers in the Land: Patterns of American Nativism, 1860–1925.* New Brunswick, NJ: Rutgers University Press, 2nd ed., 1988. ©1955.

Hutchinson, E. P. *Legislative History of American Immigration Policy, 1798–1965.* Philadelphia: University of Pennsylvania Press, 1981.

Jones, Maldwyn A. *American Immigration.* 2d ed. U. of Chicago, 1992.

LeMay, Michael C. *Anatomy of a Public Policy: The Reform of Contemporary Immigration Law.* Westport, Conn.: Greenwood.

— and Elliott R, Barkan, eds. *U.S. Immigration and Naturalization Laws and Issues: A Documentary History.* Westport, Conn.: Greenwood. 1999.

Lind, Michael. *The Next American Nation* (New York: Free Press, 1995).

Lowenstein, Sharon R. *Token Refuge: The Story of the Jewish Refugee Shelter at Oswego, 1944–1946.* Bloomington: Indiana University 1986.

McClain, Charles J. Jr. *In Search of Equality: the Chinese Struggle against Discrimination in Nineteenth-Century America.* Berkeley: University of California Press, 1994.

Mitchell, Christopher, ed. *Western Hemisphere Immigration and United States Foreign Policy.* University Park: Penn State University Press, 1992.

Nugent, Walter. *Crossings: The Great Transatlantic Migrations, 1870–1914.* Bloomington: Indiana University Press, 1992.

Peffer, George A. *If They Don't Bring Their Women Here: Regulating Chinese Female Immigration, 1852–1882.* Urbana: University of Illinois Press, 1999.

President's Commission on Immigration and Naturalization. *Whom We Shall Welcome.* Washington, DC: GPO, 1953.

Reimers, David M. *Still the Golden Door: The Third World Comes to America.* New York: Columbia University Press, 2nd ed., 1992.

—. *Unwelcome Strangers: American Identity and the Turn Against Immigration.* New York: Columbia University Press, 1998.

Sánchez, George J, *Becoming Mexican American: Ethnicity, Culture and Identity in Chicano Los Angeles, 1900–1945.* New York: Oxford University Press, 1993.

Sayler, Lucy, *Laws Harsh as Tigers: Chinese Immigrants and the Shaping of Modern Immigration Law.* Chapel Hill: University of North Carolina Press, 1995.

Schlesinger, Arthur M. *The Disuniting of America.* New York: Norton, 1998.

Schrag, Philip G. *A Well-Founded Fear: The Congressional Battle to Save Political Asylum in America,* New York, Routledge, 2000.

Schuck, Peter H. *Citizens, Strangers and In-Between: Essays on Immigration and Citizenship.* Denver: Westview, 1998.

Shankman, Andrew. *Ambivalent Friends; Afro-Americans View the Immigrant* (Westport, Conn.: Greenwood, 1982).

Solomon, Barbara Miller. *Ancestors and Immigrants.* Cambridge, Mass.: Harvard University Press, 1956.

Stephenson, George M. *A History of American Immigration* 1820–1924 (New York: Russell and Russell, 1964).

Suro, Roberto. *Watching America' Door; The Immigration Backlash and the New Policy Debate* (New York: Twentieth Century Fund, 1996).

——. *Strangers Among Us; Latinos Lives in a Changing America* (New York: Knopf, 1998).

Tanton, John, Denis McCormack and Joseph Wayne Smith, eds., *Immigration and The Social Contract; The Implosion of Western Societies* (Brodifield, Vt.: Ashegate Publishers, 1996).

Thernstrom, Stephan, ed. *The Harvard Encyclopedia of American Ethnic Groups.* Cambridge, Mass.: Harvard University Press, 1980.

U.S. Commission on Immigration Reform. *U.S. Immigration Policy: Restoring Credibility.* Washington, DC: GPO, 1994.

Ueda, Reed. *Postwar Immigrant America; A Social History* (Boston: Bedford Books, 1994).

United States Immigration Commission. *Reports of the Immigration Commission.* 41 vols. Washington, DC: GPO, 1911.

Vecoli, Rudolph J. and Suzanne Sinke, eds. *A Century of European Migrations, 1830–1930.* Urbana: University of Illinois Press, 1992.

Yans-McLaughlin, Virginia, ed. *Immigration Reconsidered: History, Sociology, and Politics.* New York: Oxford University Press, 1990.

Zolberg, Aristide R., *The Guarded Gate: The Reality of American Refugee Policy.* San Diego: Harcourt, 1987.

ONGOING SCHOLARSHIP

The best way to keep up with the literature in the field is to consult the following academic journals:

Journal of American Ethnic History.
Immigrants and Minorities (Great Britain).
IMR: International Migration Review.

INDEX

213

ABOUT THE AUTHORS

Roger Daniels is Charels Phelps Taft Professor of History at the University of Cincinnati. A former president of the Immigration History Society, he is the author of a dozen books including *Coming to America: A History of Immigration and Ethnicity in American Life* (HarperCollins, 1990) and *Not Like Us: Immigrants and Minorities in America, 1890–1924* (Ivan R. Dee, 1997).

Otis L. Graham is professor emeritus at the University of California, Santa Barbara, and distinguished visiting professor at the University of North Carolina, Wilmington. He is the author and editor of sixteen books in American history, including *An Encore for Reform: The Old Progressives and the New Deal* (Oxford University Press, 1966); *The Great Campaigns: Reform and War in America, 1900–1928* (Prentice Hall, 1973); *Toward a Planned Society: From Roosevelt to Nixon* (Oxford University Press, 1976); and *Losing Time: The Industrial Policy Debate* (Harvard University Press, 1992).

Graham was chairman of the board of the Center for Immigration Studies in Washington, D.C. (1985–95). He served as editor of *The Public Historian* (1989–97) and received the 1999 Robert Kelley Memorial Award by the National Council on Public History. He was named a Guggenheim Fellow and as a fellow at both the Woodrow Wilson Center and the Center for Advanced Study of the Behavioral Sciences at Stanford.